CREATED BY **JOSS WHEDON**

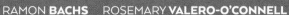

JORDIE **BELLAIRE** RAMON **BACHS** ROSEMARY **VALERO-O'CONNELL** RAÚL **ANGULO**

Buffy the Vampire Slayer™

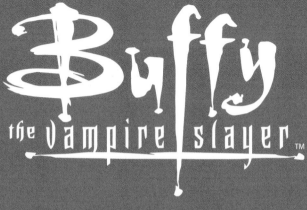

VOLUME FOUR **FRENEMIES**

RING OF FIRE

Published by
BOOM! STUDIOS

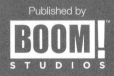

Series Designer
Michelle Ankley

Collection Designer
Scott Newman

Assistant Editor
Gavin Gronenthal

Associate Editor
Jonathan Manning

Editor
Jeanine Schaefer

Special Thanks to **Sierra Hahn**, **Becca J. Sadowsky**, and **Nicole Spiegel** & **Carol Roeder** at Twentieth Century Fox.

BOOM! Studios, 5670 Wilshire Boulevard, Suite 400, Los Angeles, CA 90036-5679. Printed in USA. First Printing.

ISBN: 978-1-68415-595-8, eISBN: 978-1-64668-007-8

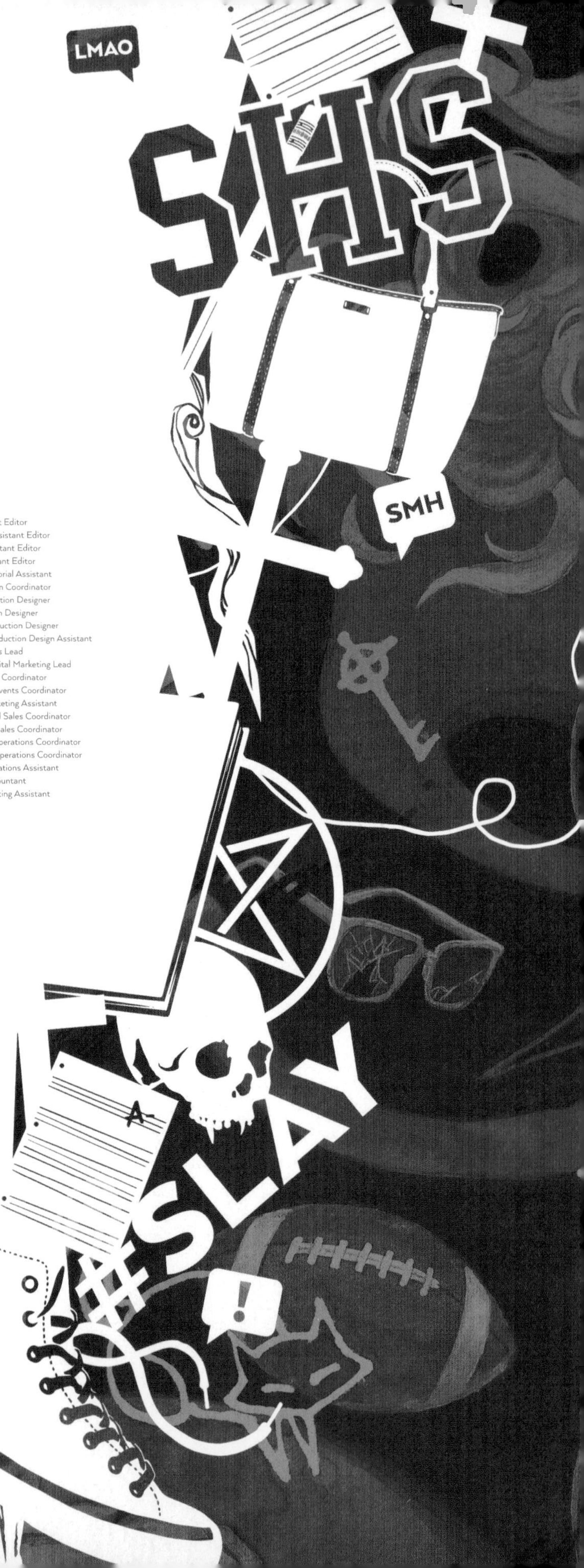

LMAO
SHS
SMH
A-
#SLAY
!

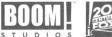

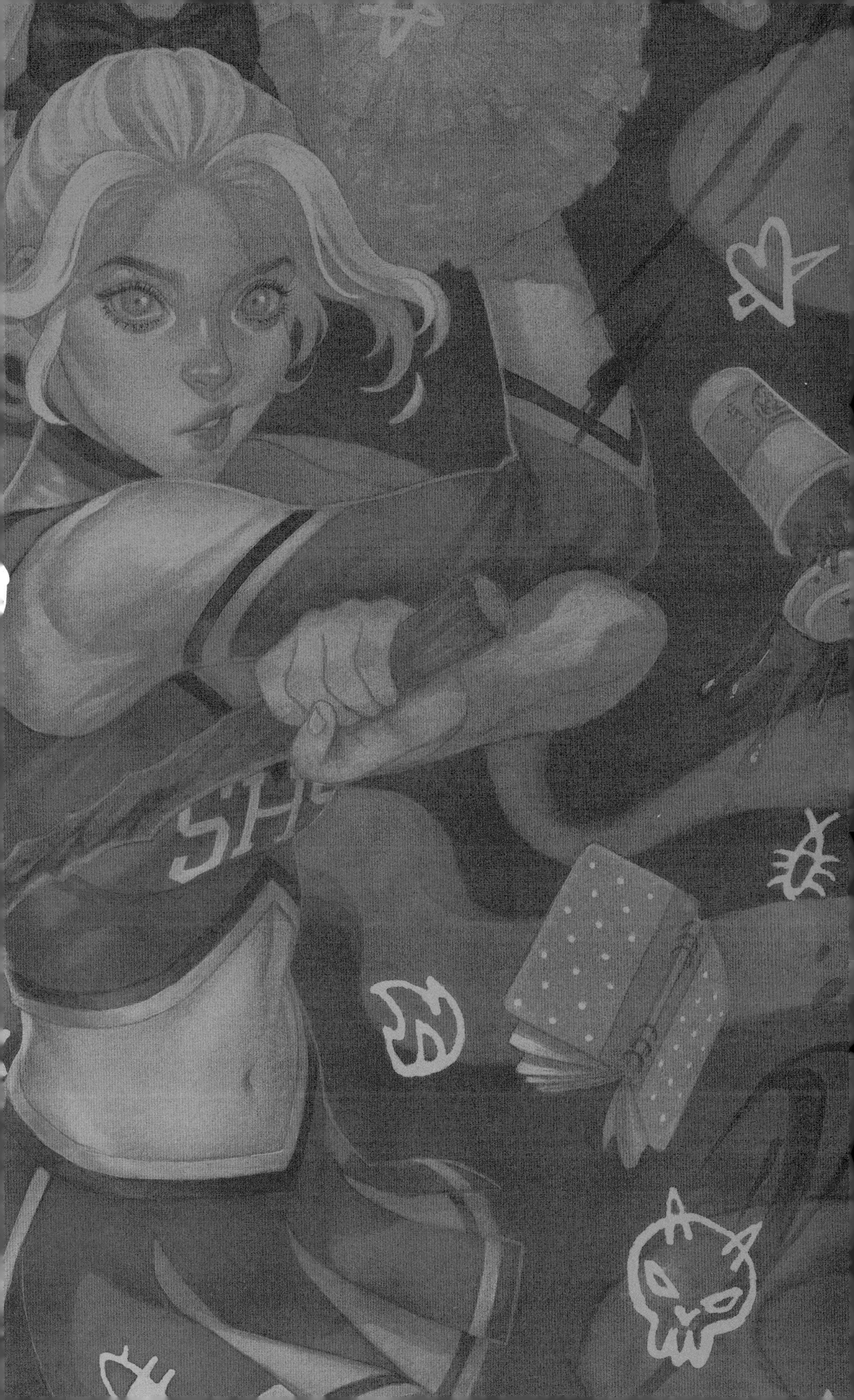
SH

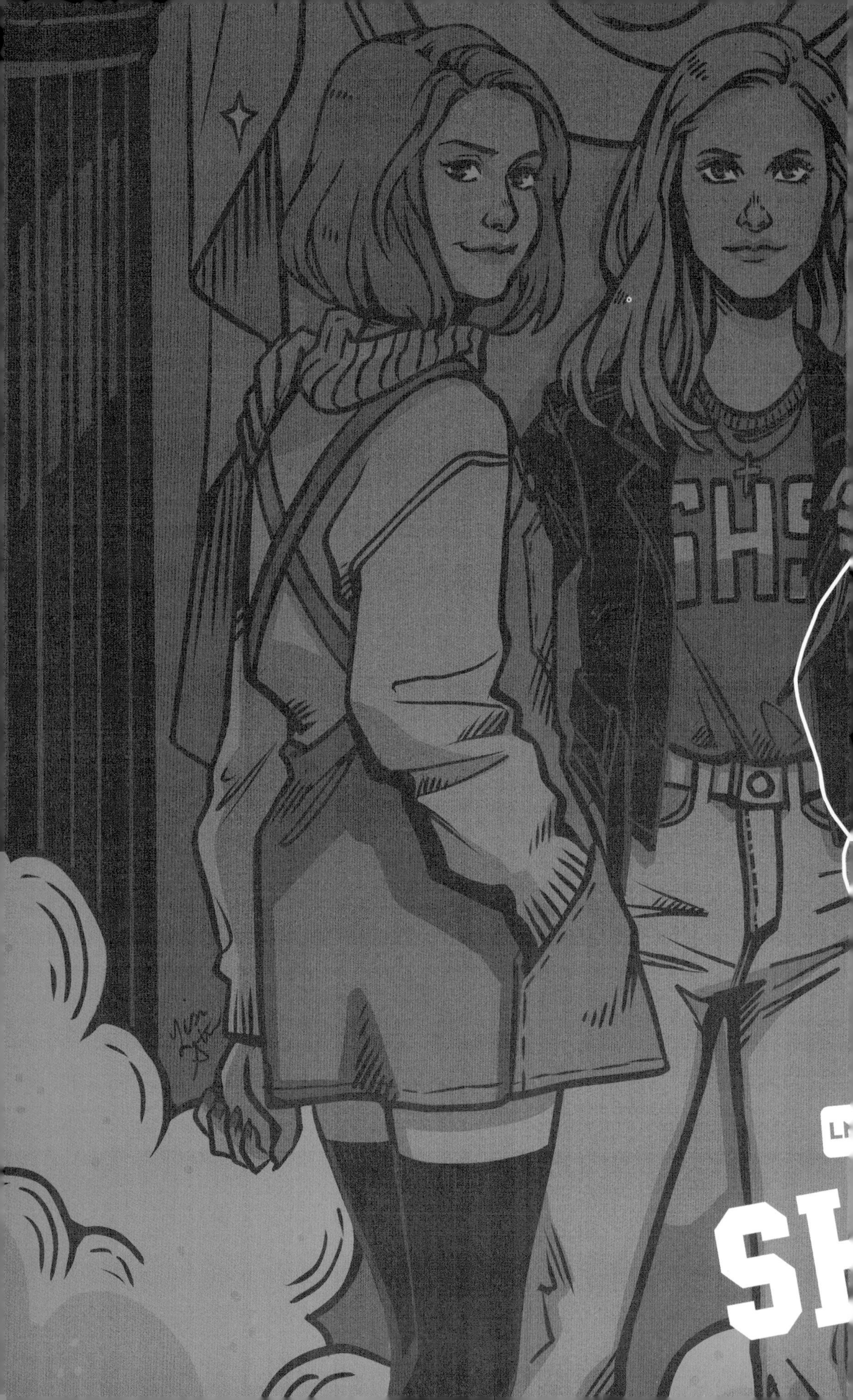

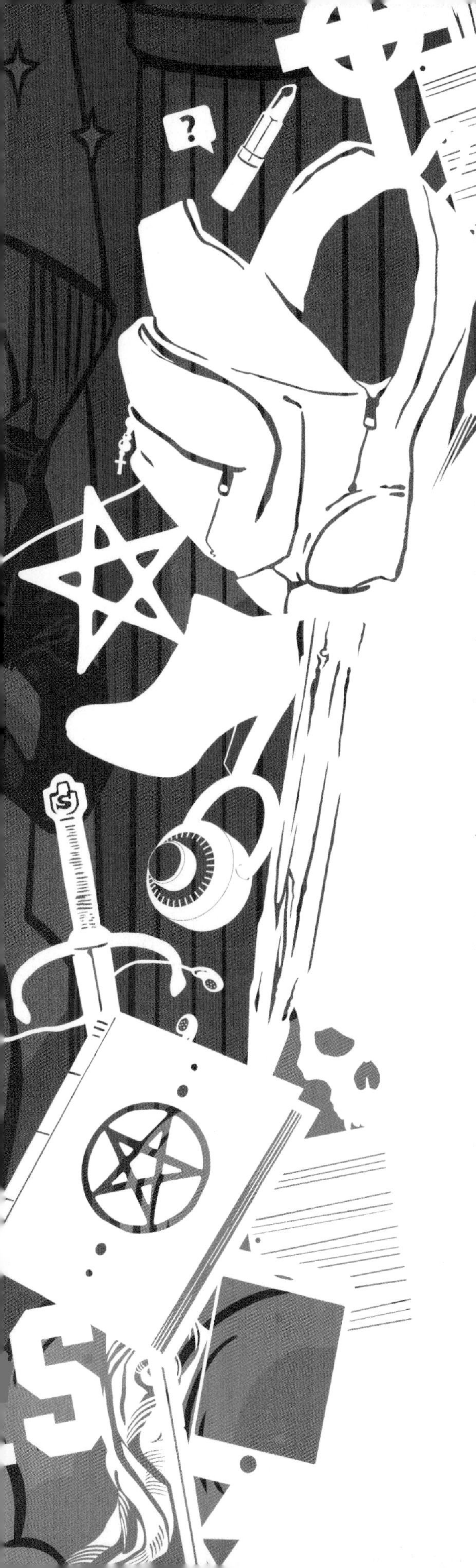

Created by

Joss Whedon

Written by

Jordie Bellaire

Illustrated by

Rosemary Valero-O'Connell (Chapter 13)

Julian Lopez (Chapter 14)

with **Moisés Hidalgo**

Ramon Bachs (Chapter 15-16)

Colored by

Raúl Angulo

With **Eleonora Bruni** (Chapter 13)

& **Francesco Segala** (Chapter 14)

Lettered by

Ed Dukeshire

Cover by

David López

THIRTEEN

Issue Thirteen Cover by **David López**

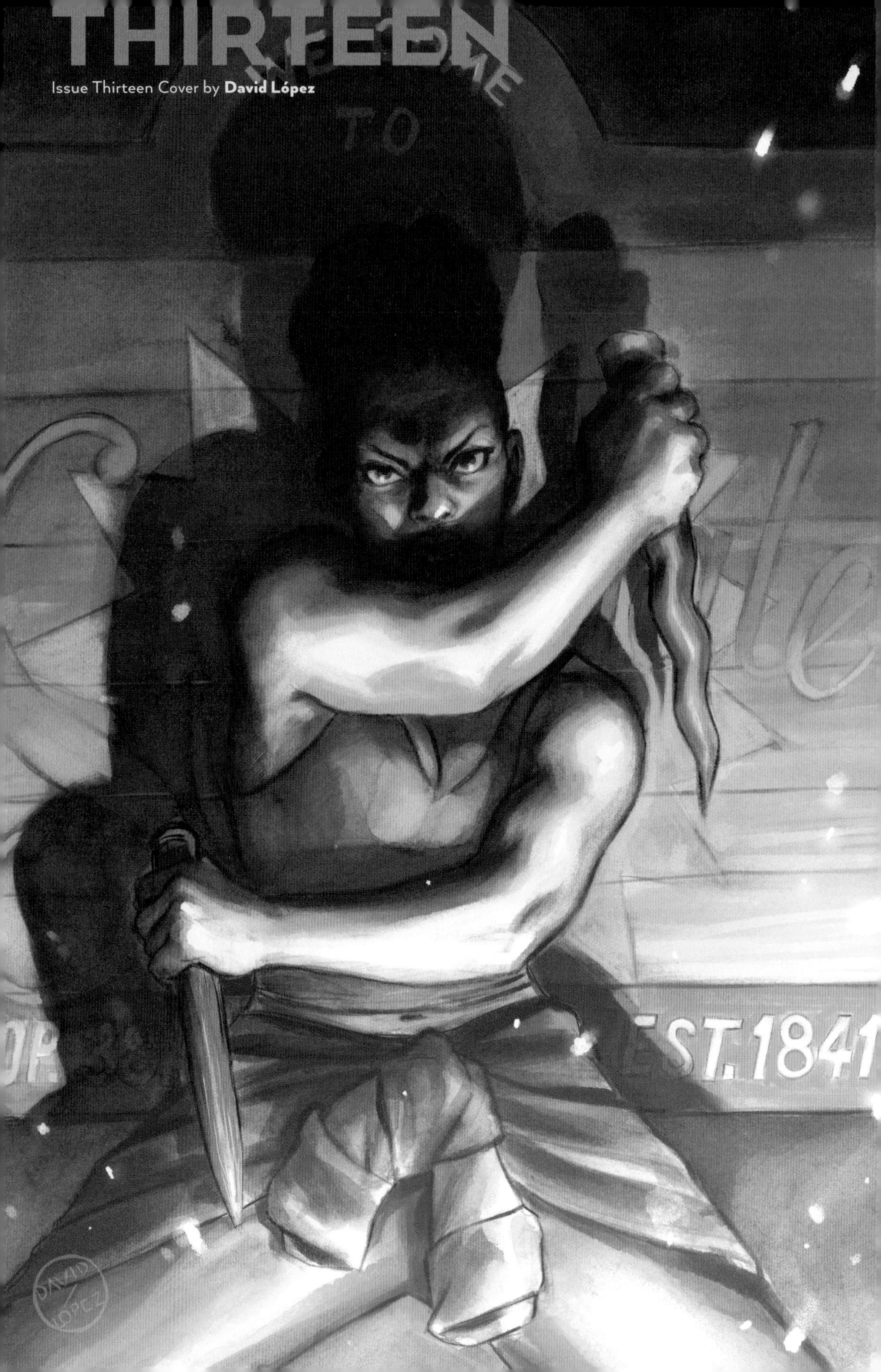

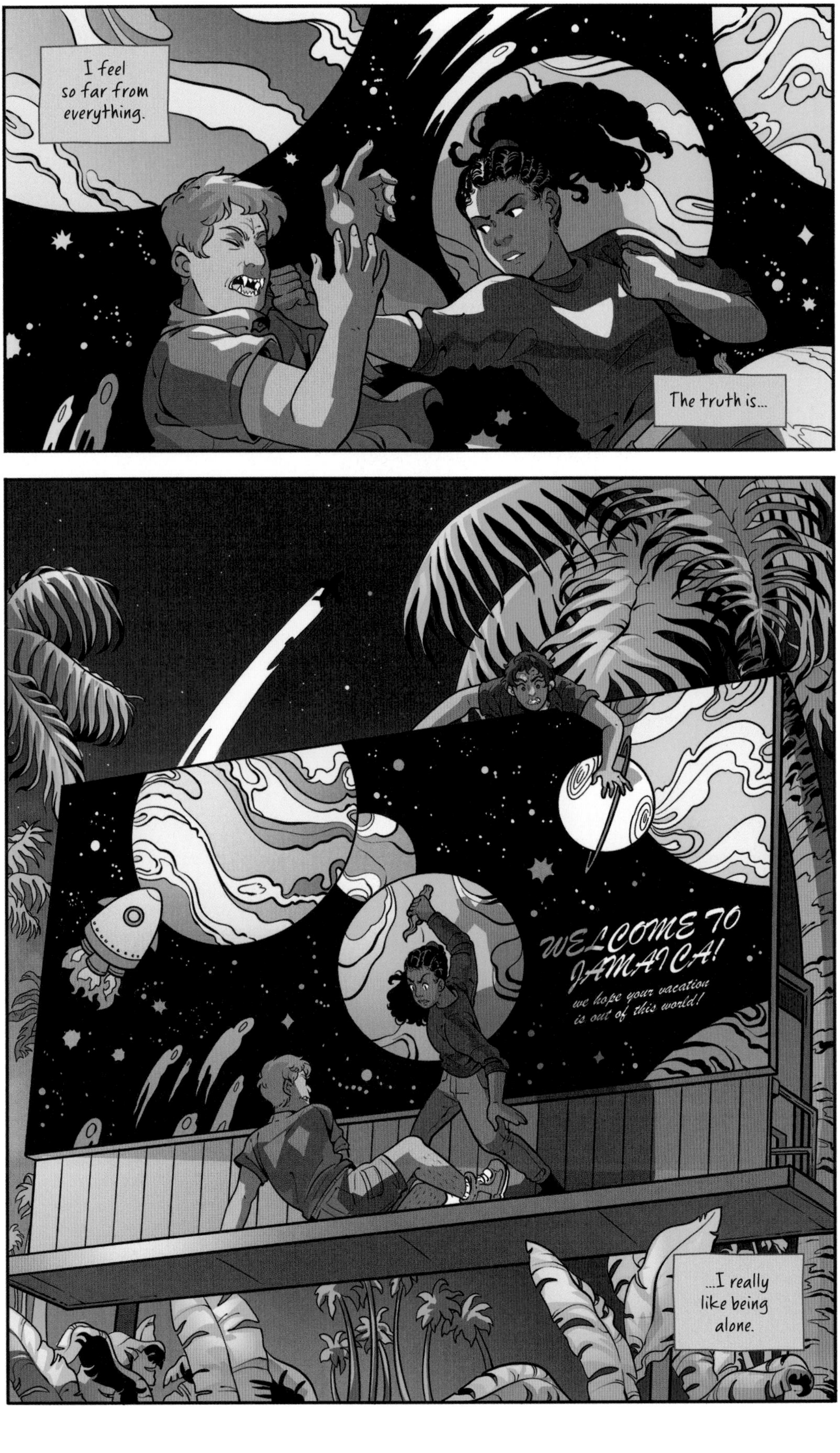
I feel so far from everything.
The truth is...
WELCOME TO JAMAICA!
we hope your vacation is out of this world!
...I really like being alone.

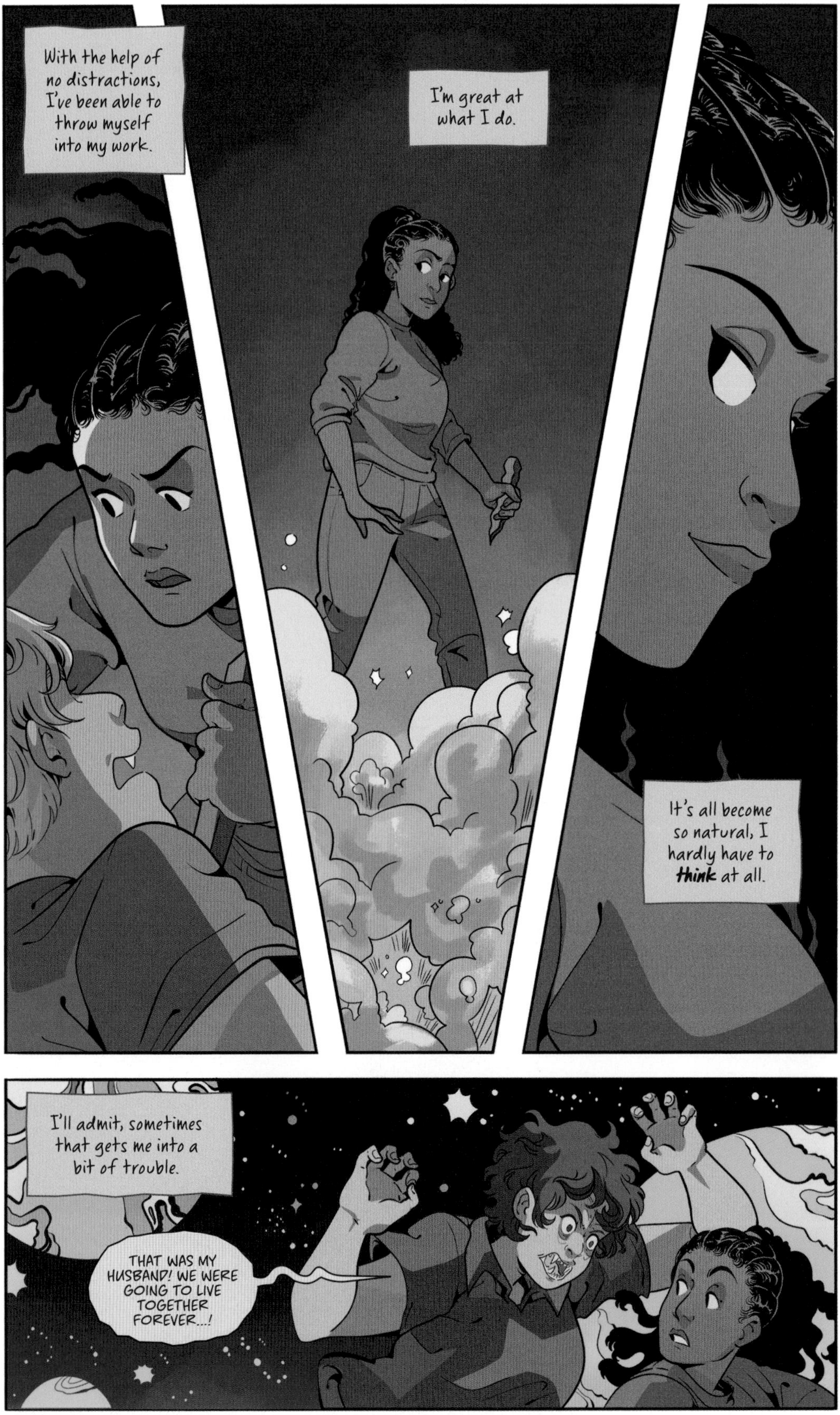
With the help of no distractions, I've been able to throw myself into my work.
I'm great at what I do.
It's all become so natural, I hardly have to **think** at all.
I'll admit, sometimes that gets me into a bit of trouble.
THAT WAS MY HUSBAND! WE WERE GOING TO LIVE TOGETHER FOREVER...!

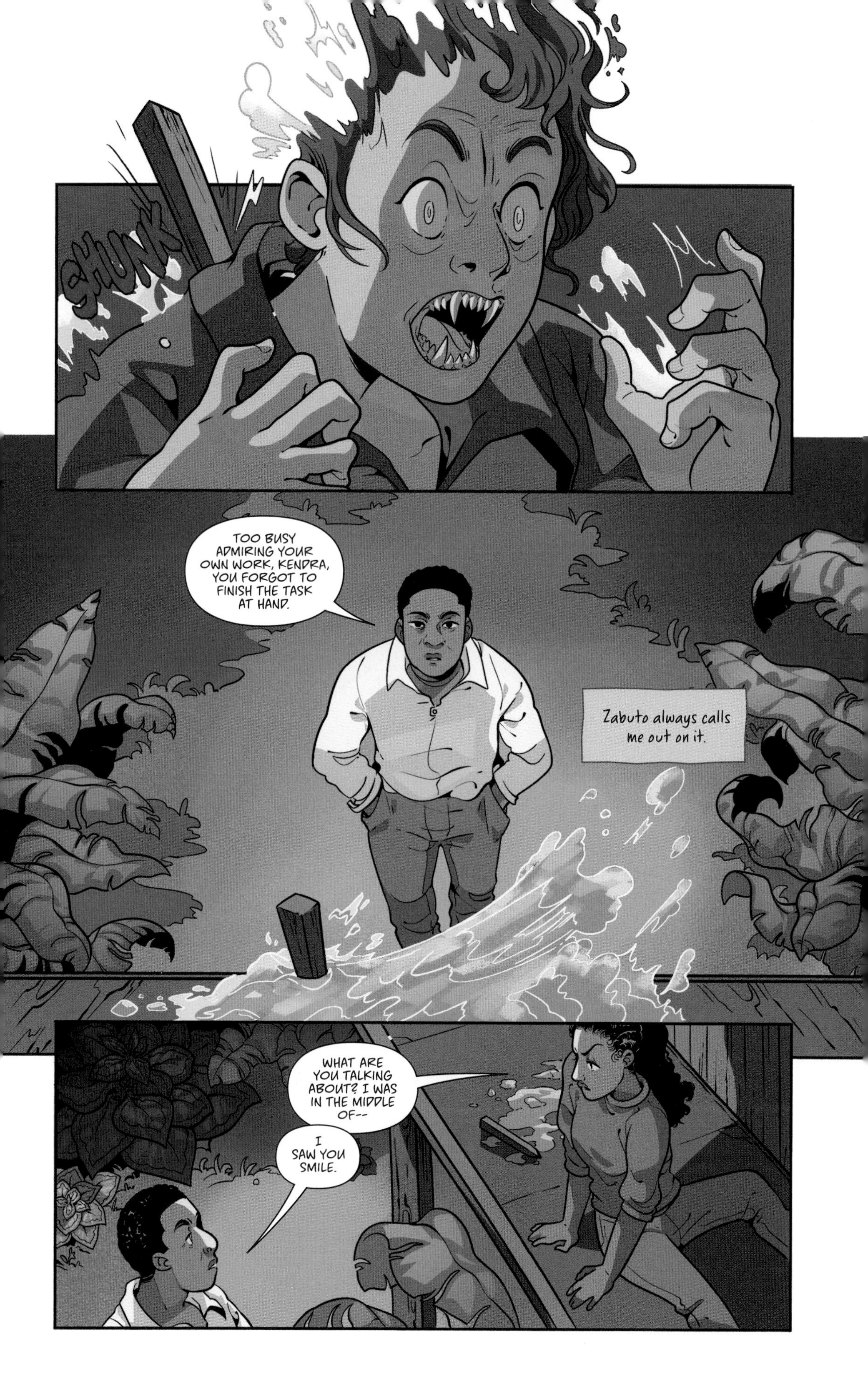
SHUNK
TOO BUSY ADMIRING YOUR OWN WORK, KENDRA, YOU FORGOT TO FINISH THE TASK AT HAND.
Zabuto always calls me out on it.
WHAT ARE YOU TALKING ABOUT? I WAS IN THE MIDDLE OF--
I SAW YOU SMILE.

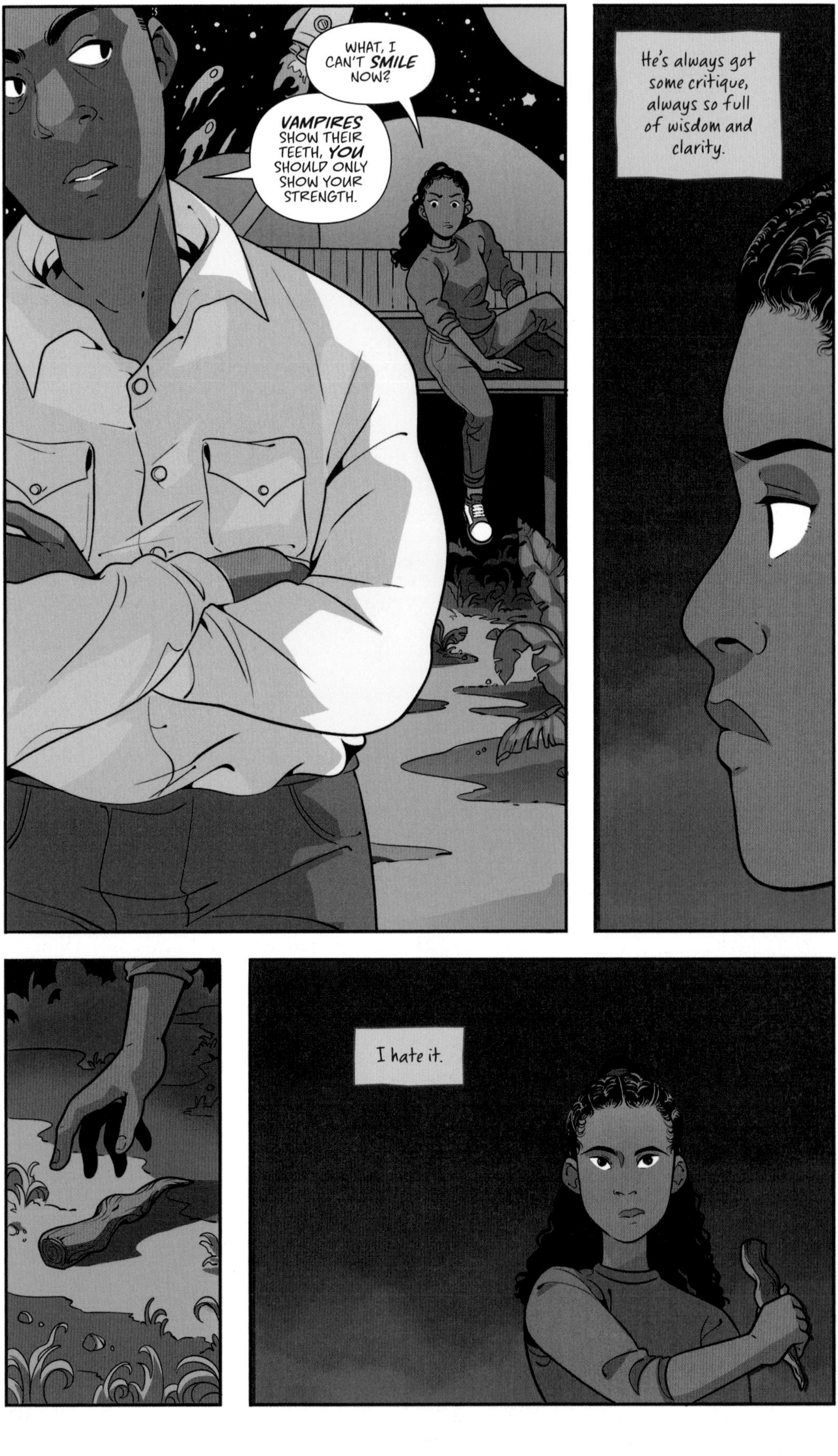
WHAT, I CAN'T SMILE NOW?
VAMPIRES SHOW THEIR TEETH, YOU SHOULD ONLY SHOW YOUR STRENGTH.
He's always got some critique, always so full of wisdom and clarity.
I hate it.

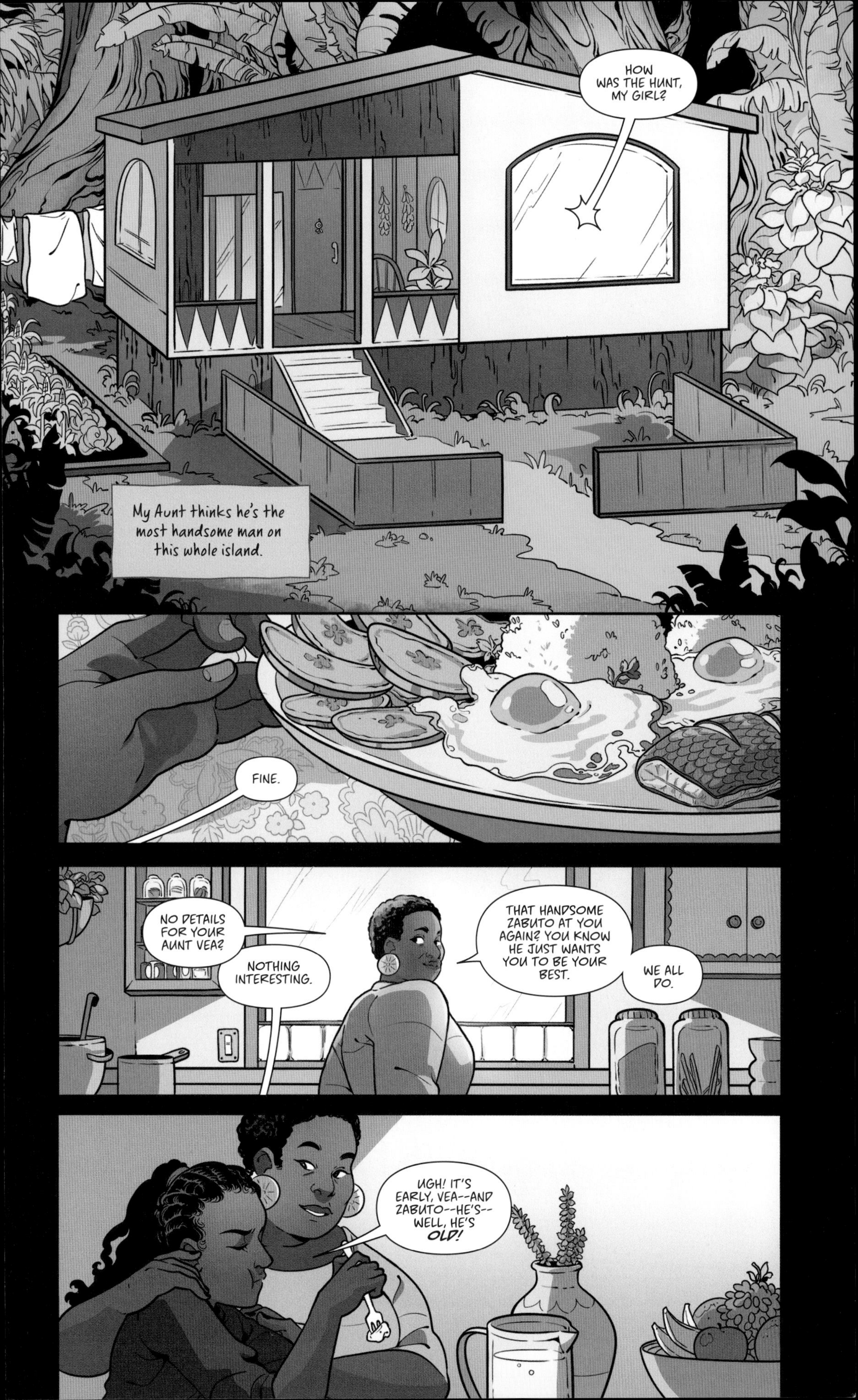
HOW WAS THE HUNT, MY GIRL?
My Aunt thinks he's the most handsome man on this whole island.
FINE.
NO DETAILS FOR YOUR AUNT VEA?
NOTHING INTERESTING.
THAT HANDSOME ZABUTO AT YOU AGAIN? YOU KNOW HE JUST WANTS YOU TO BE YOUR BEST.
WE ALL DO.
UGH! IT'S EARLY, VEA--AND ZABUTO--HE'S--WELL, HE'S OLD!

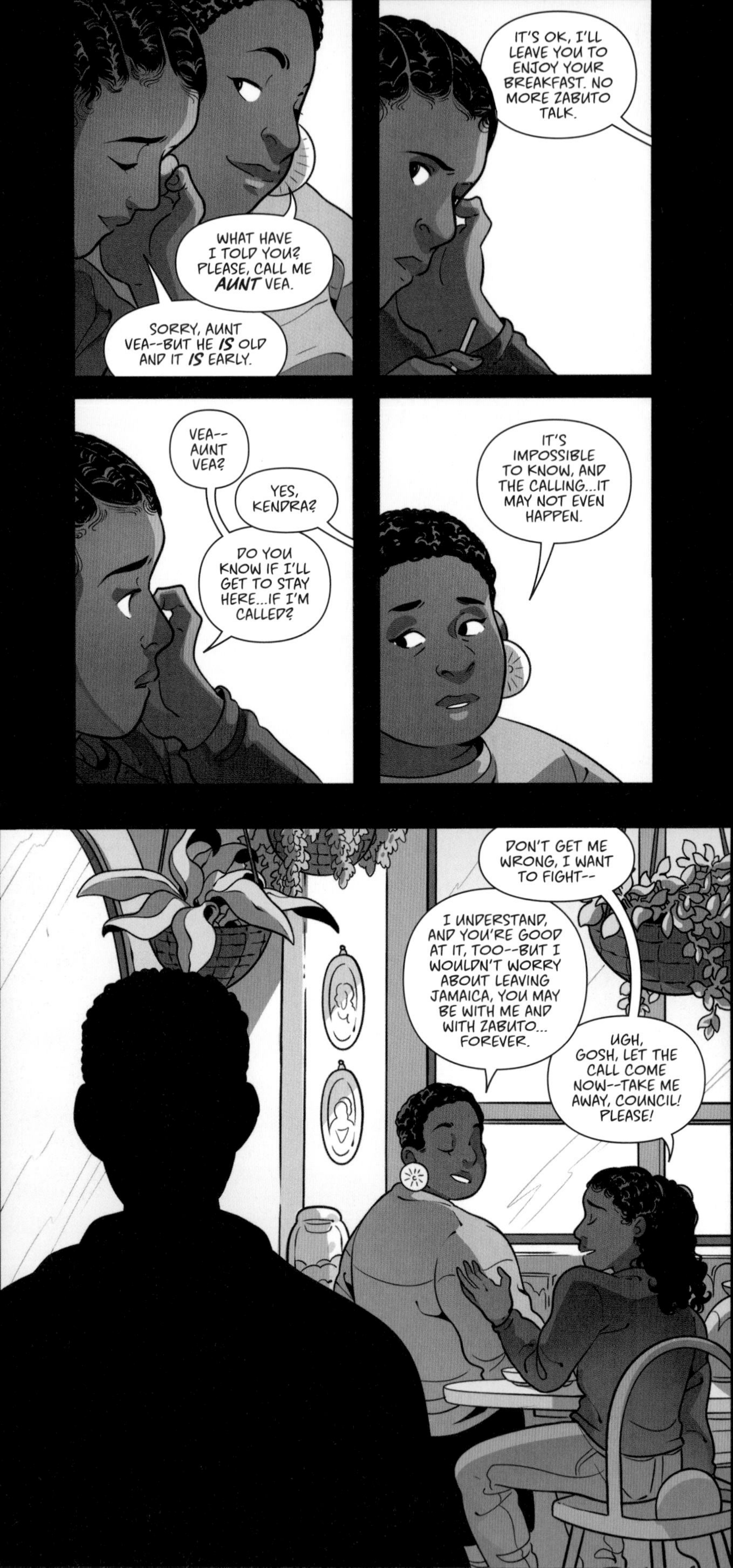
WHAT HAVE I TOLD YOU? PLEASE, CALL ME AUNT VEA.
SORRY, AUNT VEA--BUT HE IS OLD AND IT IS EARLY.
IT'S OK, I'LL LEAVE YOU TO ENJOY YOUR BREAKFAST. NO MORE ZABUTO TALK.
VEA-- AUNT VEA?
YES, KENDRA?
DO YOU KNOW IF I'LL GET TO STAY HERE...IF I'M CALLED?
IT'S IMPOSSIBLE TO KNOW, AND THE CALLING...IT MAY NOT EVEN HAPPEN.
DON'T GET ME WRONG, I WANT TO FIGHT--
I UNDERSTAND, AND YOU'RE GOOD AT IT, TOO--BUT I WOULDN'T WORRY ABOUT LEAVING JAMAICA, YOU MAY BE WITH ME AND WITH ZABUTO... FOREVER.
UGH, GOSH, LET THE CALL COME NOW--TAKE ME AWAY, COUNCIL! PLEASE!

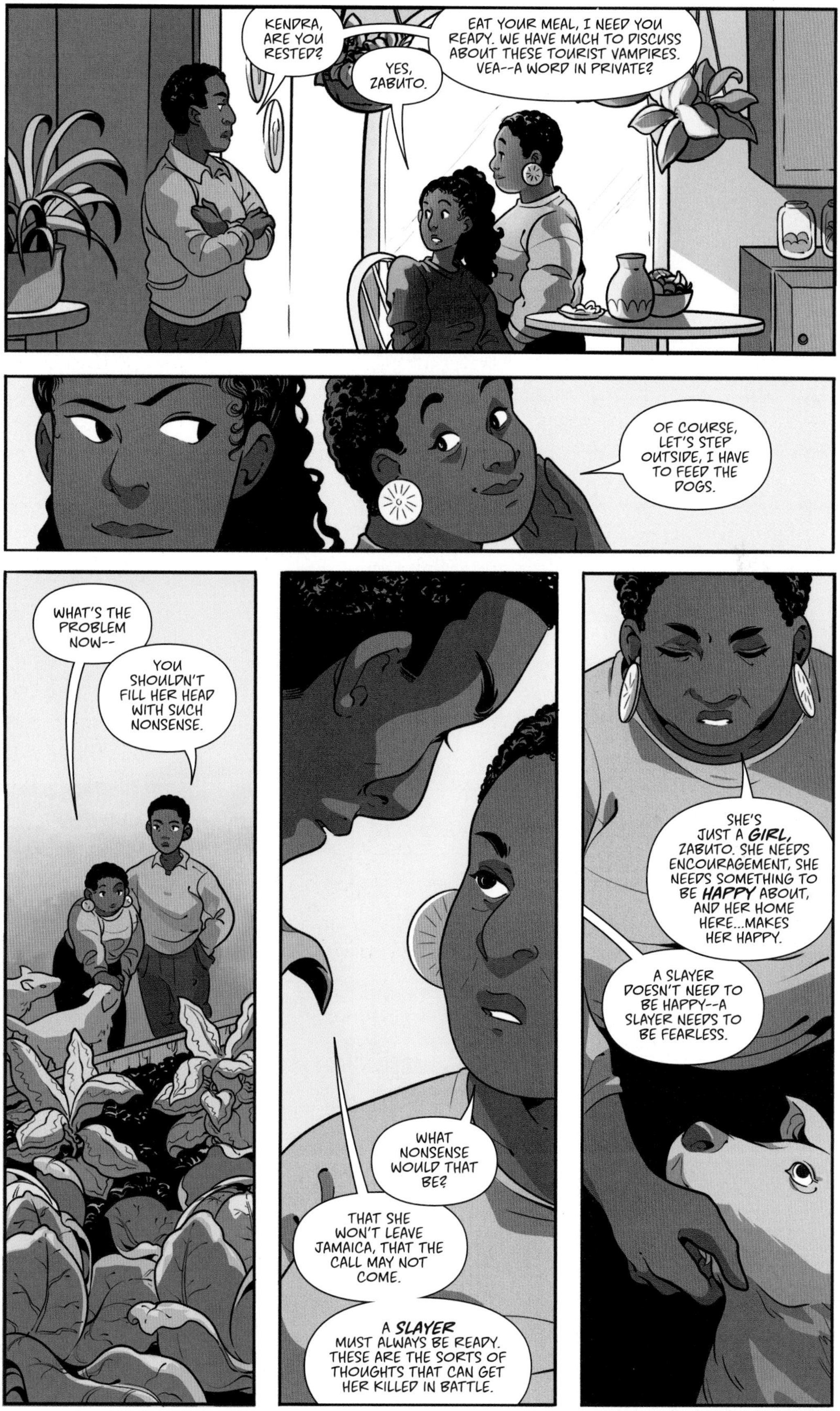
KENDRA, ARE YOU RESTED?
YES, ZABUTO.
EAT YOUR MEAL, I NEED YOU READY. WE HAVE MUCH TO DISCUSS ABOUT THESE TOURIST VAMPIRES. VEA--A WORD IN PRIVATE?
OF COURSE, LET'S STEP OUTSIDE, I HAVE TO FEED THE DOGS.
WHAT'S THE PROBLEM NOW--
YOU SHOULDN'T FILL HER HEAD WITH SUCH NONSENSE.
WHAT NONSENSE WOULD THAT BE?
THAT SHE WON'T LEAVE JAMAICA, THAT THE CALL MAY NOT COME.
A SLAYER MUST ALWAYS BE READY. THESE ARE THE SORTS OF THOUGHTS THAT CAN GET HER KILLED IN BATTLE.
SHE'S JUST A GIRL, ZABUTO. SHE NEEDS ENCOURAGEMENT, SHE NEEDS SOMETHING TO BE HAPPY ABOUT, AND HER HOME HERE...MAKES HER HAPPY.
A SLAYER DOESN'T NEED TO BE HAPPY--A SLAYER NEEDS TO BE FEARLESS.

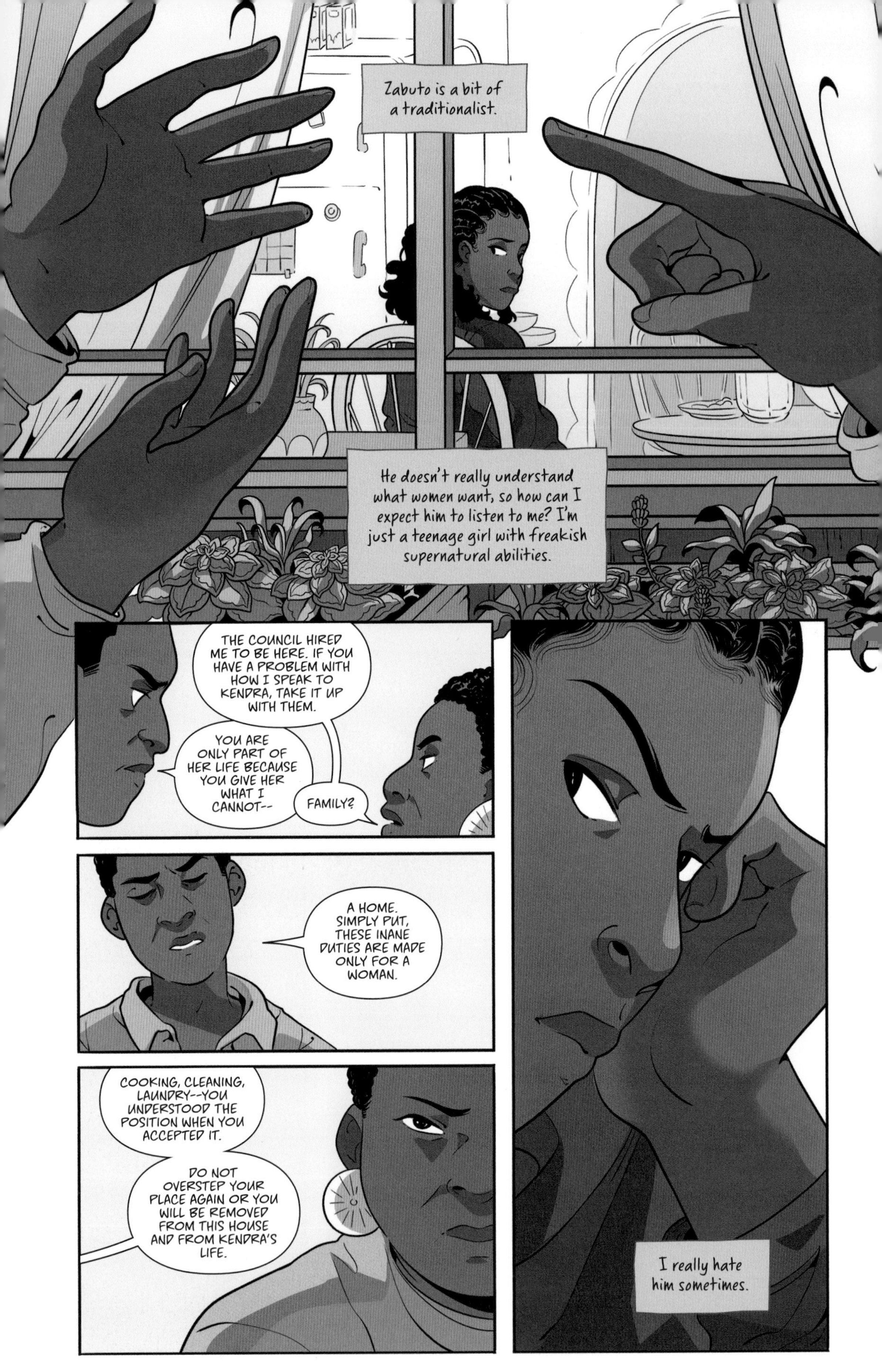
Zabuto is a bit of a traditionalist.
He doesn't really understand what women want, so how can I expect him to listen to me? I'm just a teenage girl with freakish supernatural abilities.
THE COUNCIL HIRED ME TO BE HERE. IF YOU HAVE A PROBLEM WITH HOW I SPEAK TO KENDRA, TAKE IT UP WITH THEM.
YOU ARE ONLY PART OF HER LIFE BECAUSE YOU GIVE HER WHAT I CANNOT--
FAMILY?
A HOME. SIMPLY PUT, THESE INANE DUTIES ARE MADE ONLY FOR A WOMAN.
COOKING, CLEANING, LAUNDRY--YOU UNDERSTOOD THE POSITION WHEN YOU ACCEPTED IT.
DO NOT OVERSTEP YOUR PLACE AGAIN OR YOU WILL BE REMOVED FROM THIS HOUSE AND FROM KENDRA'S LIFE.
I really hate him sometimes.

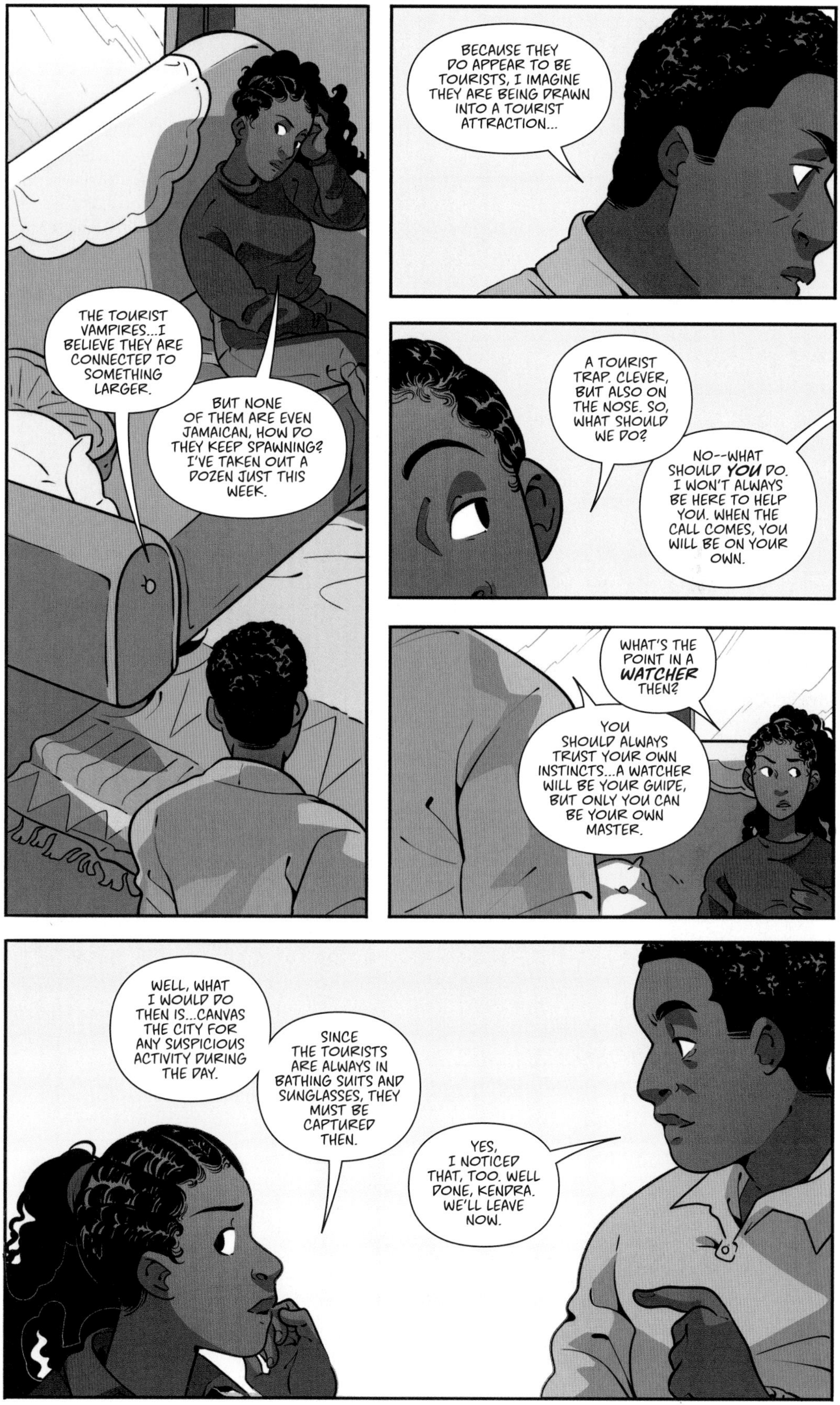
THE TOURIST VAMPIRES...I BELIEVE THEY ARE CONNECTED TO SOMETHING LARGER.
BUT NONE OF THEM ARE EVEN JAMAICAN, HOW DO THEY KEEP SPAWNING? I'VE TAKEN OUT A DOZEN JUST THIS WEEK.
BECAUSE THEY DO APPEAR TO BE TOURISTS, I IMAGINE THEY ARE BEING DRAWN INTO A TOURIST ATTRACTION...
A TOURIST TRAP. CLEVER, BUT ALSO ON THE NOSE. SO, WHAT SHOULD WE DO?
NO--WHAT SHOULD *YOU* DO. I WON'T ALWAYS BE HERE TO HELP YOU. WHEN THE CALL COMES, YOU WILL BE ON YOUR OWN.
WHAT'S THE POINT IN A ***WATCHER*** THEN?
YOU SHOULD ALWAYS TRUST YOUR OWN INSTINCTS...A WATCHER WILL BE YOUR GUIDE, BUT ONLY YOU CAN BE YOUR OWN MASTER.
WELL, WHAT I WOULD DO THEN IS...CANVAS THE CITY FOR ANY SUSPICIOUS ACTIVITY DURING THE DAY.
SINCE THE TOURISTS ARE ALWAYS IN BATHING SUITS AND SUNGLASSES, THEY MUST BE CAPTURED THEN.
YES, I NOTICED THAT, TOO. WELL DONE, KENDRA. WE'LL LEAVE NOW.

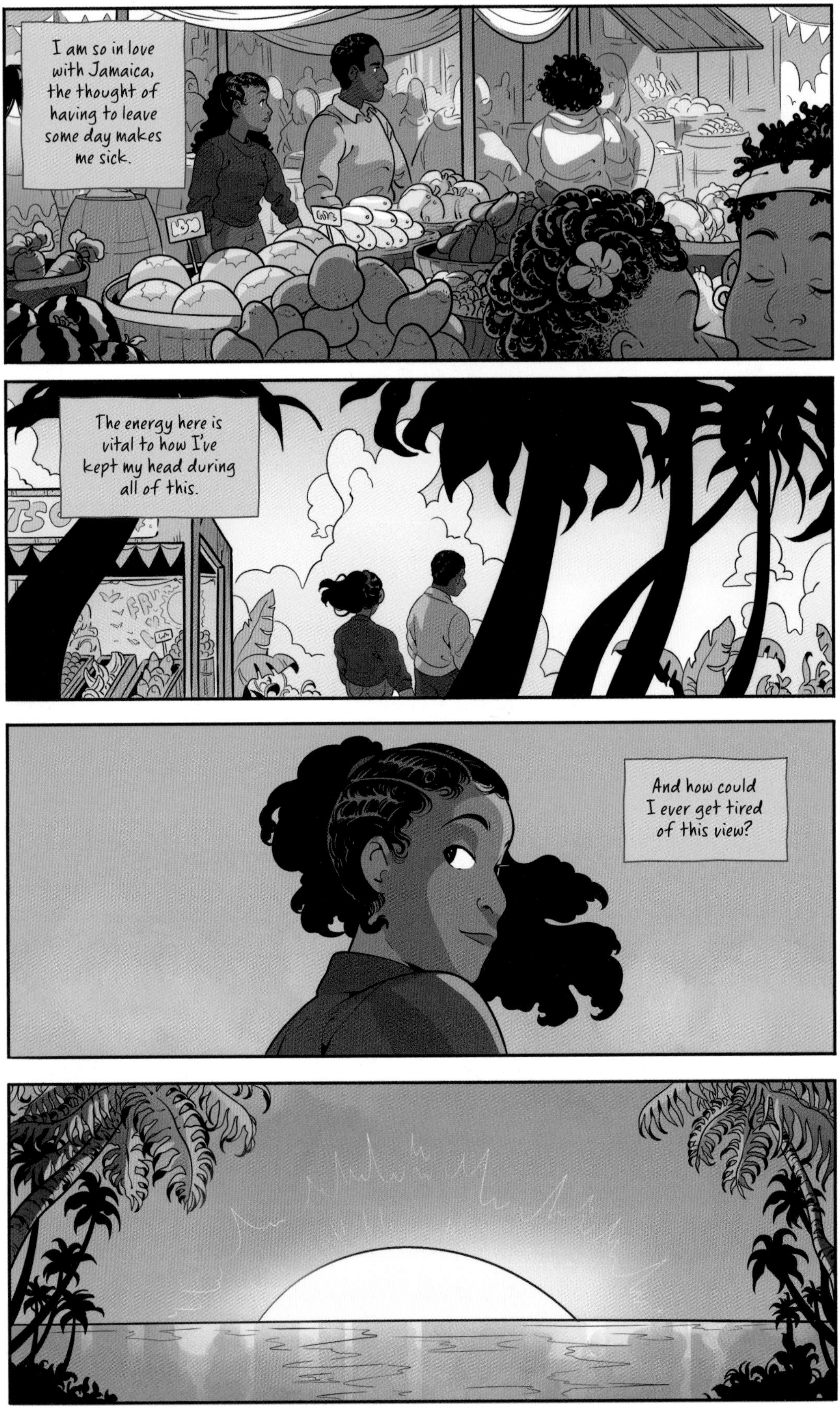
I am so in love with Jamaica, the thought of having to leave some day makes me sick.
The energy here is vital to how I've kept my head during all of this.
And how could I ever get tired of this view?

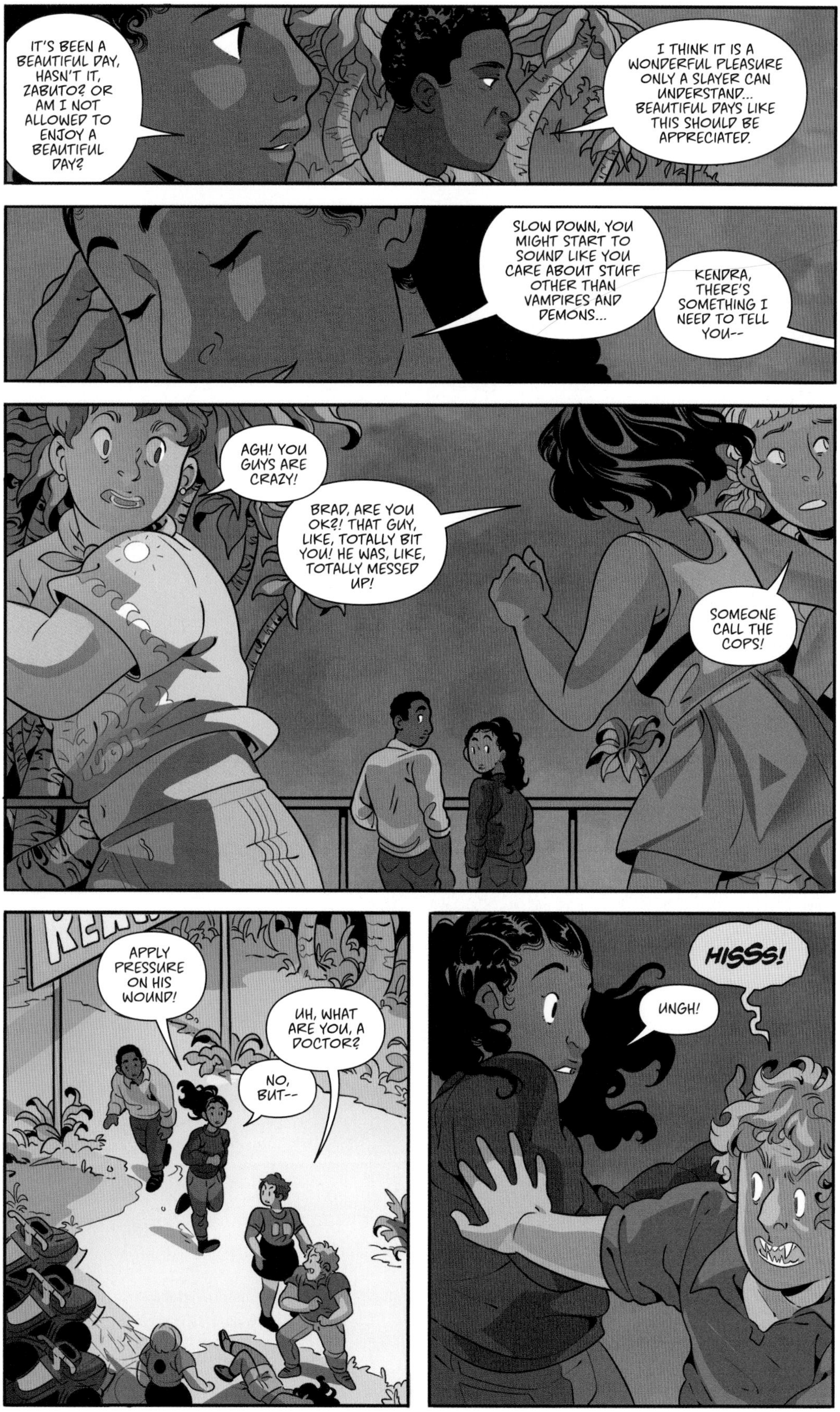

IT'S BEEN A BEAUTIFUL DAY, HASN'T IT, ZABUTO? OR AM I NOT ALLOWED TO ENJOY A BEAUTIFUL DAY?
I THINK IT IS A WONDERFUL PLEASURE ONLY A SLAYER CAN UNDERSTAND... BEAUTIFUL DAYS LIKE THIS SHOULD BE APPRECIATED.
SLOW DOWN, YOU MIGHT START TO SOUND LIKE YOU CARE ABOUT STUFF OTHER THAN VAMPIRES AND DEMONS...
KENDRA, THERE'S SOMETHING I NEED TO TELL YOU--
AGH! YOU GUYS ARE CRAZY!
BRAD, ARE YOU OK?! THAT GUY, LIKE, TOTALLY BIT YOU! HE WAS, LIKE, TOTALLY MESSED UP!
SOMEONE CALL THE COPS!
APPLY PRESSURE ON HIS WOUND!
UH, WHAT ARE YOU, A DOCTOR?
NO, BUT--
HISSS!
UNGH!

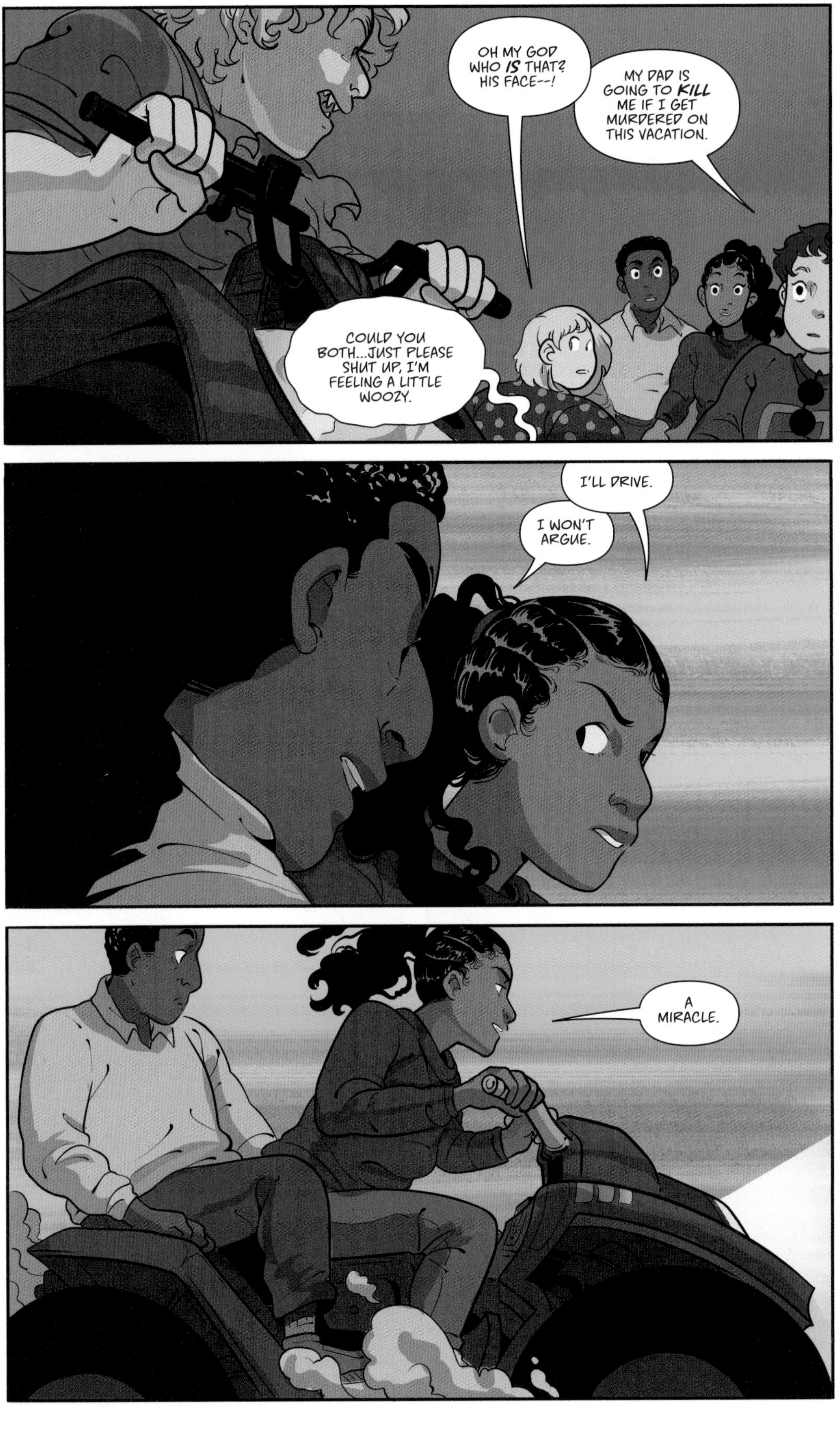
OH MY GOD WHO *IS* THAT? HIS FACE--!
MY DAD IS GOING TO **KILL** ME IF I GET MURDERED ON THIS VACATION.
COULD YOU BOTH...JUST PLEASE SHUT UP, I'M FEELING A LITTLE WOOZY.
I'LL DRIVE.
I WON'T ARGUE.
A MIRACLE.

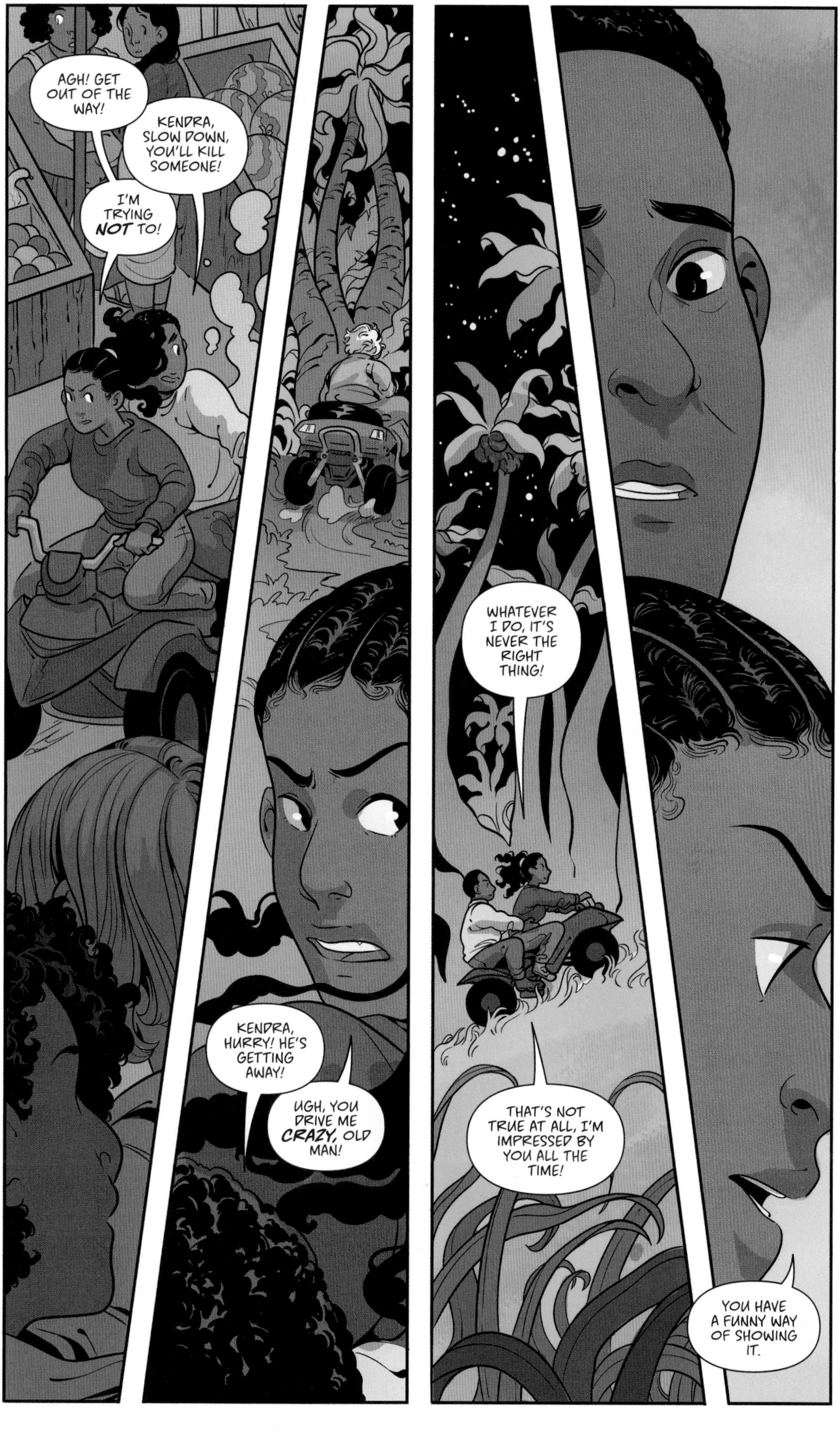
AGH! GET OUT OF THE WAY!
KENDRA, SLOW DOWN, YOU'LL KILL SOMEONE!
I'M TRYING NOT TO!
KENDRA, HURRY! HE'S GETTING AWAY!
UGH, YOU DRIVE ME CRAZY, OLD MAN!
WHATEVER I DO, IT'S NEVER THE RIGHT THING!
THAT'S NOT TRUE AT ALL, I'M IMPRESSED BY YOU ALL THE TIME!
YOU HAVE A FUNNY WAY OF SHOWING IT.

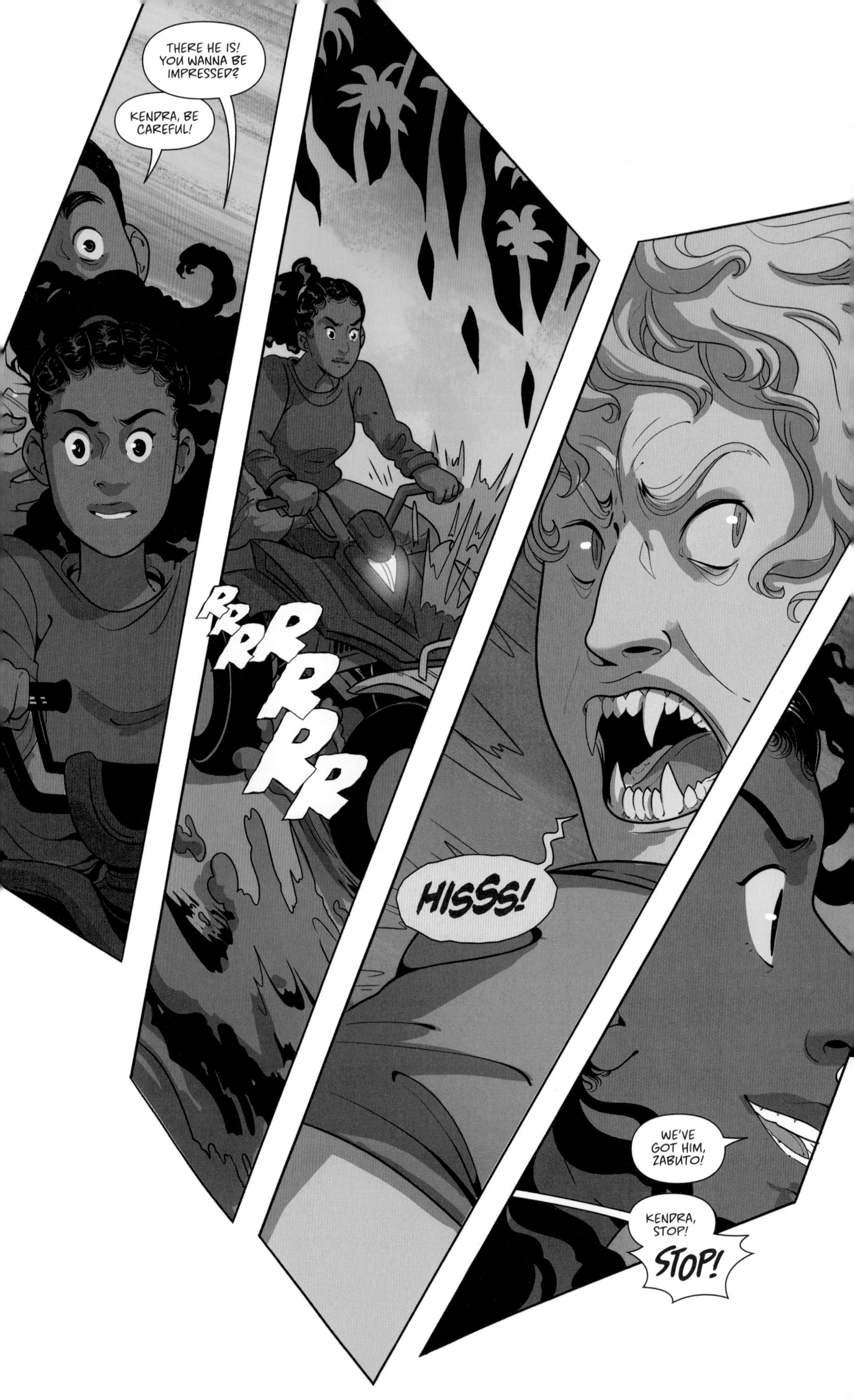
THERE HE IS! YOU WANNA BE IMPRESSED?
KENDRA, BE CAREFUL!
RRRRRRRR
HISSS!
WE'VE GOT HIM, ZABUTO!
KENDRA, STOP!
STOP!

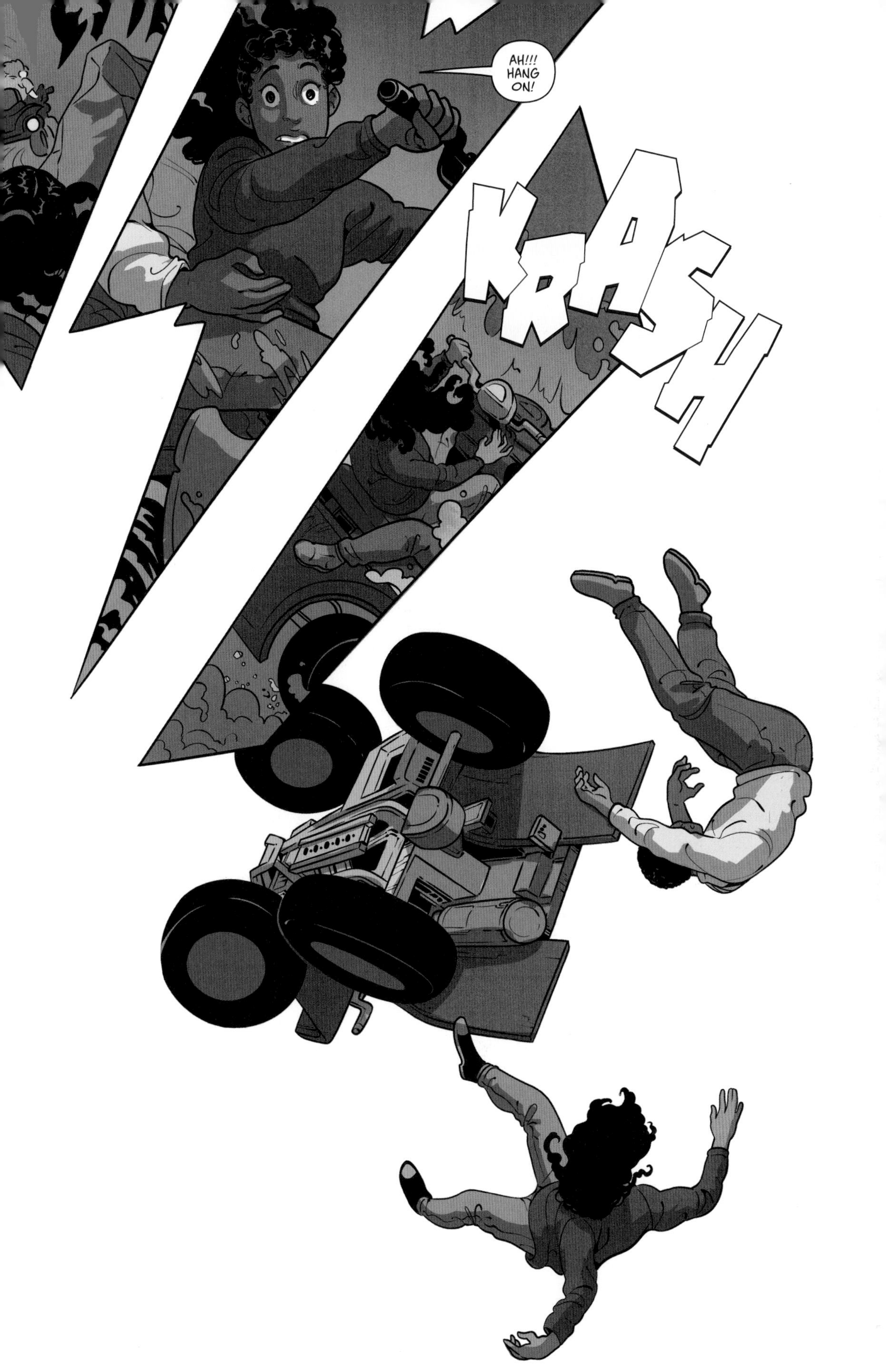
AH!!! HANG ON!
KRASH

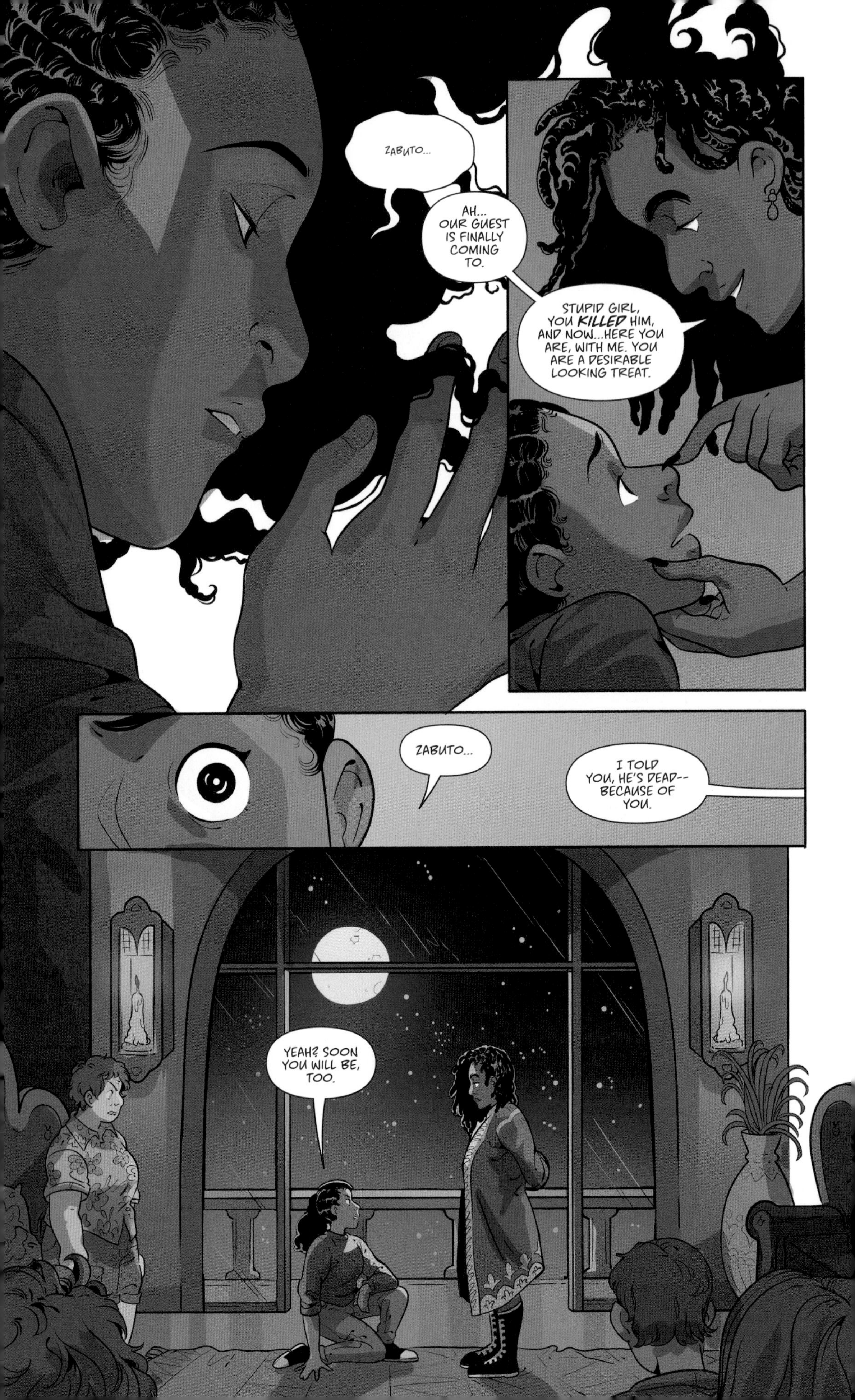
ZABUTO...
AH... OUR GUEST IS FINALLY COMING TO.
STUPID GIRL, YOU KILLED HIM, AND NOW...HERE YOU ARE, WITH ME. YOU ARE A DESIRABLE LOOKING TREAT.
ZABUTO...
I TOLD YOU, HE'S DEAD--BECAUSE OF YOU.
YEAH? SOON YOU WILL BE, TOO.

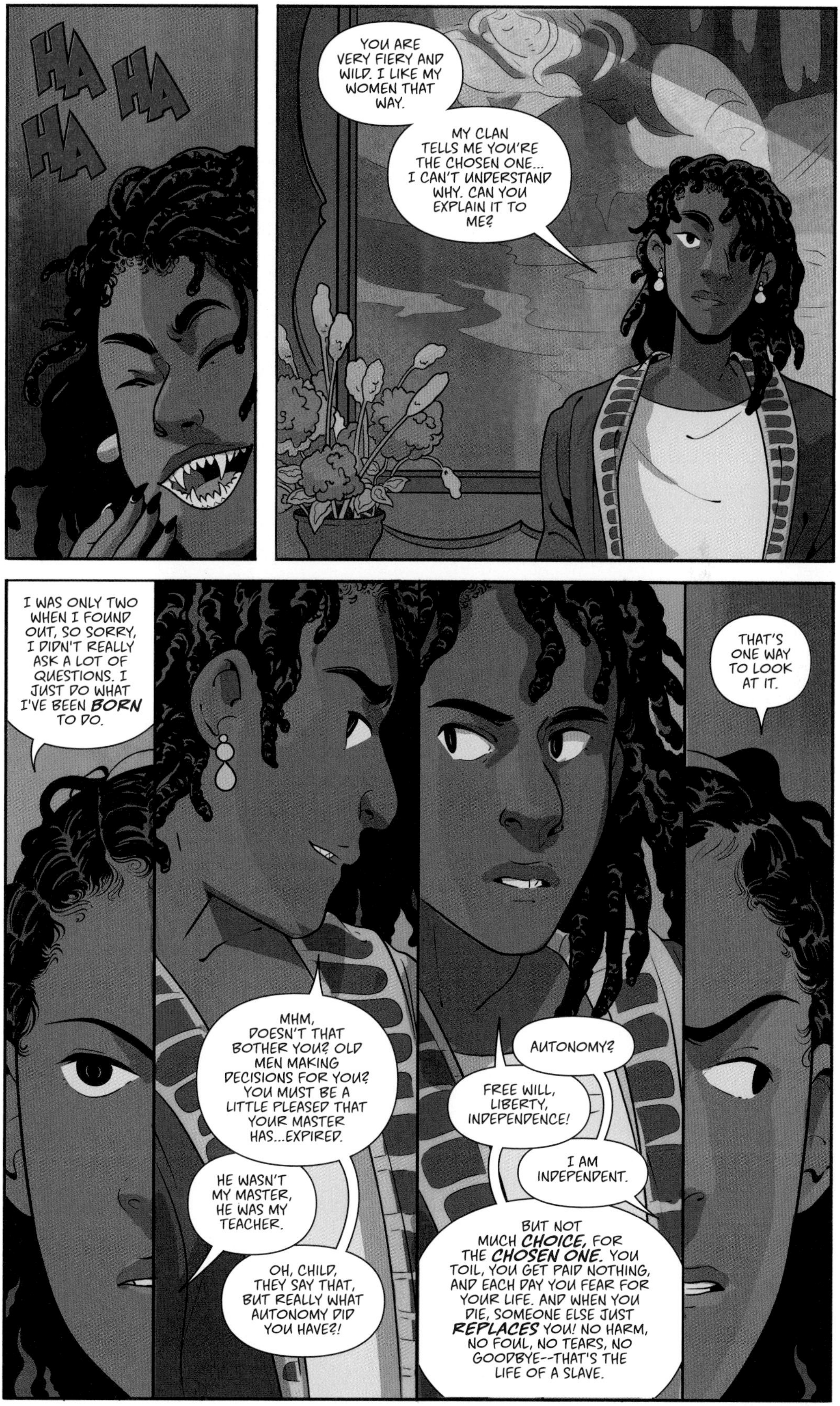
HA HA HA HA
YOU ARE VERY FIERY AND WILD. I LIKE MY WOMEN THAT WAY.
MY CLAN TELLS ME YOU'RE THE CHOSEN ONE... I CAN'T UNDERSTAND WHY. CAN YOU EXPLAIN IT TO ME?
I WAS ONLY TWO WHEN I FOUND OUT, SO SORRY, I DIDN'T REALLY ASK A LOT OF QUESTIONS. I JUST DO WHAT I'VE BEEN **BORN** TO DO.
THAT'S ONE WAY TO LOOK AT IT.
MHM, DOESN'T THAT BOTHER YOU? OLD MEN MAKING DECISIONS FOR YOU? YOU MUST BE A LITTLE PLEASED THAT YOUR MASTER HAS...EXPIRED.
HE WASN'T MY MASTER, HE WAS MY TEACHER.
OH, CHILD, THEY SAY THAT, BUT REALLY WHAT AUTONOMY DID YOU HAVE?!
AUTONOMY?
FREE WILL, LIBERTY, INDEPENDENCE!
I AM INDEPENDENT.
BUT NOT MUCH **CHOICE,** FOR THE **CHOSEN ONE.** YOU TOIL, YOU GET PAID NOTHING, AND EACH DAY YOU FEAR FOR YOUR LIFE. AND WHEN YOU DIE, SOMEONE ELSE JUST **REPLACES** YOU! NO HARM, NO FOUL, NO TEARS, NO GOODBYE--THAT'S THE LIFE OF A SLAVE.

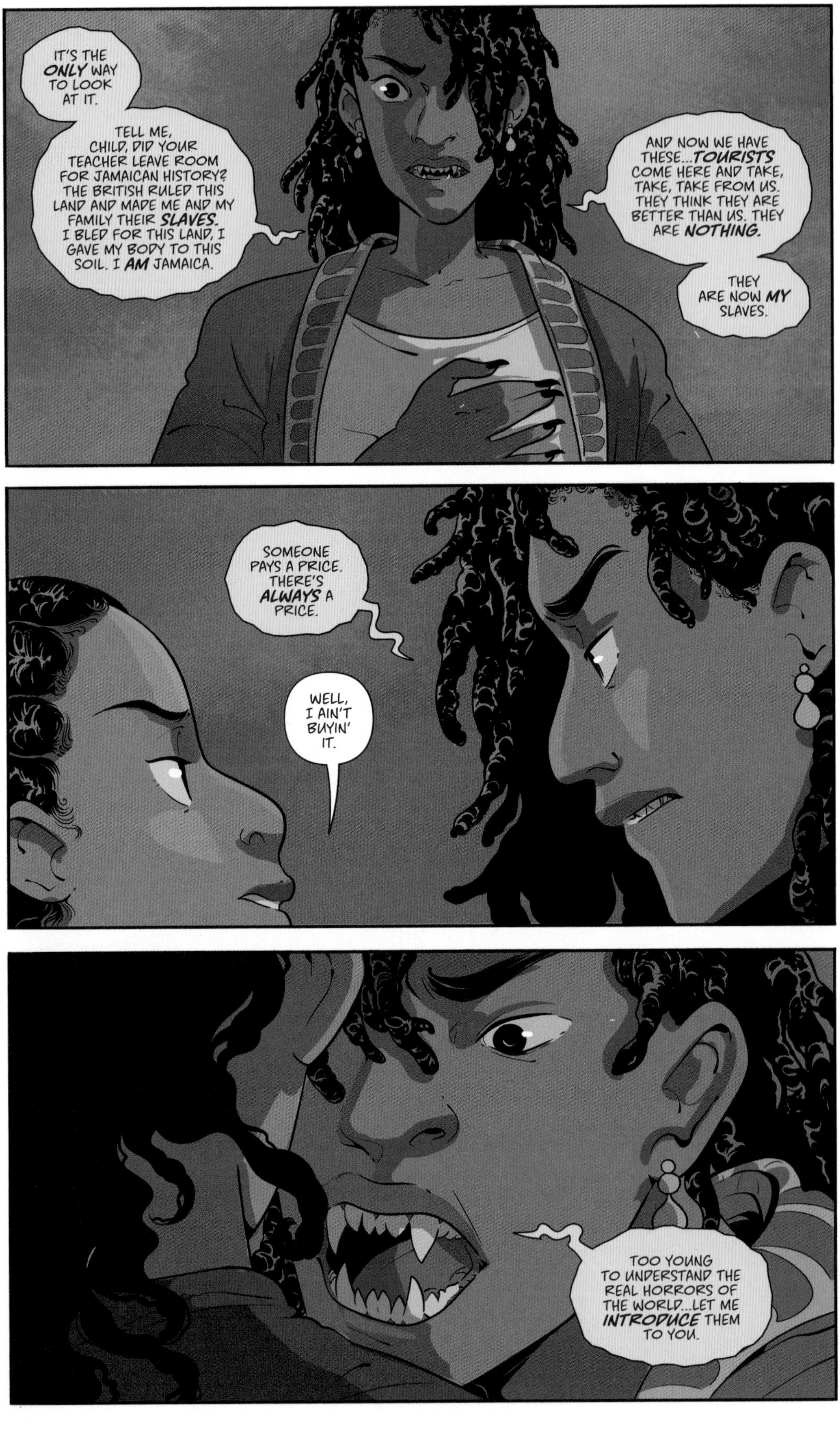
IT'S THE ONLY WAY TO LOOK AT IT.
TELL ME, CHILD, DID YOUR TEACHER LEAVE ROOM FOR JAMAICAN HISTORY? THE BRITISH RULED THIS LAND AND MADE ME AND MY FAMILY THEIR SLAVES. I BLED FOR THIS LAND, I GAVE MY BODY TO THIS SOIL. I AM JAMAICA.
AND NOW WE HAVE THESE...TOURISTS COME HERE AND TAKE, TAKE, TAKE FROM US. THEY THINK THEY ARE BETTER THAN US. THEY ARE NOTHING.
THEY ARE NOW MY SLAVES.
SOMEONE PAYS A PRICE. THERE'S ALWAYS A PRICE.
WELL, I AIN'T BUYIN' IT.
TOO YOUNG TO UNDERSTAND THE REAL HORRORS OF THE WORLD...LET ME INTRODUCE THEM TO YOU.

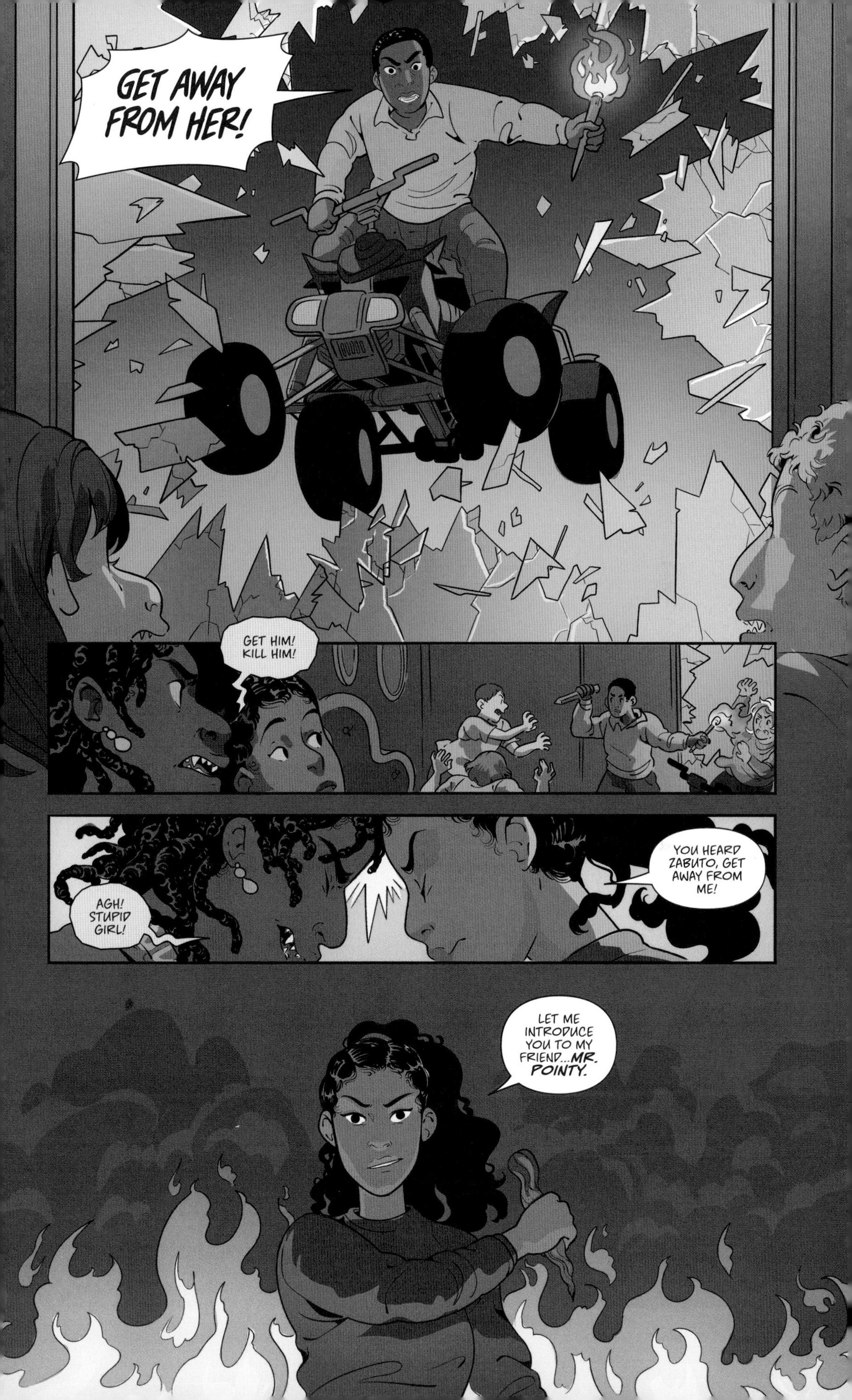

GET AWAY FROM HER!
GET HIM! KILL HIM!
YOU HEARD ZABUTO, GET AWAY FROM ME!
AGH! STUPID GIRL!
LET ME INTRODUCE YOU TO MY FRIEND...**MR. POINTY.**

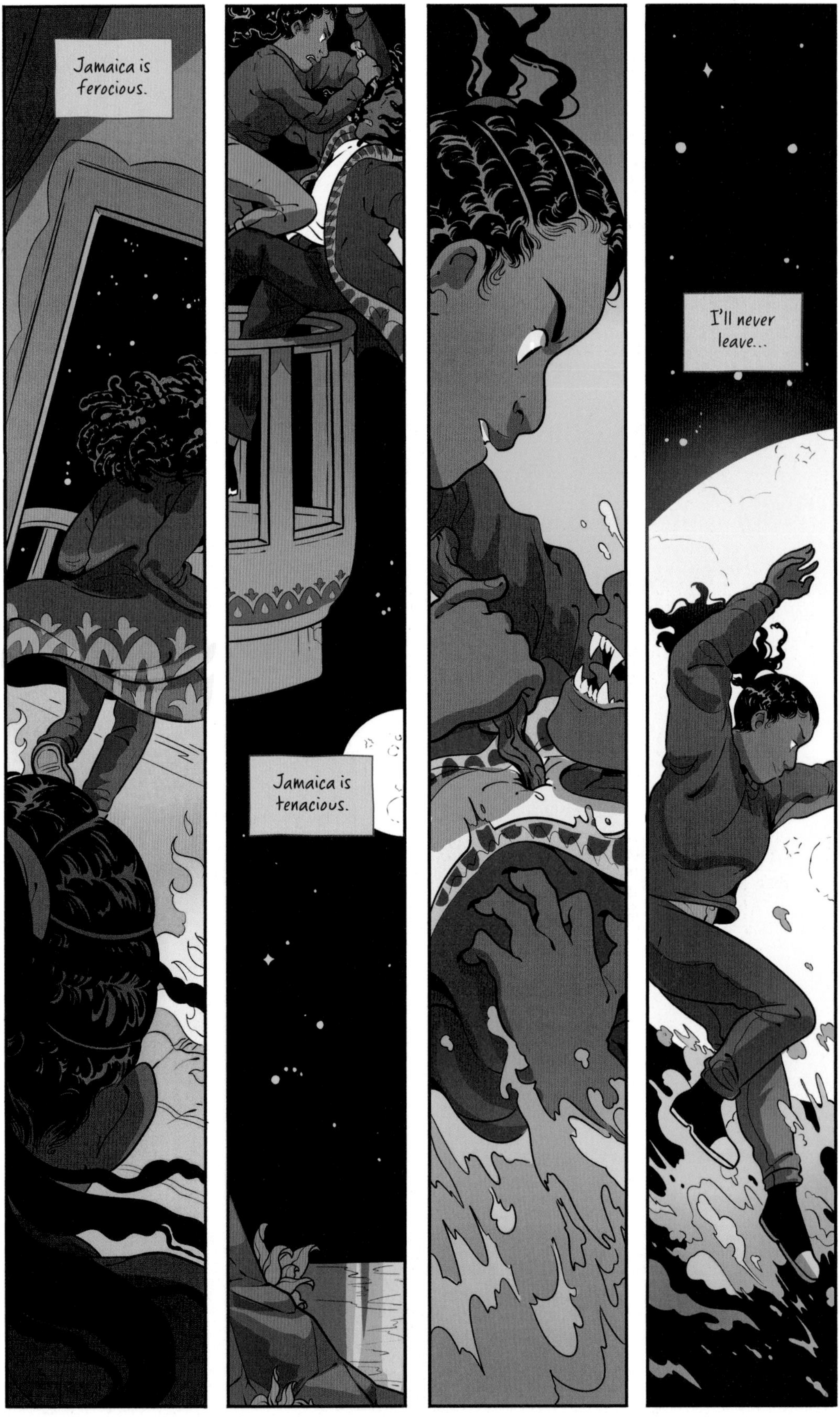
Jamaica is ferocious.
Jamaica is tenacious.
I'll never leave...

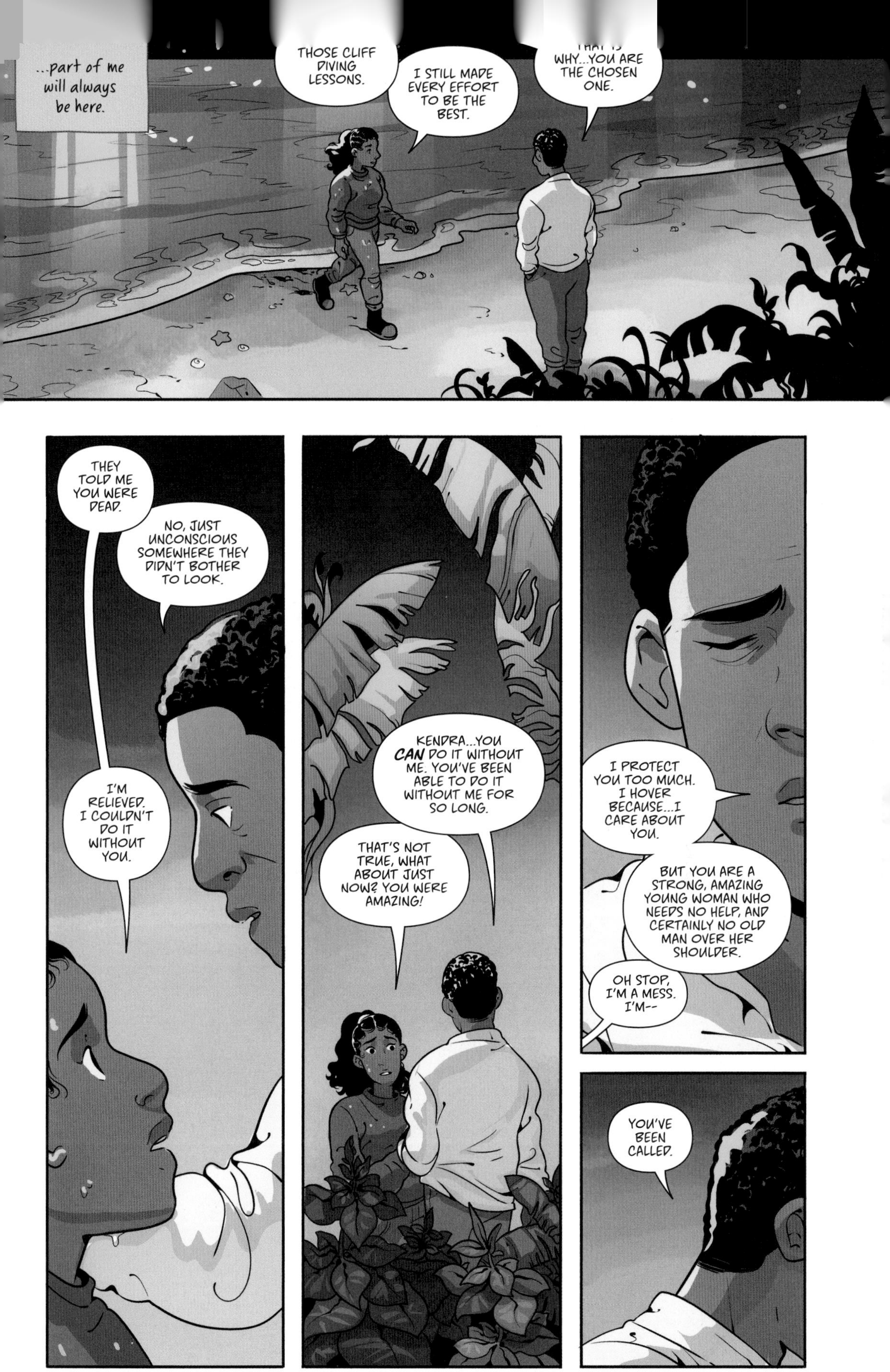
...part of me will always be here.
THOSE CLIFF DIVING LESSONS.
I STILL MADE EVERY EFFORT TO BE THE BEST.
WHY...YOU ARE THE CHOSEN ONE.
THEY TOLD ME YOU WERE DEAD.
NO, JUST UNCONSCIOUS SOMEWHERE THEY DIDN'T BOTHER TO LOOK.
I'M RELIEVED. I COULDN'T DO IT WITHOUT YOU.
KENDRA...YOU **CAN** DO IT WITHOUT ME. YOU'VE BEEN ABLE TO DO IT WITHOUT ME FOR SO LONG.
THAT'S NOT TRUE, WHAT ABOUT JUST NOW? YOU WERE AMAZING!
I PROTECT YOU TOO MUCH. I HOVER BECAUSE...I CARE ABOUT YOU.
BUT YOU ARE A STRONG, AMAZING YOUNG WOMAN WHO NEEDS NO HELP, AND CERTAINLY NO OLD MAN OVER HER SHOULDER.
OH STOP, I'M A MESS. I'M--
YOU'VE BEEN CALLED.

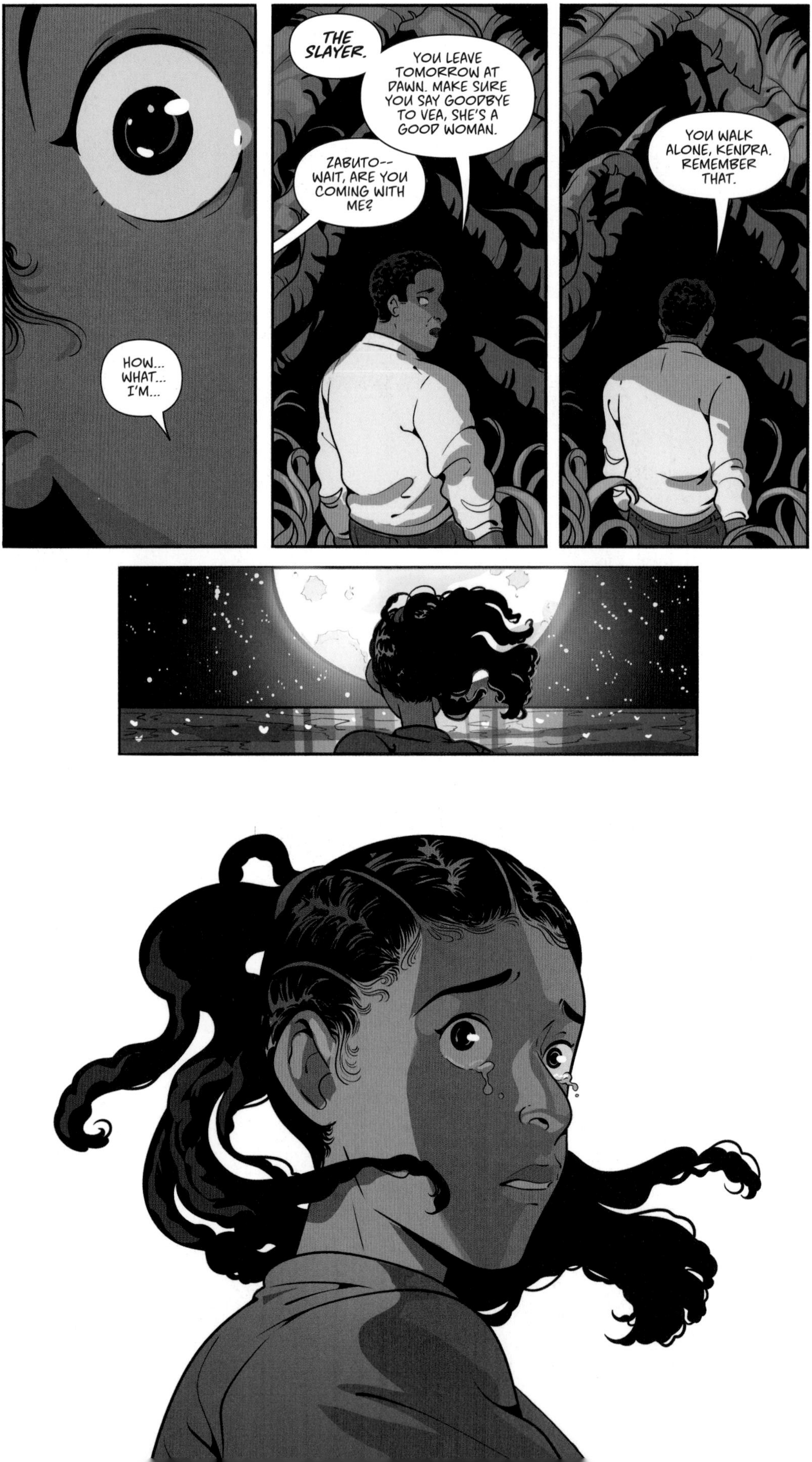
HOW... WHAT... I'M...
THE SLAYER.
YOU LEAVE TOMORROW AT DAWN. MAKE SURE YOU SAY GOODBYE TO VEA, SHE'S A GOOD WOMAN.
ZABUTO-- WAIT, ARE YOU COMING WITH ME?
YOU WALK ALONE, KENDRA. REMEMBER THAT.

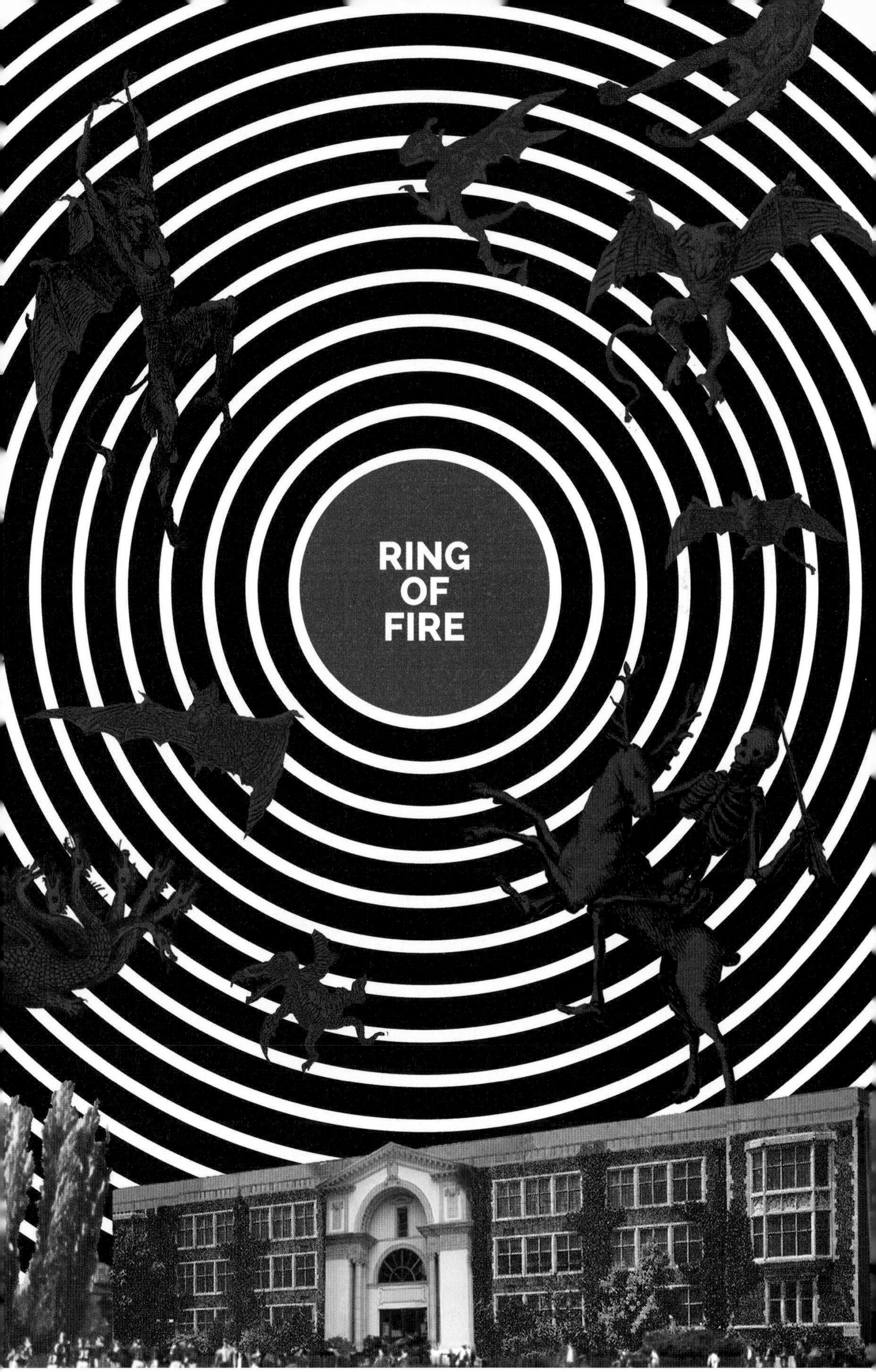
RING
OF
FIRE

Issue Thirteen Ring of Fire Cover by **Becca Carey**

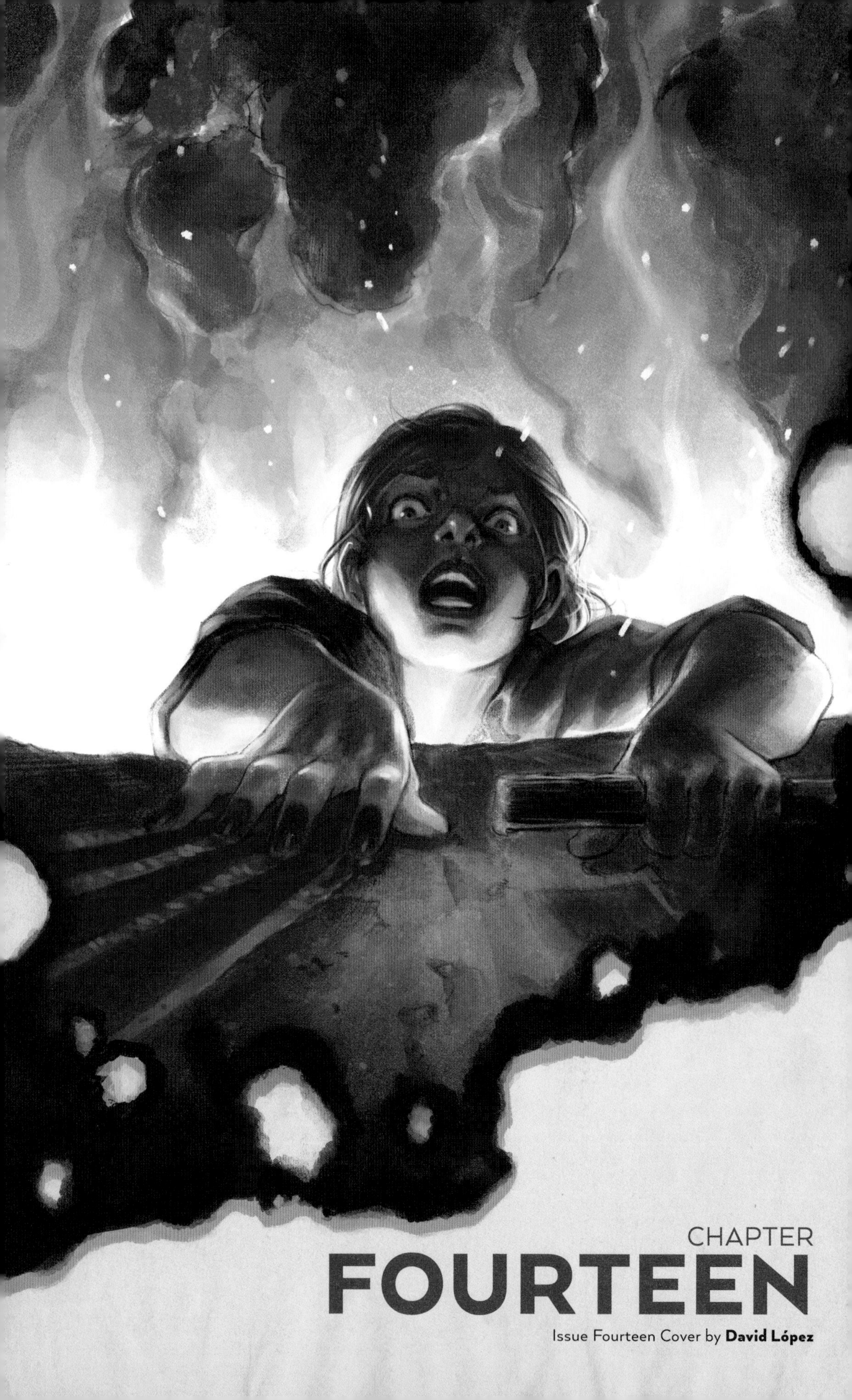

CHAPTER
FOURTEEN

Issue Fourteen Cover by **David López**

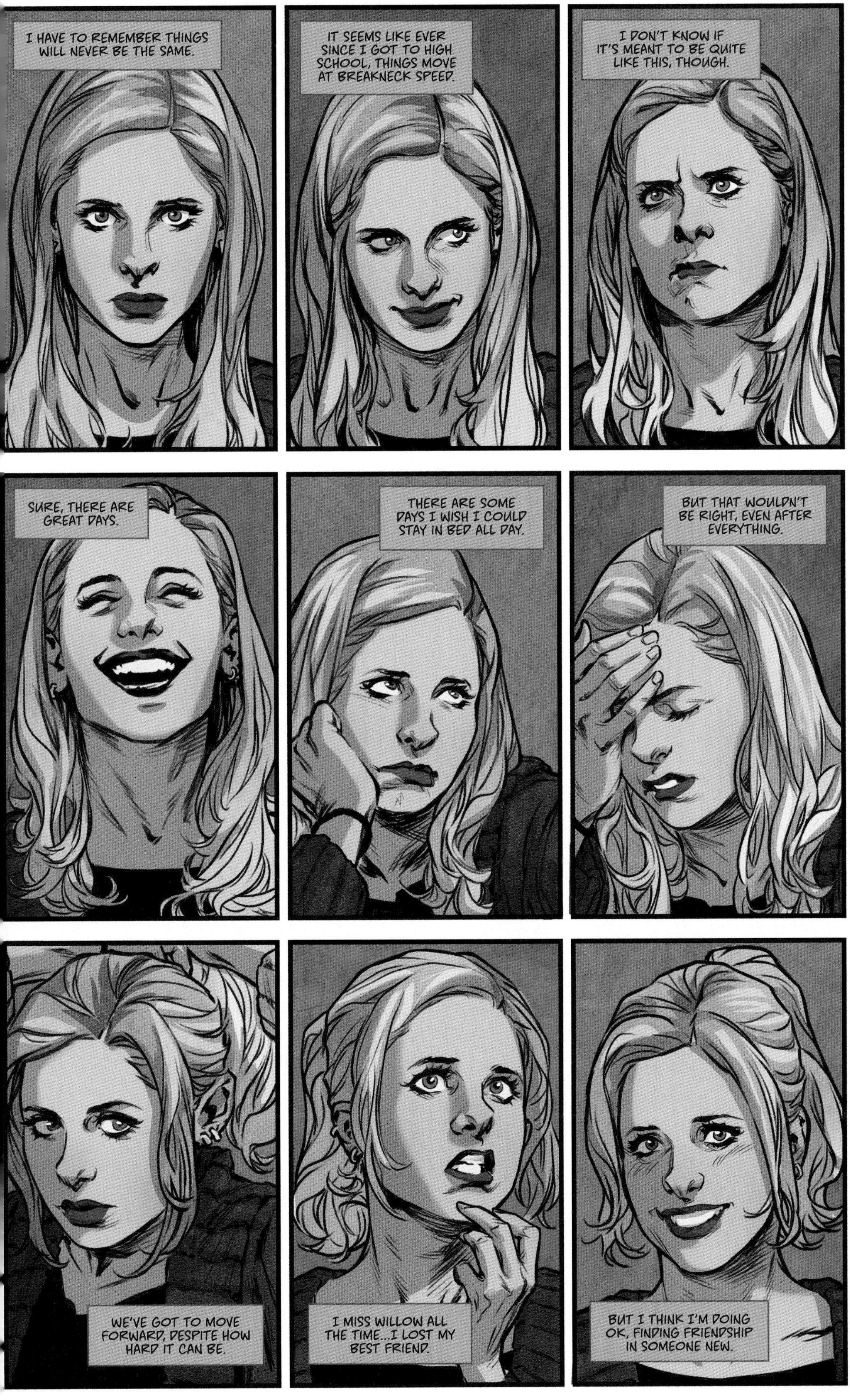
I HAVE TO REMEMBER THINGS WILL NEVER BE THE SAME.
IT SEEMS LIKE EVER SINCE I GOT TO HIGH SCHOOL, THINGS MOVE AT BREAKNECK SPEED.
I DON'T KNOW IF IT'S MEANT TO BE QUITE LIKE THIS, THOUGH.
SURE, THERE ARE GREAT DAYS.
THERE ARE SOME DAYS I WISH I COULD STAY IN BED ALL DAY.
BUT THAT WOULDN'T BE RIGHT, EVEN AFTER EVERYTHING.
WE'VE GOT TO MOVE FORWARD, DESPITE HOW HARD IT CAN BE.
I MISS WILLOW ALL THE TIME...I LOST MY BEST FRIEND.
BUT I THINK I'M DOING OK, FINDING FRIENDSHIP IN SOMEONE NEW.

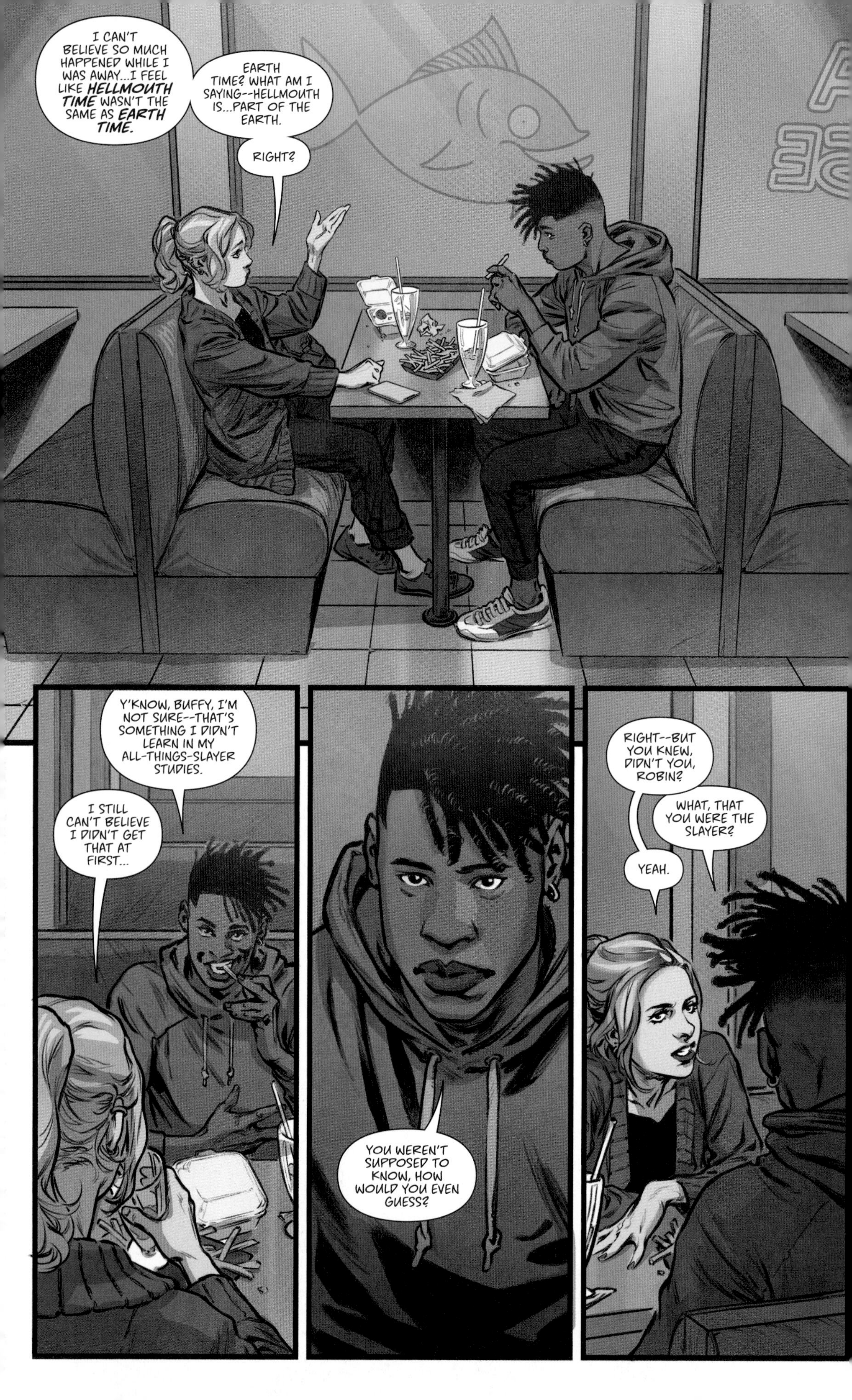
I CAN'T BELIEVE SO MUCH HAPPENED WHILE I WAS AWAY...I FEEL LIKE HELLMOUTH TIME WASN'T THE SAME AS EARTH TIME.
EARTH TIME? WHAT AM I SAYING--HELLMOUTH IS...PART OF THE EARTH.
RIGHT?
Y'KNOW, BUFFY, I'M NOT SURE--THAT'S SOMETHING I DIDN'T LEARN IN MY ALL-THINGS-SLAYER STUDIES.
I STILL CAN'T BELIEVE I DIDN'T GET THAT AT FIRST...
YOU WEREN'T SUPPOSED TO KNOW, HOW WOULD YOU EVEN GUESS?
RIGHT--BUT YOU KNEW, DIDN'T YOU, ROBIN?
WHAT, THAT YOU WERE THE SLAYER?
YEAH.

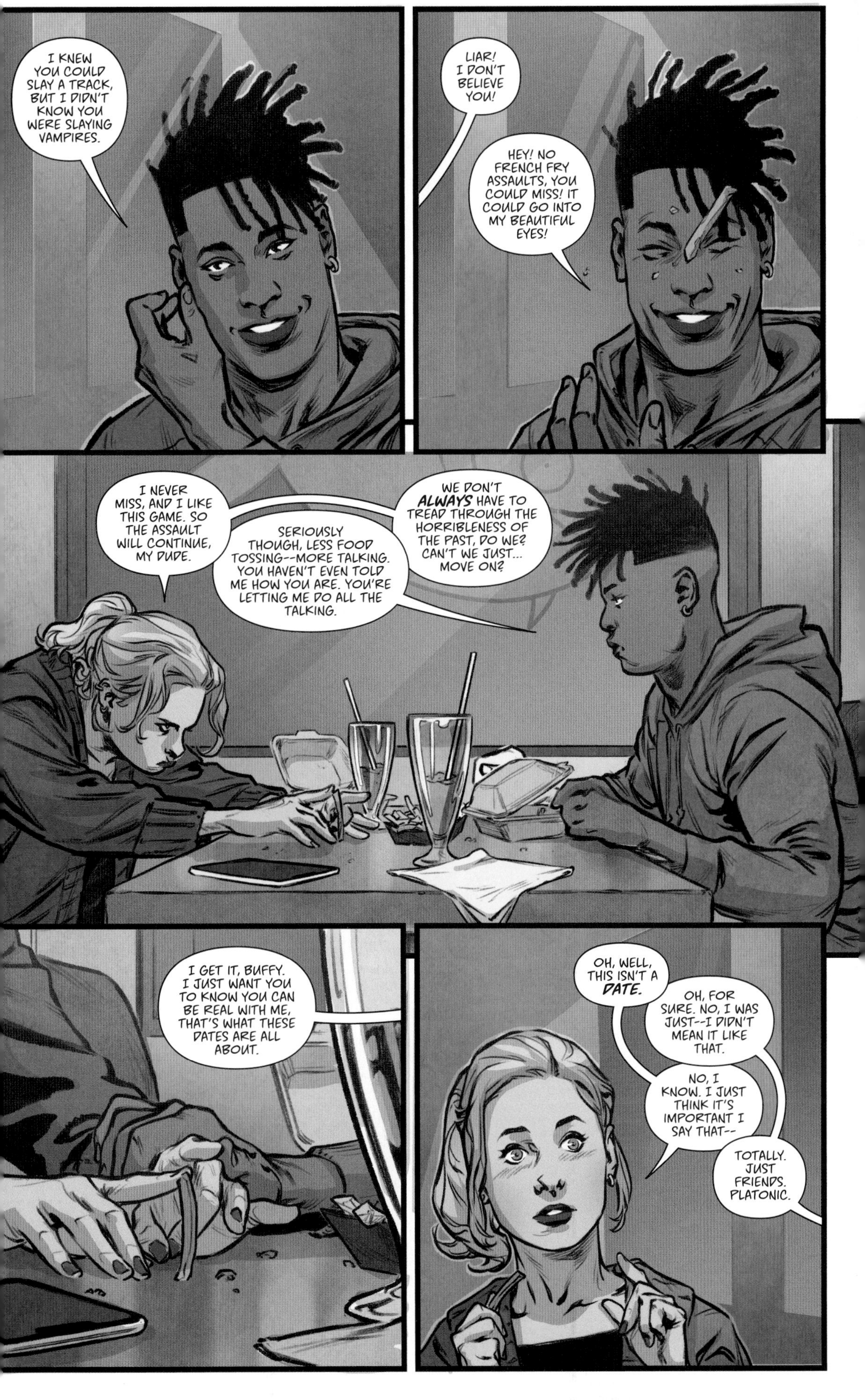
I KNEW YOU COULD SLAY A TRACK, BUT I DIDN'T KNOW YOU WERE SLAYING VAMPIRES.
LIAR! I DON'T BELIEVE YOU!
HEY! NO FRENCH FRY ASSAULTS, YOU COULD MISS! IT COULD GO INTO MY BEAUTIFUL EYES!
I NEVER MISS, AND I LIKE THIS GAME. SO THE ASSAULT WILL CONTINUE, MY DUDE.
SERIOUSLY THOUGH, LESS FOOD TOSSING--MORE TALKING. YOU HAVEN'T EVEN TOLD ME HOW YOU ARE. YOU'RE LETTING ME DO ALL THE TALKING.
WE DON'T **ALWAYS** HAVE TO TREAD THROUGH THE HORRIBLENESS OF THE PAST, DO WE? CAN'T WE JUST... MOVE ON?
I GET IT, BUFFY. I JUST WANT YOU TO KNOW YOU CAN BE REAL WITH ME, THAT'S WHAT THESE DATES ARE ALL ABOUT.
OH, WELL, THIS ISN'T A ***DATE.***
OH, FOR SURE. NO, I WAS JUST--I DIDN'T MEAN IT LIKE THAT.
NO, I KNOW. I JUST THINK IT'S IMPORTANT I SAY THAT--
TOTALLY. JUST FRIENDS. PLATONIC.

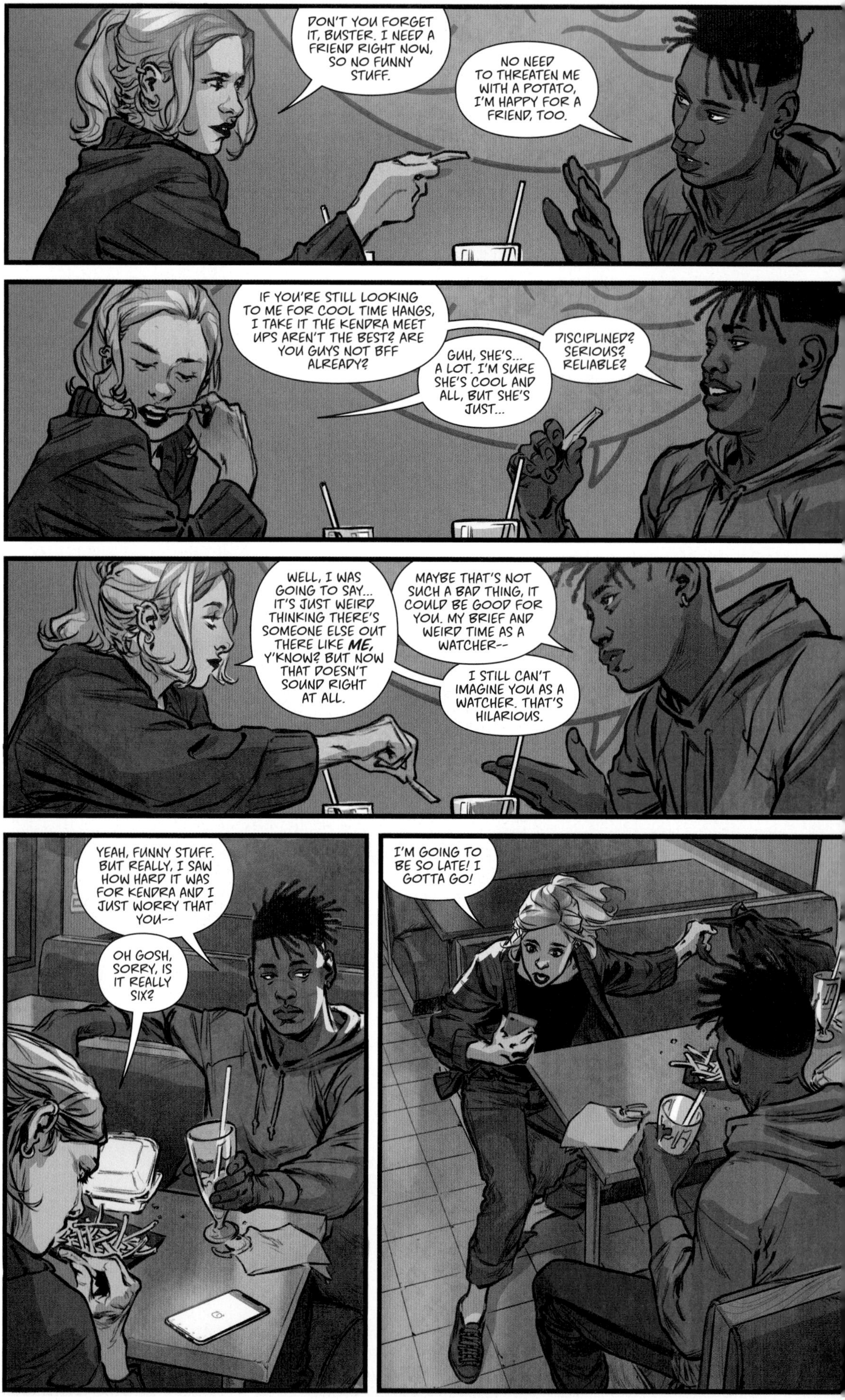
DON'T YOU FORGET IT, BUSTER. I NEED A FRIEND RIGHT NOW, SO NO FUNNY STUFF.
NO NEED TO THREATEN ME WITH A POTATO, I'M HAPPY FOR A FRIEND, TOO.
IF YOU'RE STILL LOOKING TO ME FOR COOL TIME HANGS, I TAKE IT THE KENDRA MEET UPS AREN'T THE BEST? ARE YOU GUYS NOT BFF ALREADY?
GUH, SHE'S... A LOT. I'M SURE SHE'S COOL AND ALL, BUT SHE'S JUST...
DISCIPLINED? SERIOUS? RELIABLE?
WELL, I WAS GOING TO SAY... IT'S JUST WEIRD THINKING THERE'S SOMEONE ELSE OUT THERE LIKE *ME,* Y'KNOW? BUT NOW THAT DOESN'T SOUND RIGHT AT ALL.
MAYBE THAT'S NOT SUCH A BAD THING, IT COULD BE GOOD FOR YOU. MY BRIEF AND WEIRD TIME AS A WATCHER--
I STILL CAN'T IMAGINE YOU AS A WATCHER. THAT'S HILARIOUS.
YEAH, FUNNY STUFF. BUT REALLY, I SAW HOW HARD IT WAS FOR KENDRA AND I JUST WORRY THAT YOU--
OH GOSH, SORRY, IS IT REALLY SIX?
I'M GOING TO BE SO LATE! I GOTTA GO!

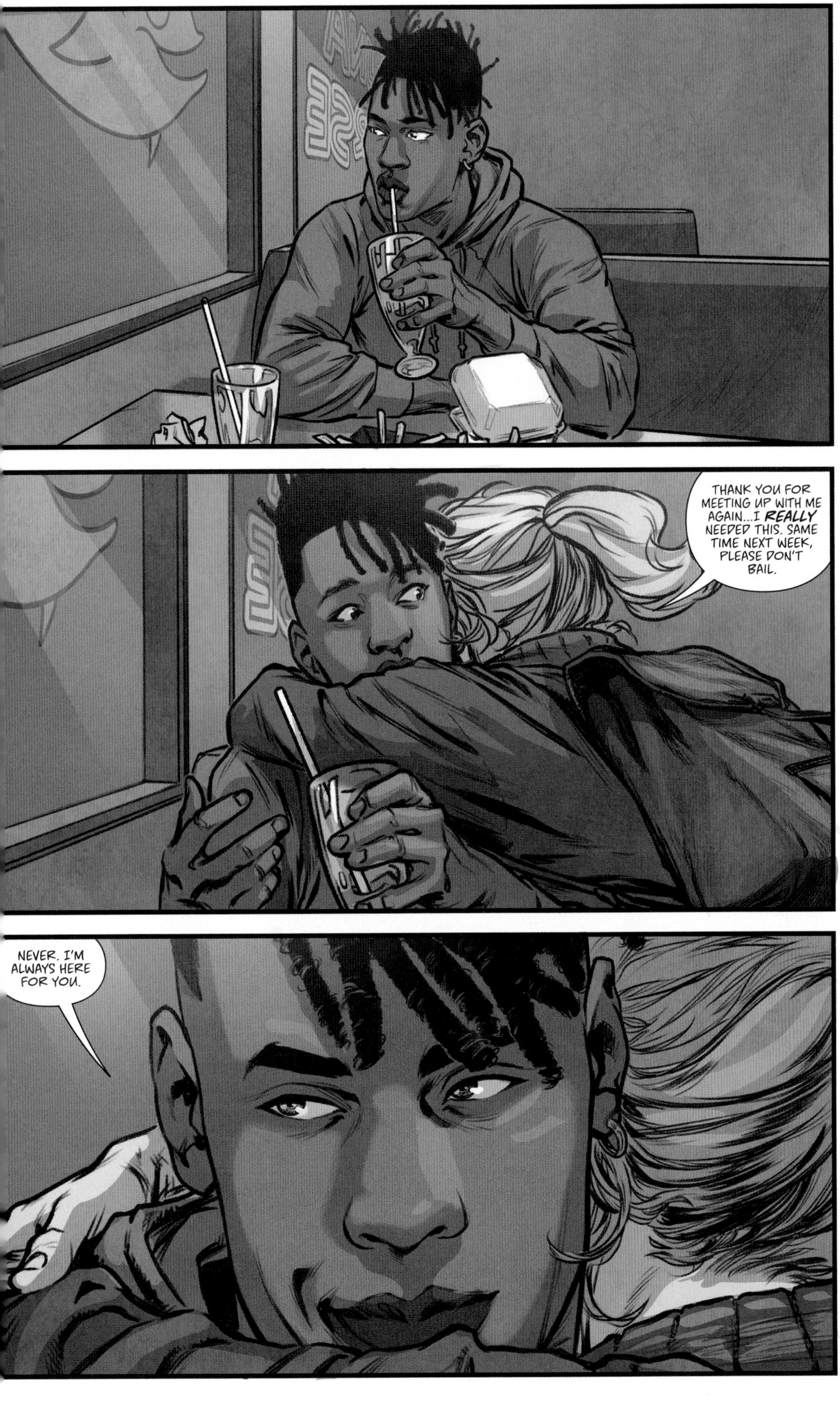
THANK YOU FOR MEETING UP WITH ME AGAIN...I **REALLY** NEEDED THIS. SAME TIME NEXT WEEK, PLEASE DON'T BAIL.
NEVER. I'M ALWAYS HERE FOR YOU.

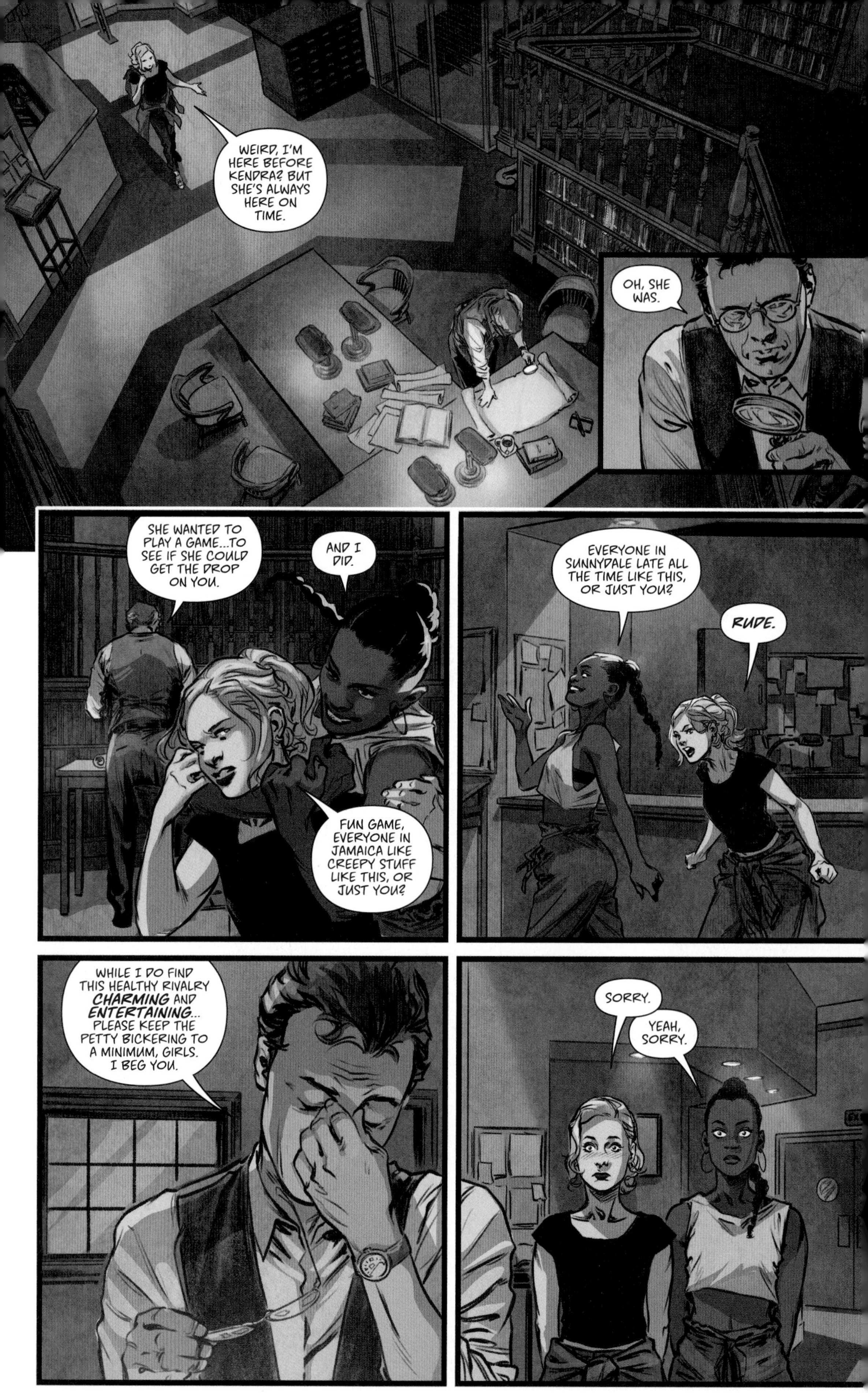
WEIRD, I'M HERE BEFORE KENDRA? BUT SHE'S ALWAYS HERE ON TIME.
OH, SHE WAS.
SHE WANTED TO PLAY A GAME...TO SEE IF SHE COULD GET THE DROP ON YOU.
AND I DID.
FUN GAME, EVERYONE IN JAMAICA LIKE CREEPY STUFF LIKE THIS, OR JUST YOU?
EVERYONE IN SUNNYDALE LATE ALL THE TIME LIKE THIS, OR JUST YOU?
RUDE.
WHILE I DO FIND THIS HEALTHY RIVALRY CHARMING AND ENTERTAINING... PLEASE KEEP THE PETTY BICKERING TO A MINIMUM, GIRLS. I BEG YOU.
SORRY.
YEAH, SORRY.

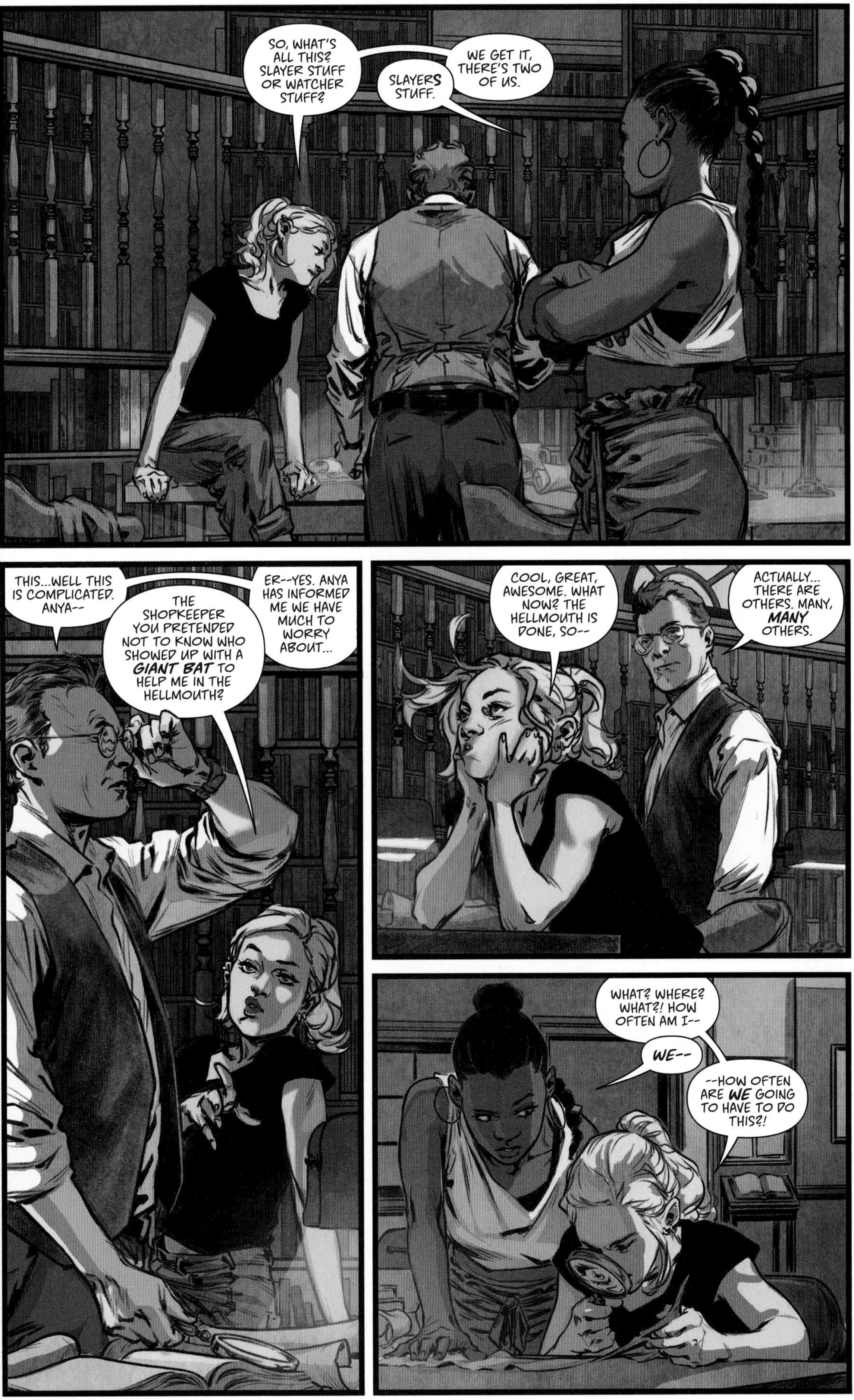
SO, WHAT'S ALL THIS? SLAYER STUFF OR WATCHER STUFF?
SLAYERS STUFF.
WE GET IT, THERE'S TWO OF US.
THIS...WELL THIS IS COMPLICATED. ANYA--
THE SHOPKEEPER YOU PRETENDED NOT TO KNOW WHO SHOWED UP WITH A GIANT BAT TO HELP ME IN THE HELLMOUTH?
ER--YES. ANYA HAS INFORMED ME WE HAVE MUCH TO WORRY ABOUT...
COOL, GREAT, AWESOME. WHAT NOW? THE HELLMOUTH IS DONE, SO--
ACTUALLY... THERE ARE OTHERS. MANY, MANY OTHERS.
WHAT? WHERE? WHAT?! HOW OFTEN AM I--
WE--
--HOW OFTEN ARE WE GOING TO HAVE TO DO THIS?!

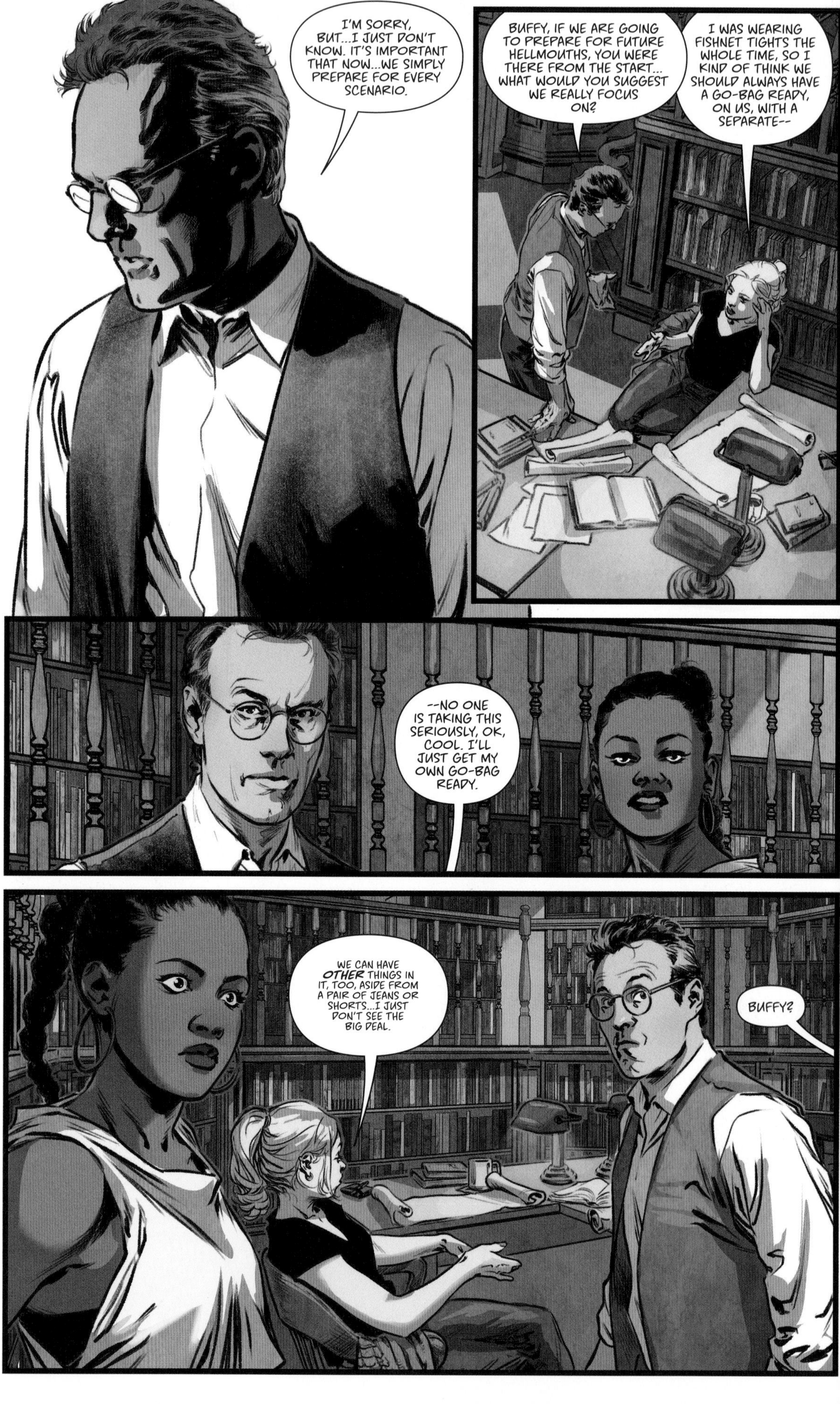
I'M SORRY, BUT...I JUST DON'T KNOW. IT'S IMPORTANT THAT NOW...WE SIMPLY PREPARE FOR EVERY SCENARIO.
BUFFY, IF WE ARE GOING TO PREPARE FOR FUTURE HELLMOUTHS, YOU WERE THERE FROM THE START... WHAT WOULD YOU SUGGEST WE REALLY FOCUS ON?
I WAS WEARING FISHNET TIGHTS THE WHOLE TIME, SO I KIND OF THINK WE SHOULD ALWAYS HAVE A GO-BAG READY, ON US, WITH A SEPARATE--
--NO ONE IS TAKING THIS SERIOUSLY, OK, COOL. I'LL JUST GET MY OWN GO-BAG READY.
WE CAN HAVE **OTHER** THINGS IN IT, TOO, ASIDE FROM A PAIR OF JEANS OR SHORTS...I JUST DON'T SEE THE BIG DEAL.
BUFFY?

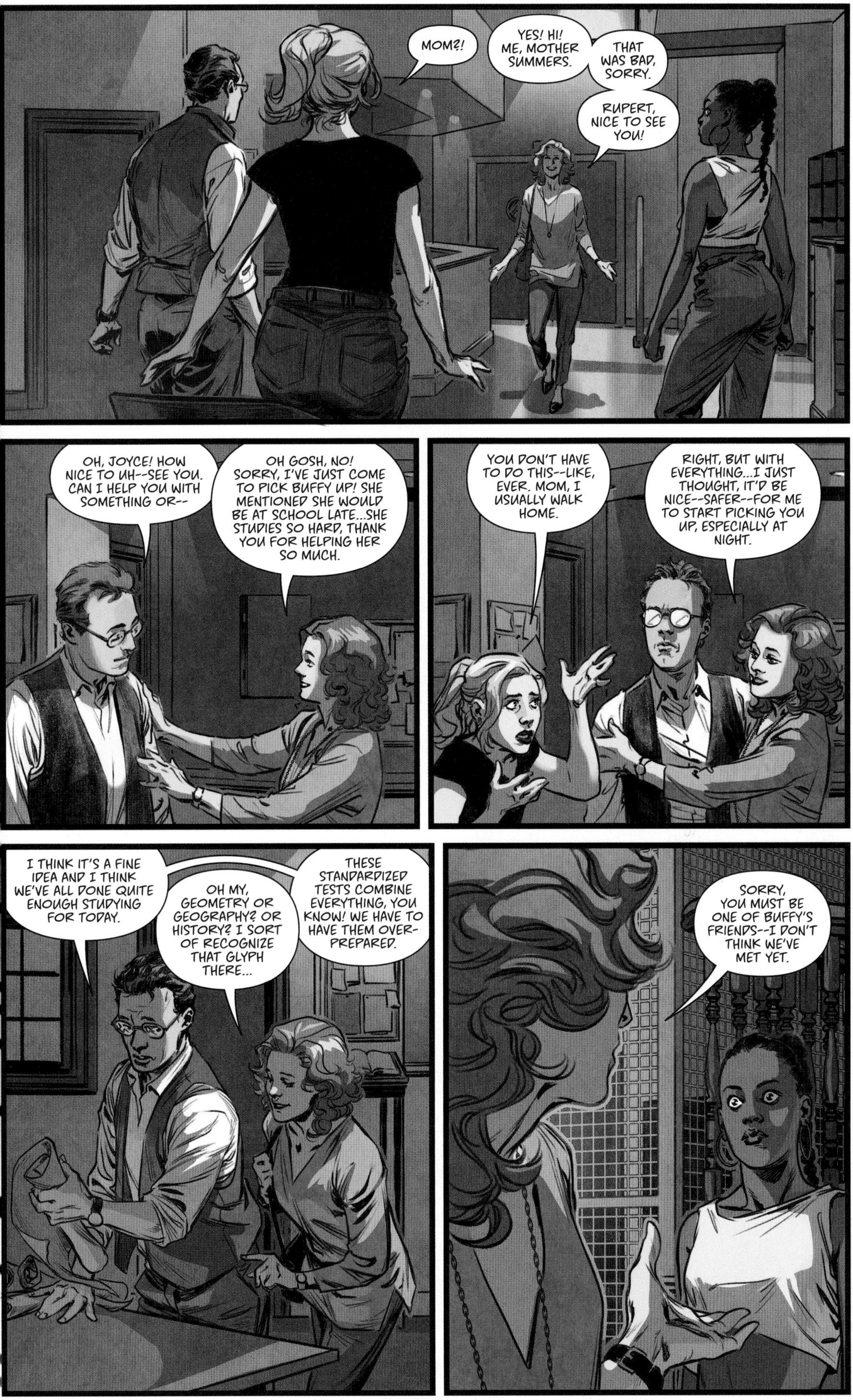
MOM?!
YES! HI! ME, MOTHER SUMMERS.
THAT WAS BAD, SORRY.
RUPERT, NICE TO SEE YOU!
OH, JOYCE! HOW NICE TO UH--SEE YOU. CAN I HELP YOU WITH SOMETHING OR--
OH GOSH, NO! SORRY, I'VE JUST COME TO PICK BUFFY UP! SHE MENTIONED SHE WOULD BE AT SCHOOL LATE...SHE STUDIES SO HARD, THANK YOU FOR HELPING HER SO MUCH.
YOU DON'T HAVE TO DO THIS--LIKE, EVER. MOM, I USUALLY WALK HOME.
RIGHT, BUT WITH EVERYTHING...I JUST THOUGHT, IT'D BE NICE--SAFER--FOR ME TO START PICKING YOU UP, ESPECIALLY AT NIGHT.
I THINK IT'S A FINE IDEA AND I THINK WE'VE ALL DONE QUITE ENOUGH STUDYING FOR TODAY.
OH MY, GEOMETRY OR GEOGRAPHY? OR HISTORY? I SORT OF RECOGNIZE THAT GLYPH THERE...
THESE STANDARDIZED TESTS COMBINE EVERYTHING, YOU KNOW! WE HAVE TO HAVE THEM OVER-PREPARED.
SORRY, YOU MUST BE ONE OF BUFFY'S FRIENDS--I DON'T THINK WE'VE MET YET.

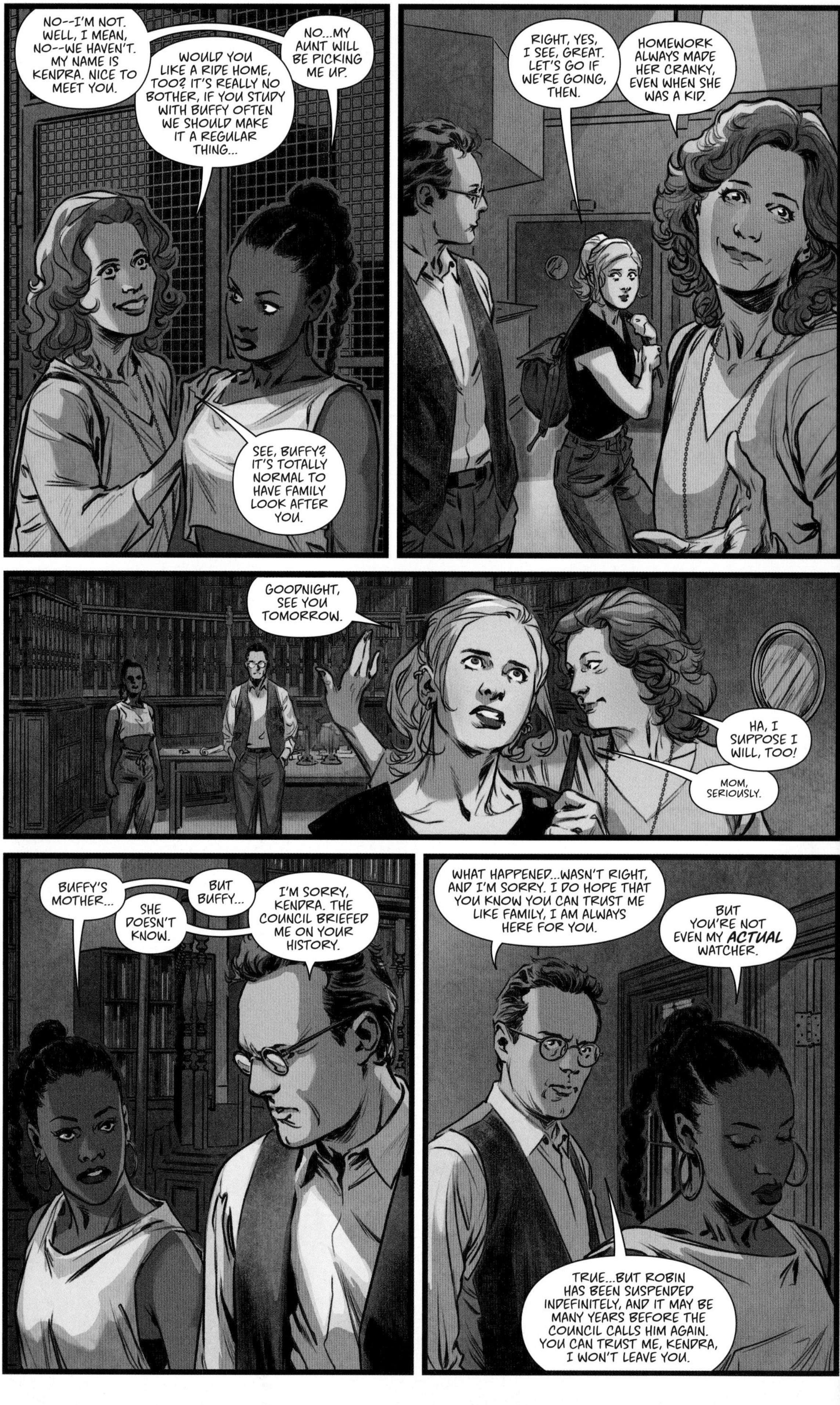
NO--I'M NOT. WELL, I MEAN, NO--WE HAVEN'T. MY NAME IS KENDRA. NICE TO MEET YOU.
WOULD YOU LIKE A RIDE HOME, TOO? IT'S REALLY NO BOTHER, IF YOU STUDY WITH BUFFY OFTEN WE SHOULD MAKE IT A REGULAR THING...
NO...MY AUNT WILL BE PICKING ME UP.
SEE, BUFFY? IT'S TOTALLY NORMAL TO HAVE FAMILY LOOK AFTER YOU.
RIGHT, YES, I SEE, GREAT. LET'S GO IF WE'RE GOING, THEN.
HOMEWORK ALWAYS MADE HER CRANKY, EVEN WHEN SHE WAS A KID.
GOODNIGHT, SEE YOU TOMORROW.
HA, I SUPPOSE I WILL, TOO!
MOM, SERIOUSLY.
BUFFY'S MOTHER...
BUT BUFFY...
SHE DOESN'T KNOW.
I'M SORRY, KENDRA. THE COUNCIL BRIEFED ME ON YOUR HISTORY.
WHAT HAPPENED...WASN'T RIGHT, AND I'M SORRY. I DO HOPE THAT YOU KNOW YOU CAN TRUST ME LIKE FAMILY, I AM ALWAYS HERE FOR YOU.
BUT YOU'RE NOT EVEN MY ***ACTUAL*** WATCHER.
TRUE...BUT ROBIN HAS BEEN SUSPENDED INDEFINITELY, AND IT MAY BE MANY YEARS BEFORE THE COUNCIL CALLS HIM AGAIN. YOU CAN TRUST ME, KENDRA, I WON'T LEAVE YOU.

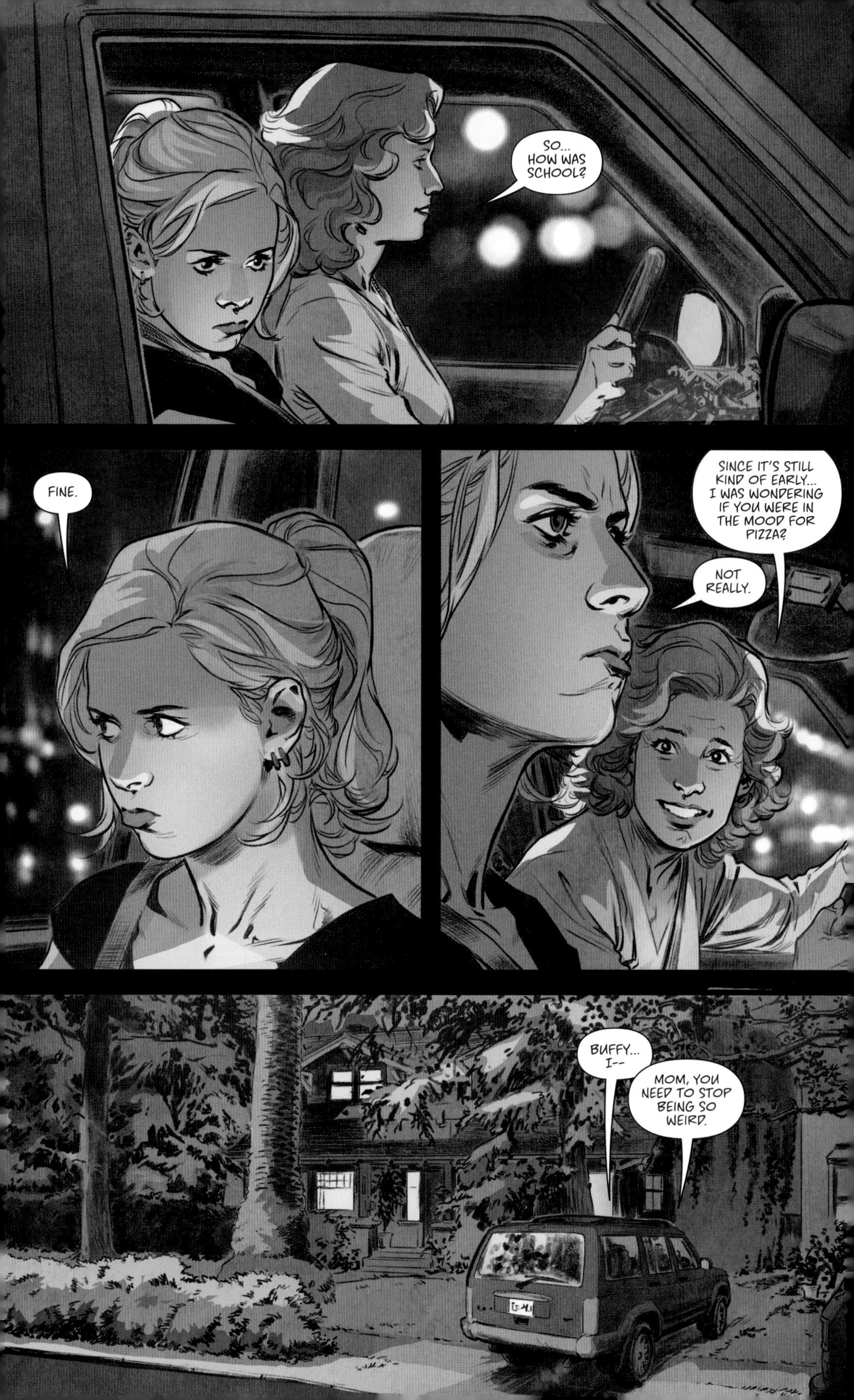
SO... HOW WAS SCHOOL?
FINE.
SINCE IT'S STILL KIND OF EARLY... I WAS WONDERING IF YOU WERE IN THE MOOD FOR PIZZA?
NOT REALLY.
BUFFY... I--
MOM, YOU NEED TO STOP BEING SO WEIRD.

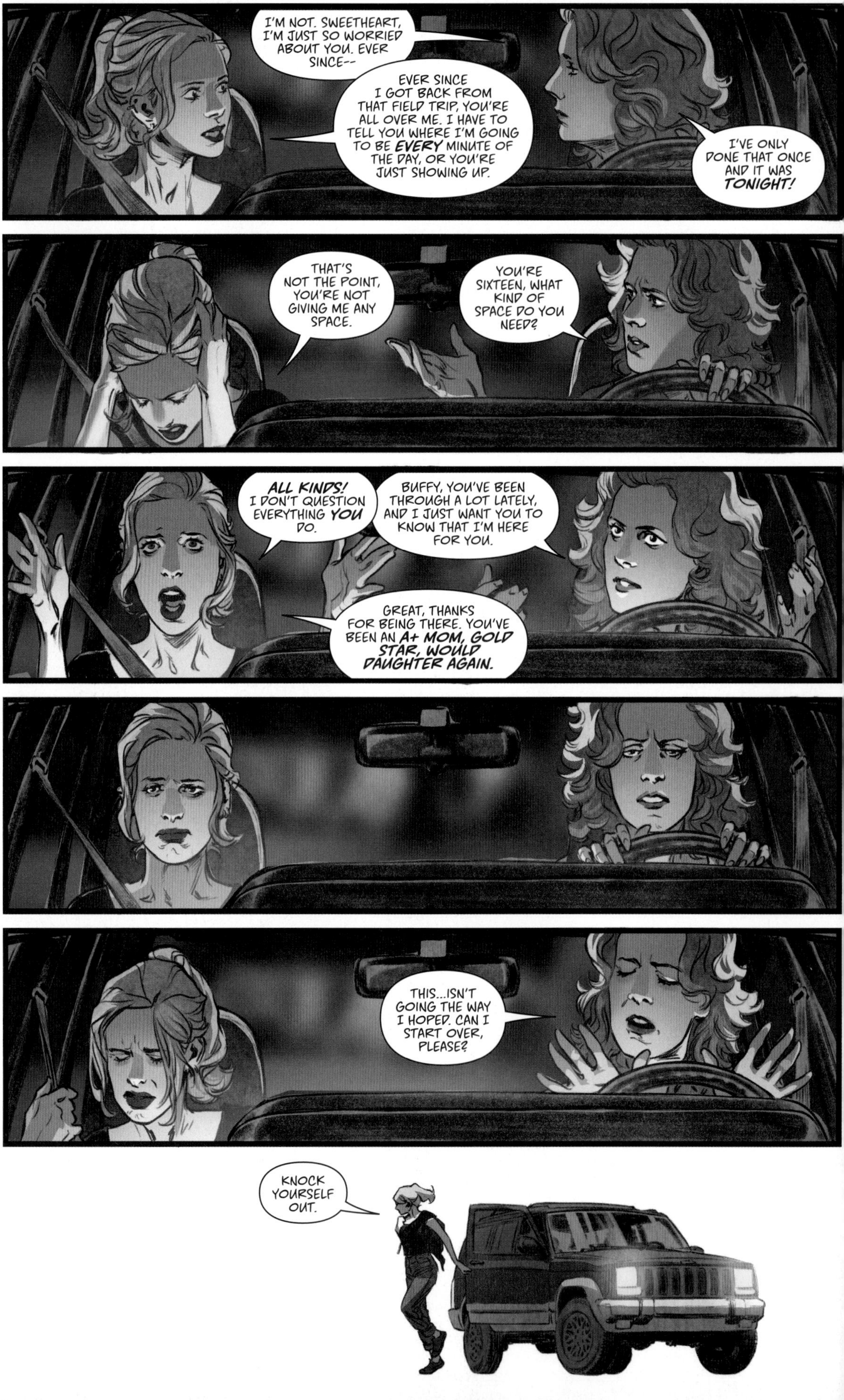
I'M NOT. SWEETHEART, I'M JUST SO WORRIED ABOUT YOU. EVER SINCE--
EVER SINCE I GOT BACK FROM THAT FIELD TRIP, YOU'RE ALL OVER ME. I HAVE TO TELL YOU WHERE I'M GOING TO BE EVERY MINUTE OF THE DAY, OR YOU'RE JUST SHOWING UP.
I'VE ONLY DONE THAT ONCE AND IT WAS TONIGHT!
THAT'S NOT THE POINT, YOU'RE NOT GIVING ME ANY SPACE.
YOU'RE SIXTEEN, WHAT KIND OF SPACE DO YOU NEED?
ALL KINDS! I DON'T QUESTION EVERYTHING YOU DO.
BUFFY, YOU'VE BEEN THROUGH A LOT LATELY, AND I JUST WANT YOU TO KNOW THAT I'M HERE FOR YOU.
GREAT, THANKS FOR BEING THERE. YOU'VE BEEN AN A+ MOM, GOLD STAR, WOULD DAUGHTER AGAIN.
THIS...ISN'T GOING THE WAY I HOPED. CAN I START OVER, PLEASE?
KNOCK YOURSELF OUT.

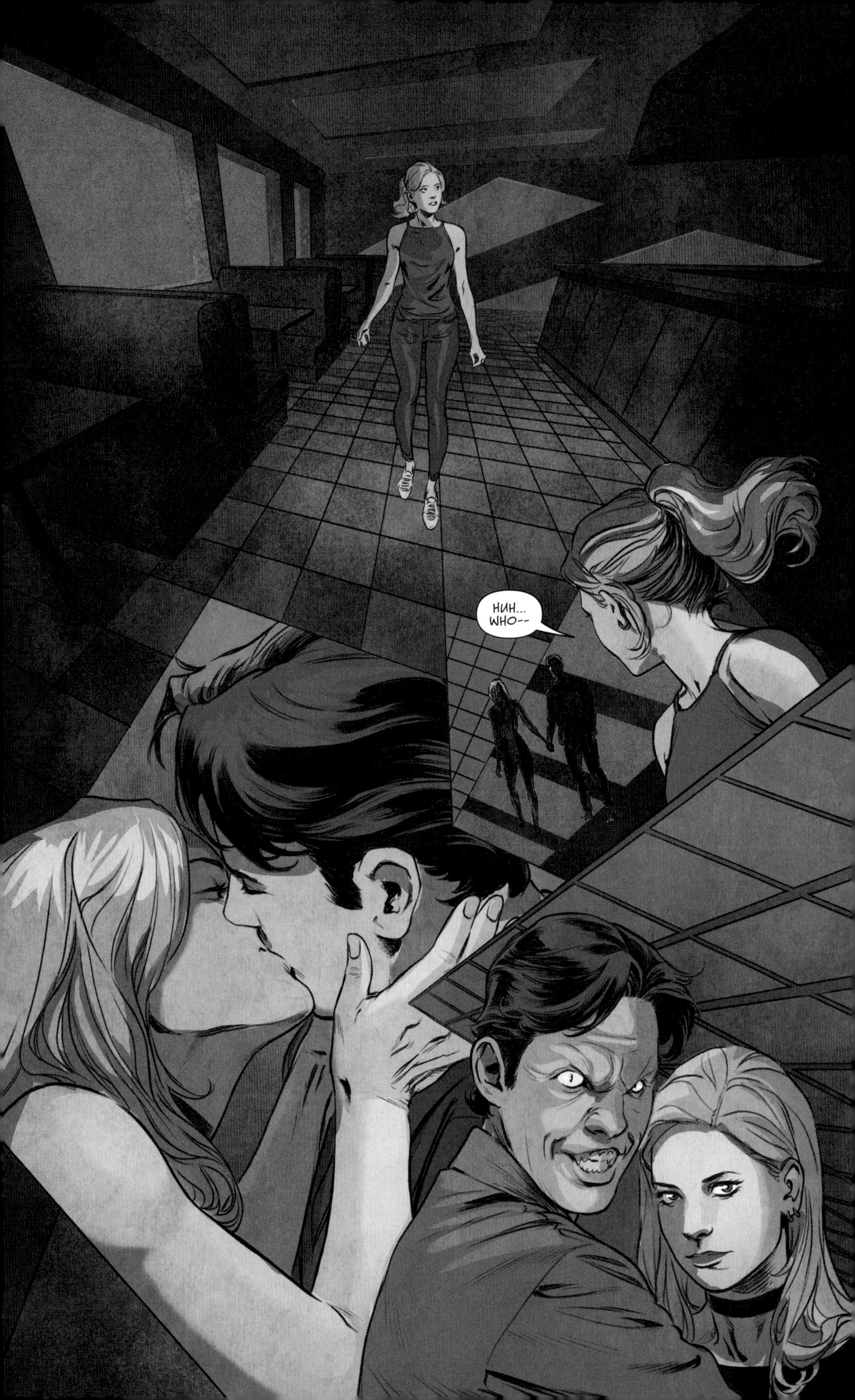
HUH... WHO--

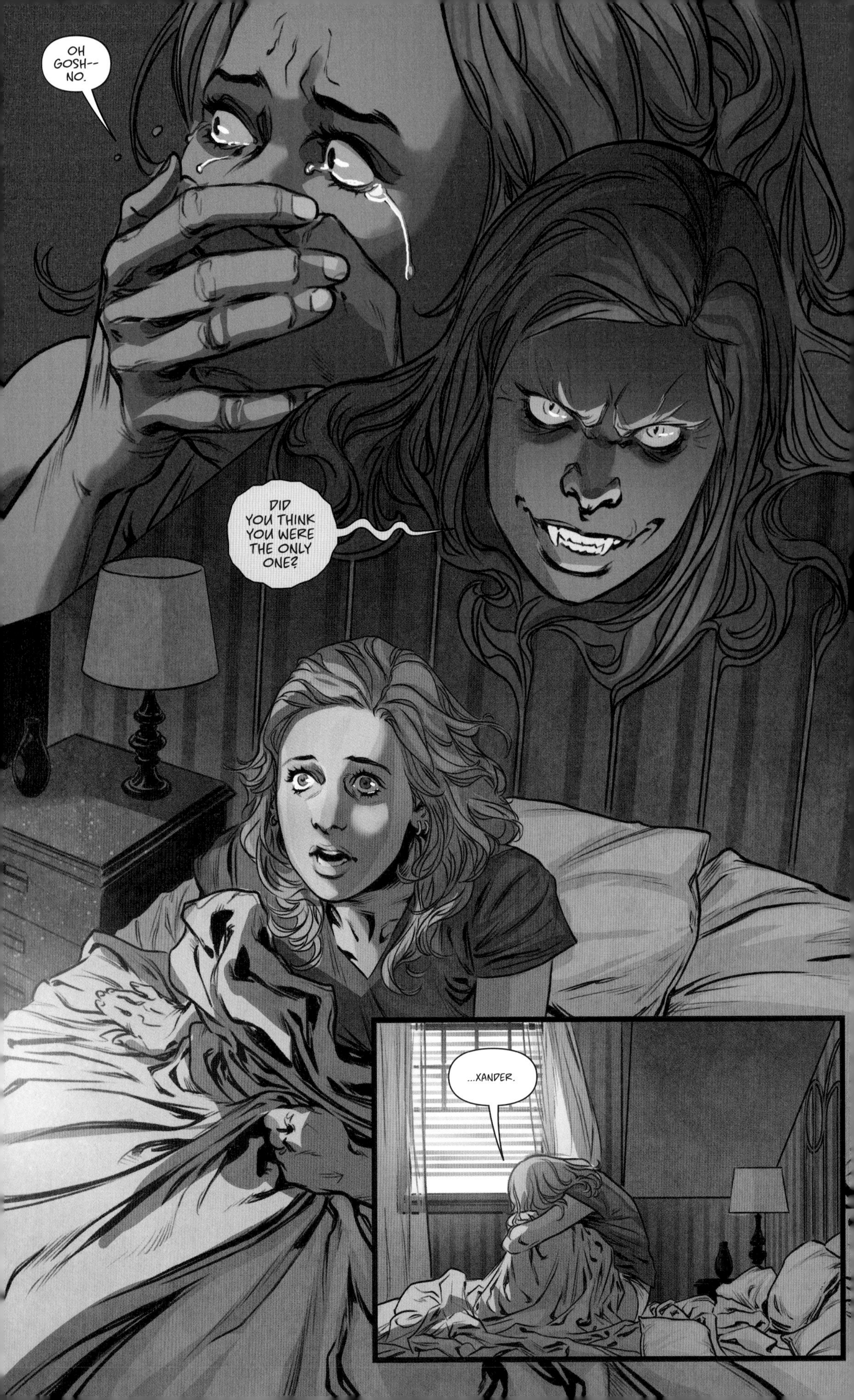
OH GOSH-- NO.
DID YOU THINK YOU WERE THE ONLY ONE?
...XANDER.

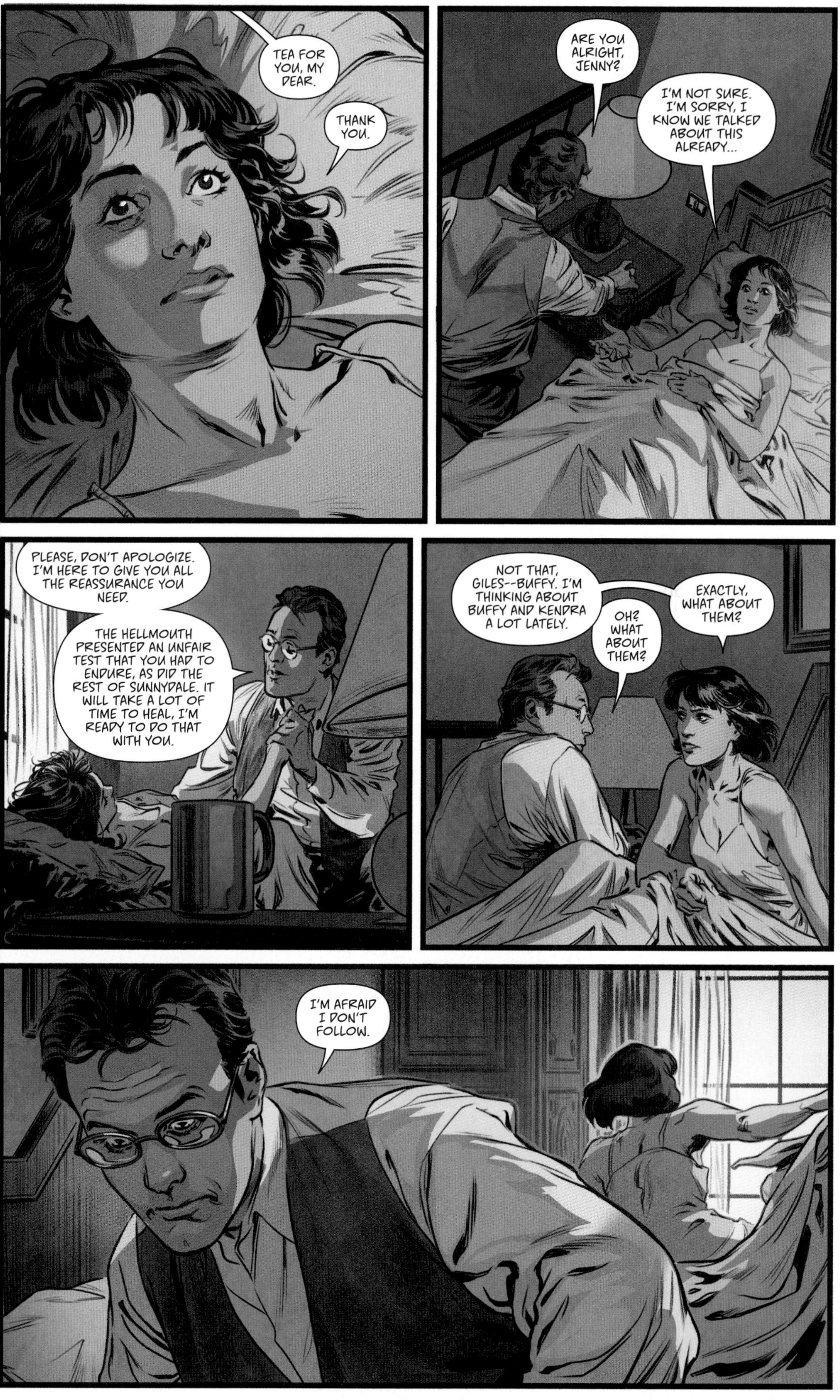
TEA FOR YOU, MY DEAR.
THANK YOU.
ARE YOU ALRIGHT, JENNY?
I'M NOT SURE. I'M SORRY, I KNOW WE TALKED ABOUT THIS ALREADY...
PLEASE, DON'T APOLOGIZE. I'M HERE TO GIVE YOU ALL THE REASSURANCE YOU NEED.
THE HELLMOUTH PRESENTED AN UNFAIR TEST THAT YOU HAD TO ENDURE, AS DID THE REST OF SUNNYDALE. IT WILL TAKE A LOT OF TIME TO HEAL, I'M READY TO DO THAT WITH YOU.
NOT THAT, GILES--BUFFY. I'M THINKING ABOUT BUFFY AND KENDRA A LOT LATELY.
OH? WHAT ABOUT THEM?
EXACTLY, WHAT ABOUT THEM?
I'M AFRAID I DON'T FOLLOW.

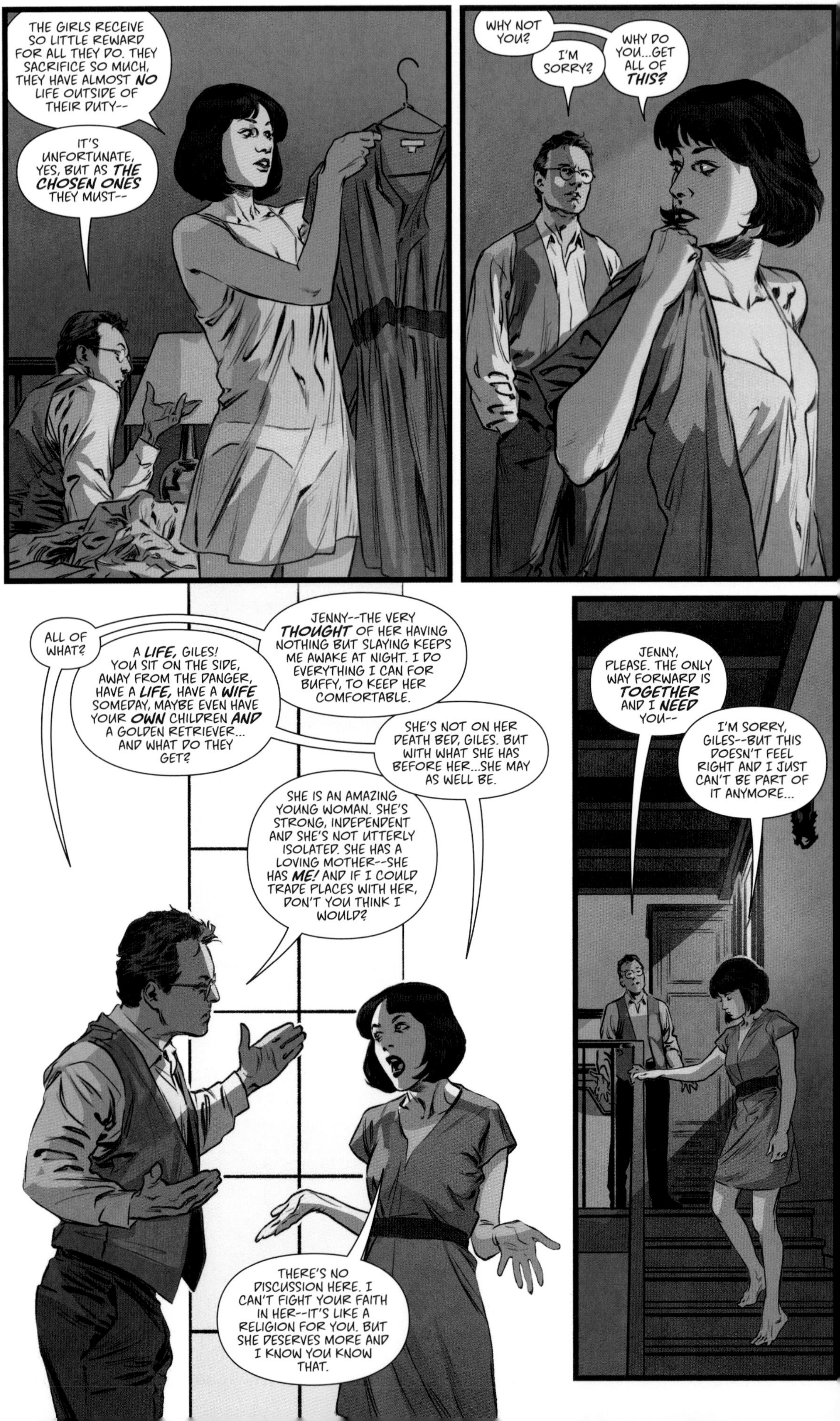
THE GIRLS RECEIVE SO LITTLE REWARD FOR ALL THEY DO. THEY SACRIFICE SO MUCH, THEY HAVE ALMOST NO LIFE OUTSIDE OF THEIR DUTY--
IT'S UNFORTUNATE, YES, BUT AS THE CHOSEN ONES THEY MUST--
WHY NOT YOU?
I'M SORRY?
WHY DO YOU...GET ALL OF THIS?
ALL OF WHAT?
A LIFE, GILES! YOU SIT ON THE SIDE, AWAY FROM THE DANGER, HAVE A LIFE, HAVE A WIFE SOMEDAY, MAYBE EVEN HAVE YOUR OWN CHILDREN AND A GOLDEN RETRIEVER... AND WHAT DO THEY GET?
JENNY--THE VERY THOUGHT OF HER HAVING NOTHING BUT SLAYING KEEPS ME AWAKE AT NIGHT. I DO EVERYTHING I CAN FOR BUFFY, TO KEEP HER COMFORTABLE.
SHE'S NOT ON HER DEATH BED, GILES. BUT WITH WHAT SHE HAS BEFORE HER...SHE MAY AS WELL BE.
SHE IS AN AMAZING YOUNG WOMAN. SHE'S STRONG, INDEPENDENT AND SHE'S NOT UTTERLY ISOLATED. SHE HAS A LOVING MOTHER--SHE HAS ME! AND IF I COULD TRADE PLACES WITH HER, DON'T YOU THINK I WOULD?
THERE'S NO DISCUSSION HERE. I CAN'T FIGHT YOUR FAITH IN HER--IT'S LIKE A RELIGION FOR YOU. BUT SHE DESERVES MORE AND I KNOW YOU KNOW THAT.
JENNY, PLEASE. THE ONLY WAY FORWARD IS TOGETHER AND I NEED YOU--
I'M SORRY, GILES--BUT THIS DOESN'T FEEL RIGHT AND I JUST CAN'T BE PART OF IT ANYMORE...

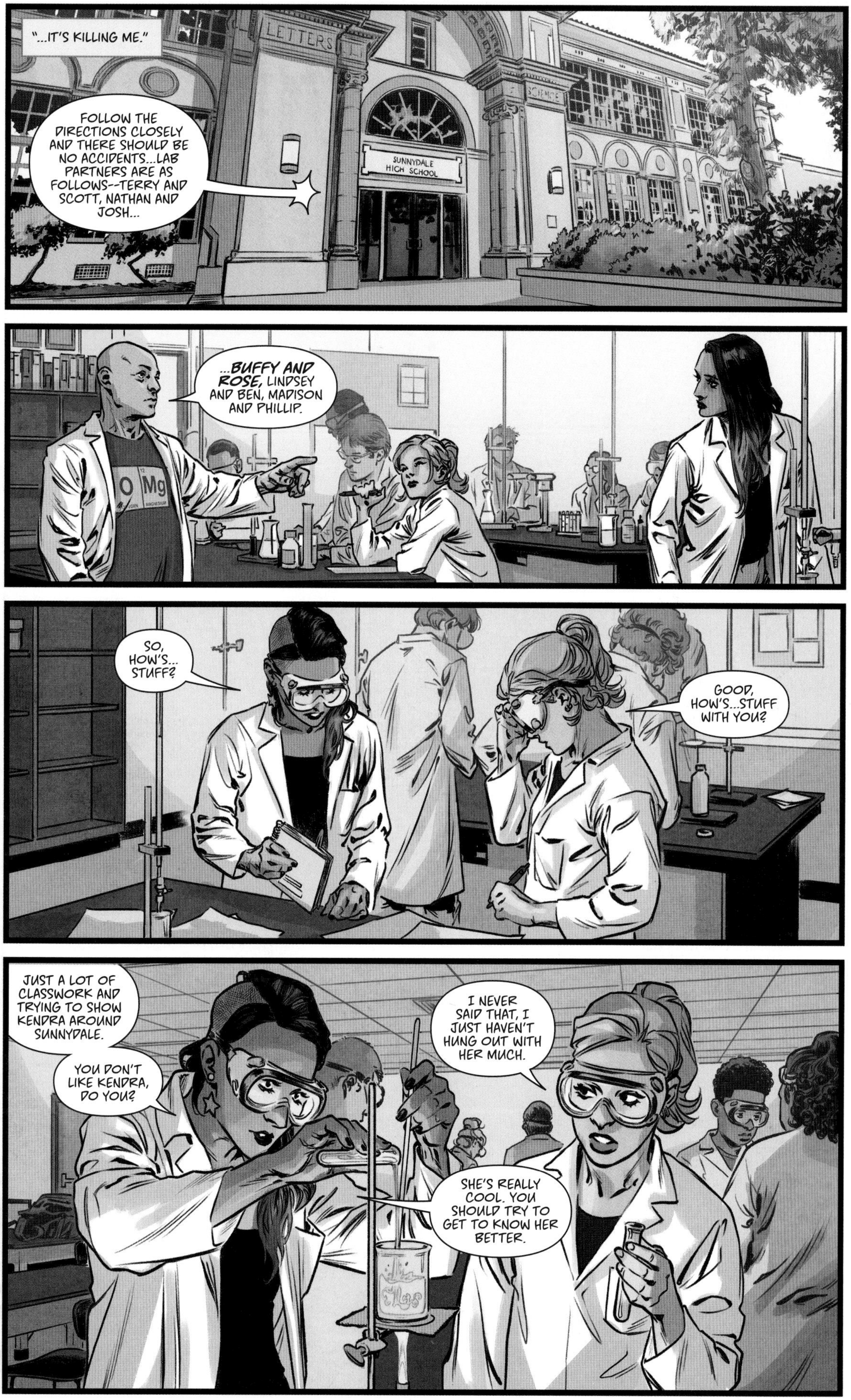
"...IT'S KILLING ME."
LETTERS
SUNNYDALE HIGH SCHOOL
FOLLOW THE DIRECTIONS CLOSELY AND THERE SHOULD BE NO ACCIDENTS...LAB PARTNERS ARE AS FOLLOWS--TERRY AND SCOTT, NATHAN AND JOSH...
...**BUFFY AND ROSE**, LINDSEY AND BEN, MADISON AND PHILLIP.
O Mg
SO, HOW'S... STUFF?
GOOD, HOW'S...STUFF WITH YOU?
JUST A LOT OF CLASSWORK AND TRYING TO SHOW KENDRA AROUND SUNNYDALE.
YOU DON'T LIKE KENDRA, DO YOU?
I NEVER SAID THAT, I JUST HAVEN'T HUNG OUT WITH HER MUCH.
SHE'S REALLY COOL. YOU SHOULD TRY TO GET TO KNOW HER BETTER.

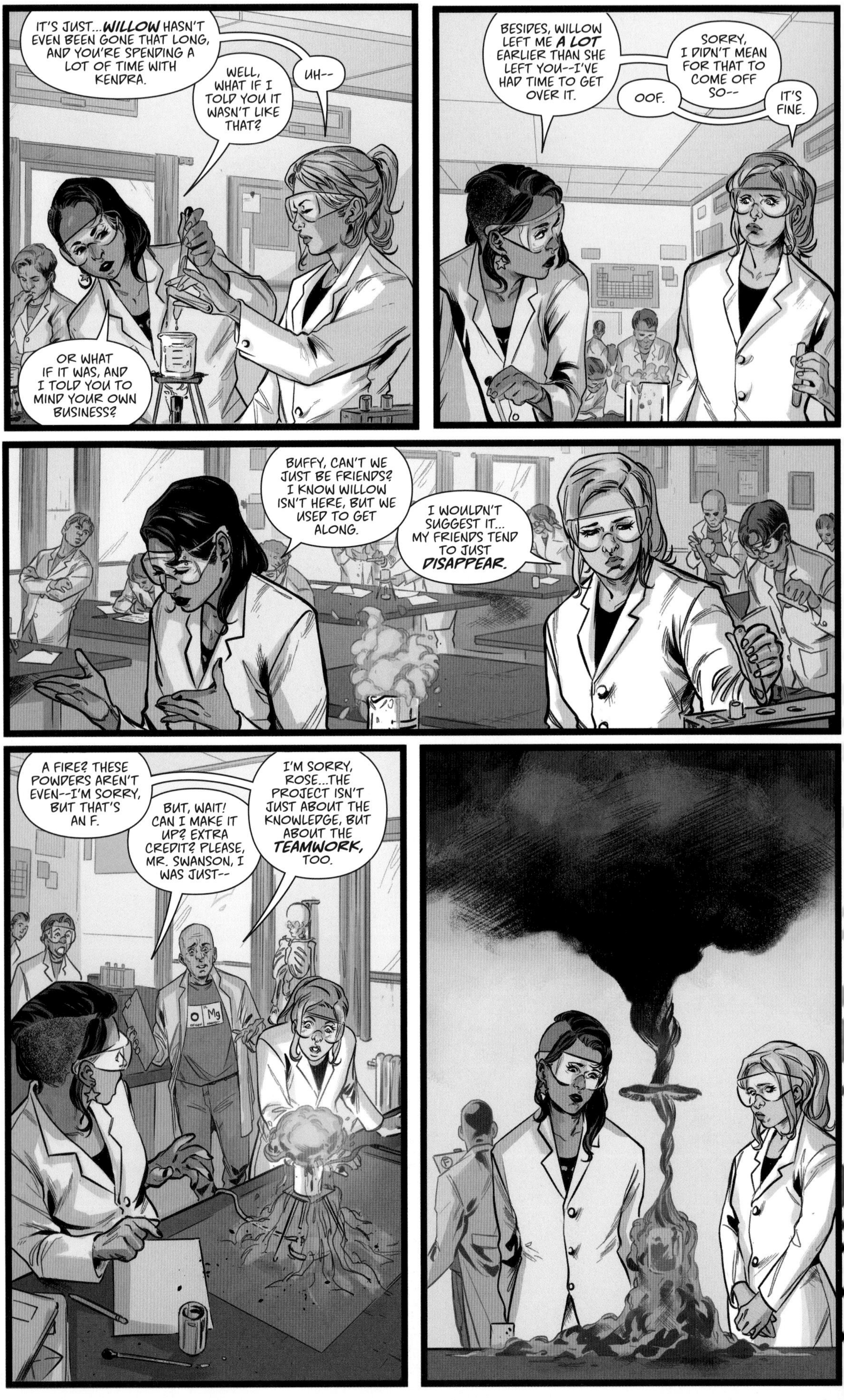
IT'S JUST...WILLOW HASN'T EVEN BEEN GONE THAT LONG, AND YOU'RE SPENDING A LOT OF TIME WITH KENDRA.
UH--
WELL, WHAT IF I TOLD YOU IT WASN'T LIKE THAT?
OR WHAT IF IT WAS, AND I TOLD YOU TO MIND YOUR OWN BUSINESS?
BESIDES, WILLOW LEFT ME A LOT EARLIER THAN SHE LEFT YOU--I'VE HAD TIME TO GET OVER IT.
OOF.
SORRY, I DIDN'T MEAN FOR THAT TO COME OFF SO--
IT'S FINE.
BUFFY, CAN'T WE JUST BE FRIENDS? I KNOW WILLOW ISN'T HERE, BUT WE USED TO GET ALONG.
I WOULDN'T SUGGEST IT... MY FRIENDS TEND TO JUST DISAPPEAR.
A FIRE? THESE POWDERS AREN'T EVEN--I'M SORRY, BUT THAT'S AN F.
BUT, WAIT! CAN I MAKE IT UP? EXTRA CREDIT? PLEASE, MR. SWANSON, I WAS JUST--
I'M SORRY, ROSE...THE PROJECT ISN'T JUST ABOUT THE KNOWLEDGE, BUT ABOUT THE TEAMWORK, TOO.

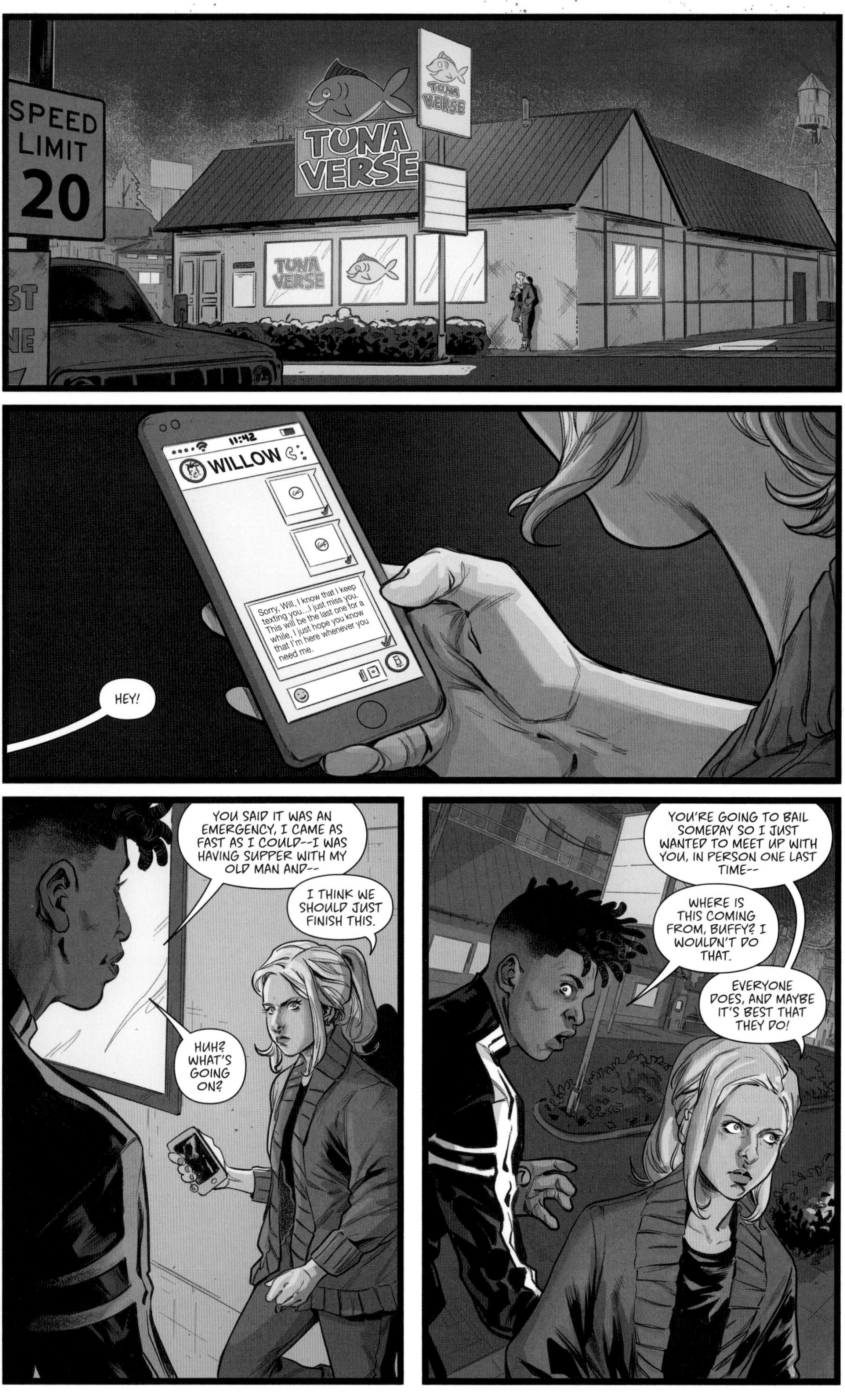
SPEED LIMIT 20
TUNA VERSE
TUNA VERSE
TUNA VERSE
11:42
WILLOW
Sorry, Will, I know that I keep texting you...I just miss you. This will be the last one for a while, I just hope you know that I'm here whenever you need me.
HEY!
YOU SAID IT WAS AN EMERGENCY, I CAME AS FAST AS I COULD--I WAS HAVING SUPPER WITH MY OLD MAN AND--
I THINK WE SHOULD JUST FINISH THIS.
HUH? WHAT'S GOING ON?
YOU'RE GOING TO BAIL SOMEDAY SO I JUST WANTED TO MEET UP WITH YOU, IN PERSON ONE LAST TIME--
WHERE IS THIS COMING FROM, BUFFY? I WOULDN'T DO THAT.
EVERYONE DOES, AND MAYBE IT'S BEST THAT THEY DO!

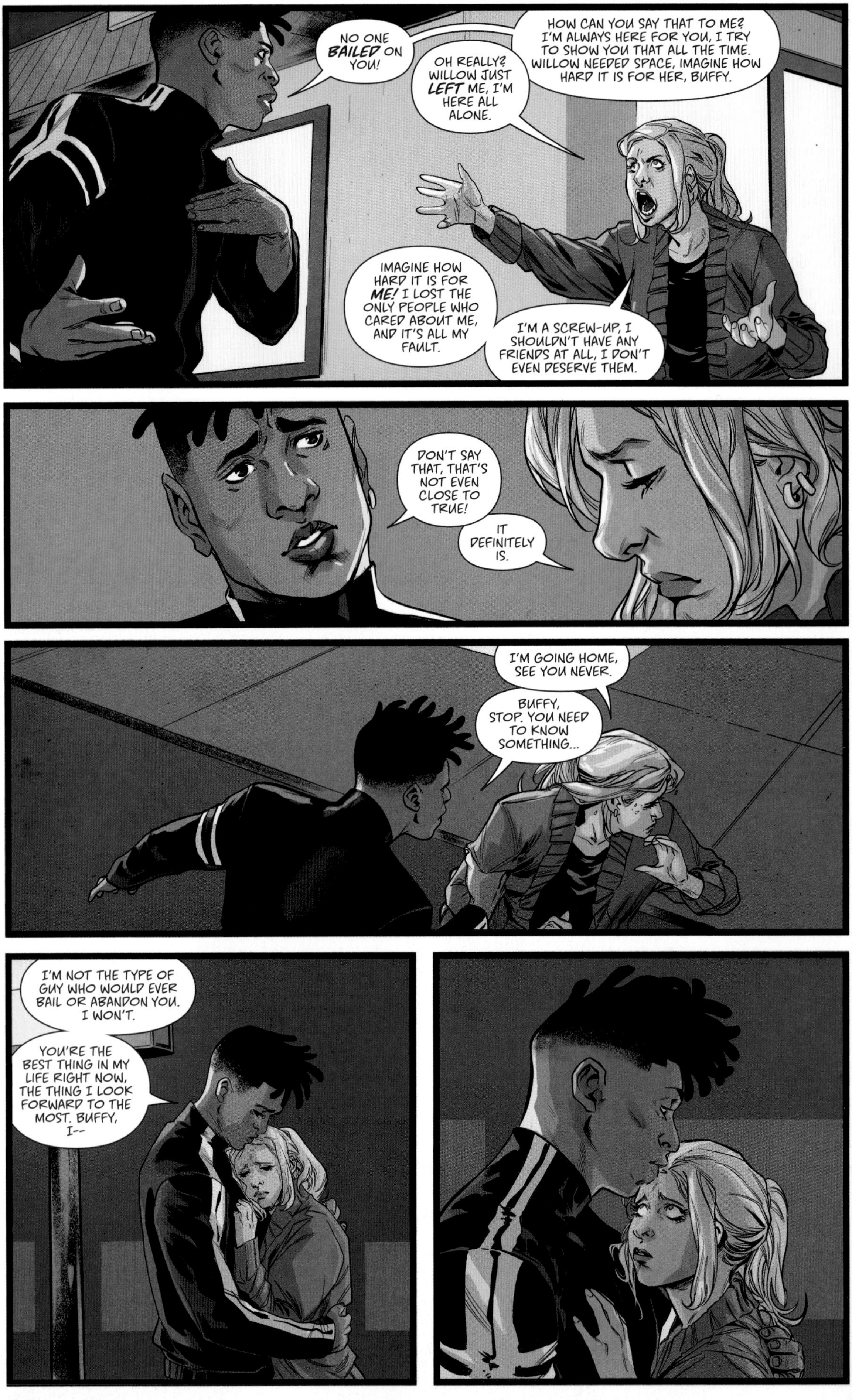
NO ONE **BAILED** ON YOU!
HOW CAN YOU SAY THAT TO ME? I'M ALWAYS HERE FOR YOU, I TRY TO SHOW YOU THAT ALL THE TIME. WILLOW NEEDED SPACE, IMAGINE HOW HARD IT IS FOR HER, BUFFY.
OH REALLY? WILLOW JUST **LEFT** ME, I'M HERE ALL ALONE.
IMAGINE HOW HARD IT IS FOR **ME!** I LOST THE ONLY PEOPLE WHO CARED ABOUT ME, AND IT'S ALL MY FAULT.
I'M A SCREW-UP, I SHOULDN'T HAVE ANY FRIENDS AT ALL, I DON'T EVEN DESERVE THEM.
DON'T SAY THAT, THAT'S NOT EVEN CLOSE TO TRUE!
IT DEFINITELY IS.
I'M GOING HOME, SEE YOU NEVER.
BUFFY, STOP. YOU NEED TO KNOW SOMETHING...
I'M NOT THE TYPE OF GUY WHO WOULD EVER BAIL OR ABANDON YOU. I WON'T.
YOU'RE THE BEST THING IN MY LIFE RIGHT NOW, THE THING I LOOK FORWARD TO THE MOST. BUFFY, I--

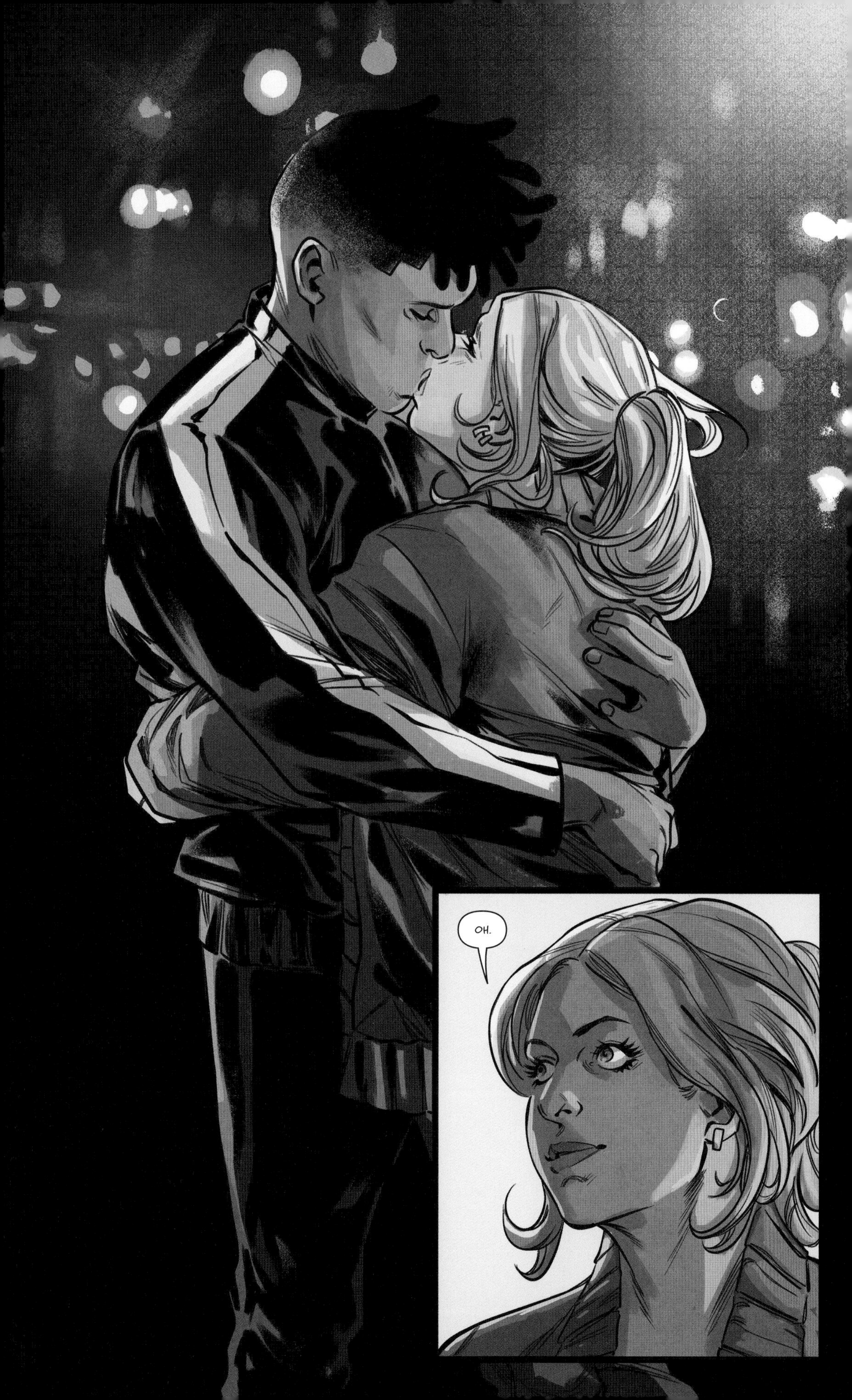
OH.

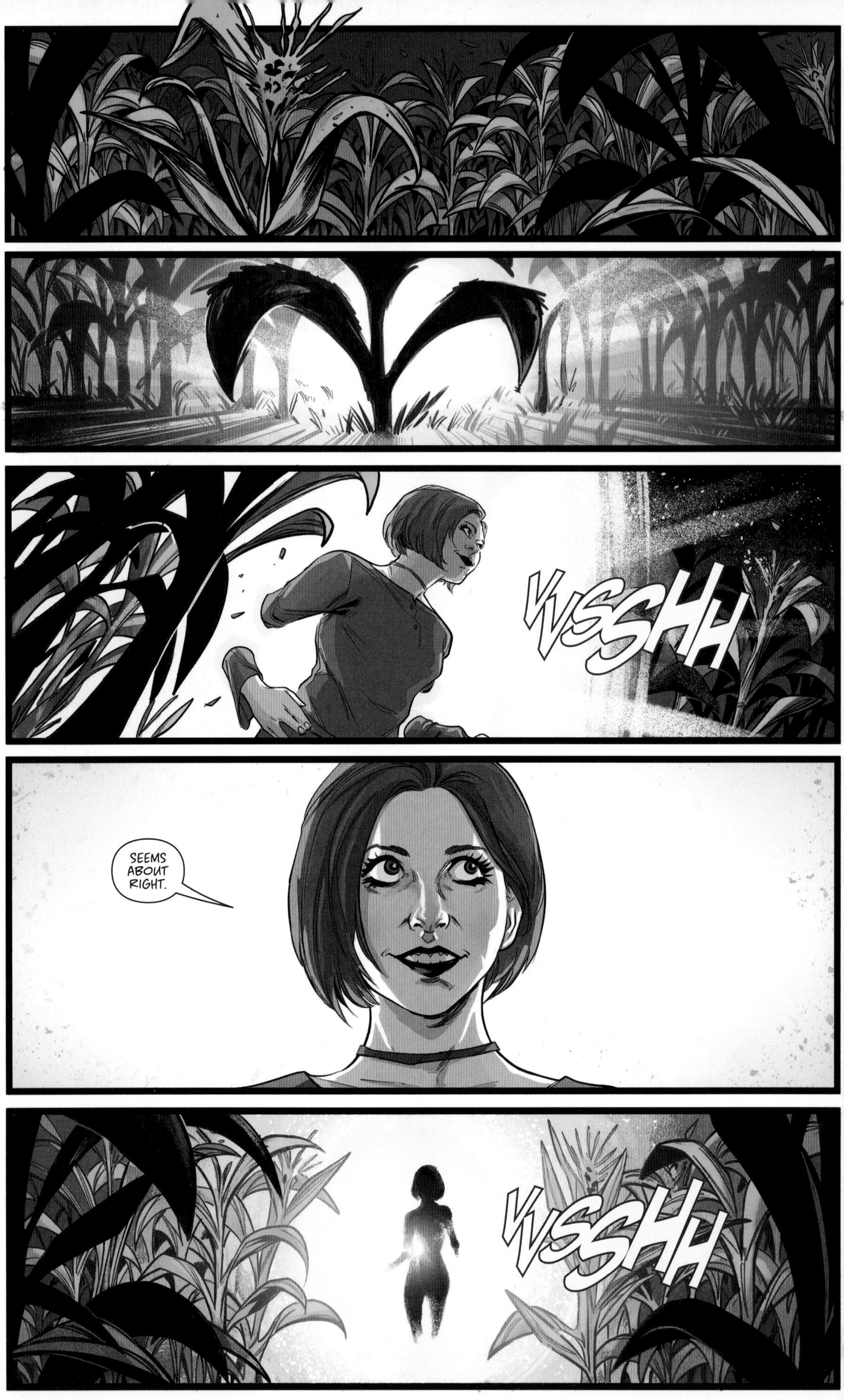
VVSSHH
SEEMS ABOUT RIGHT.
VVSSHH

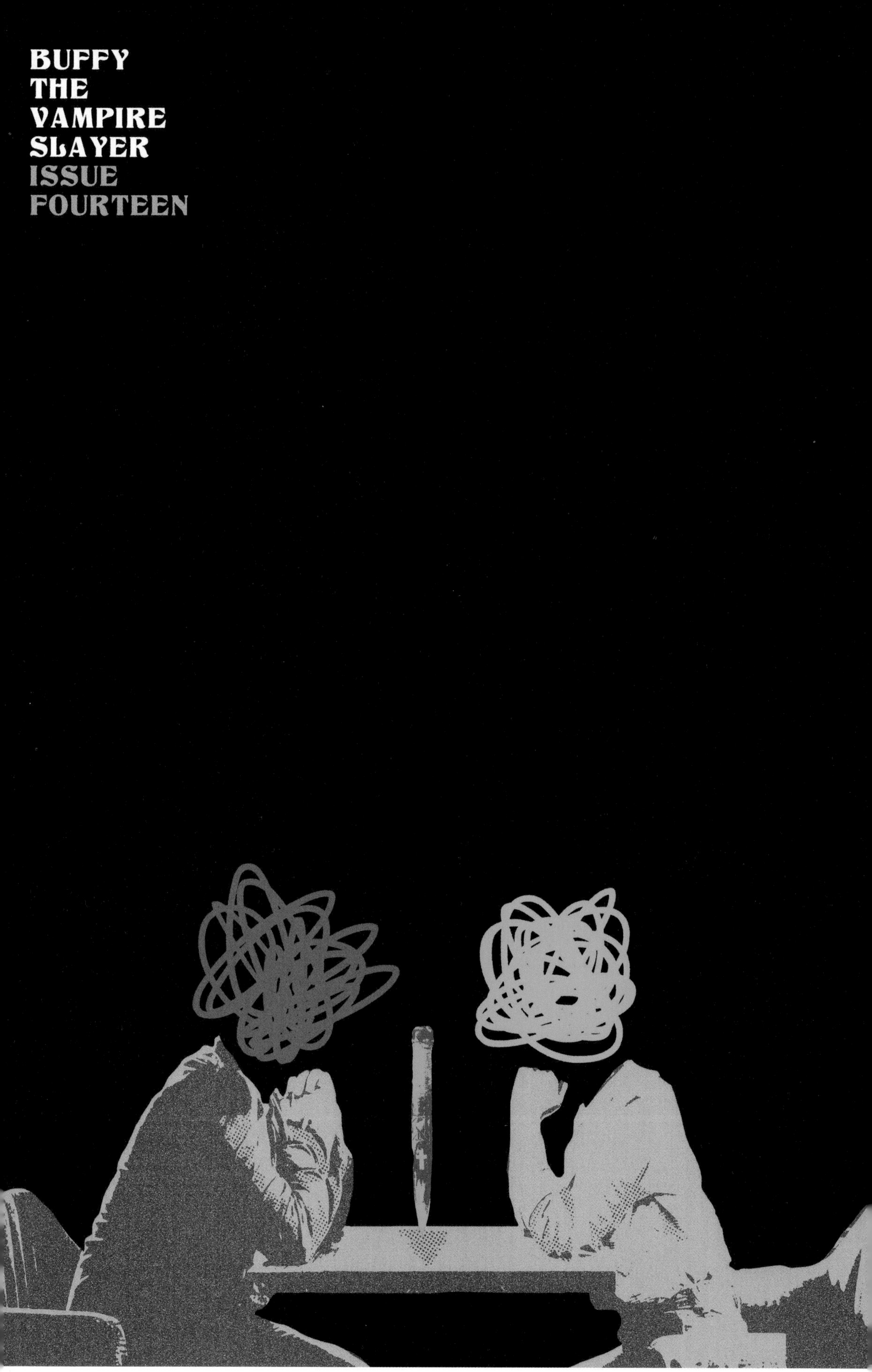
BUFFY
THE
VAMPIRE
SLAYER
ISSUE
FOURTEEN

Issue Fourteen Ring of Fire Cover by **Becca Carey**

CHAPTER
FIFTEEN

Issue Fifteen Cover by **David López**

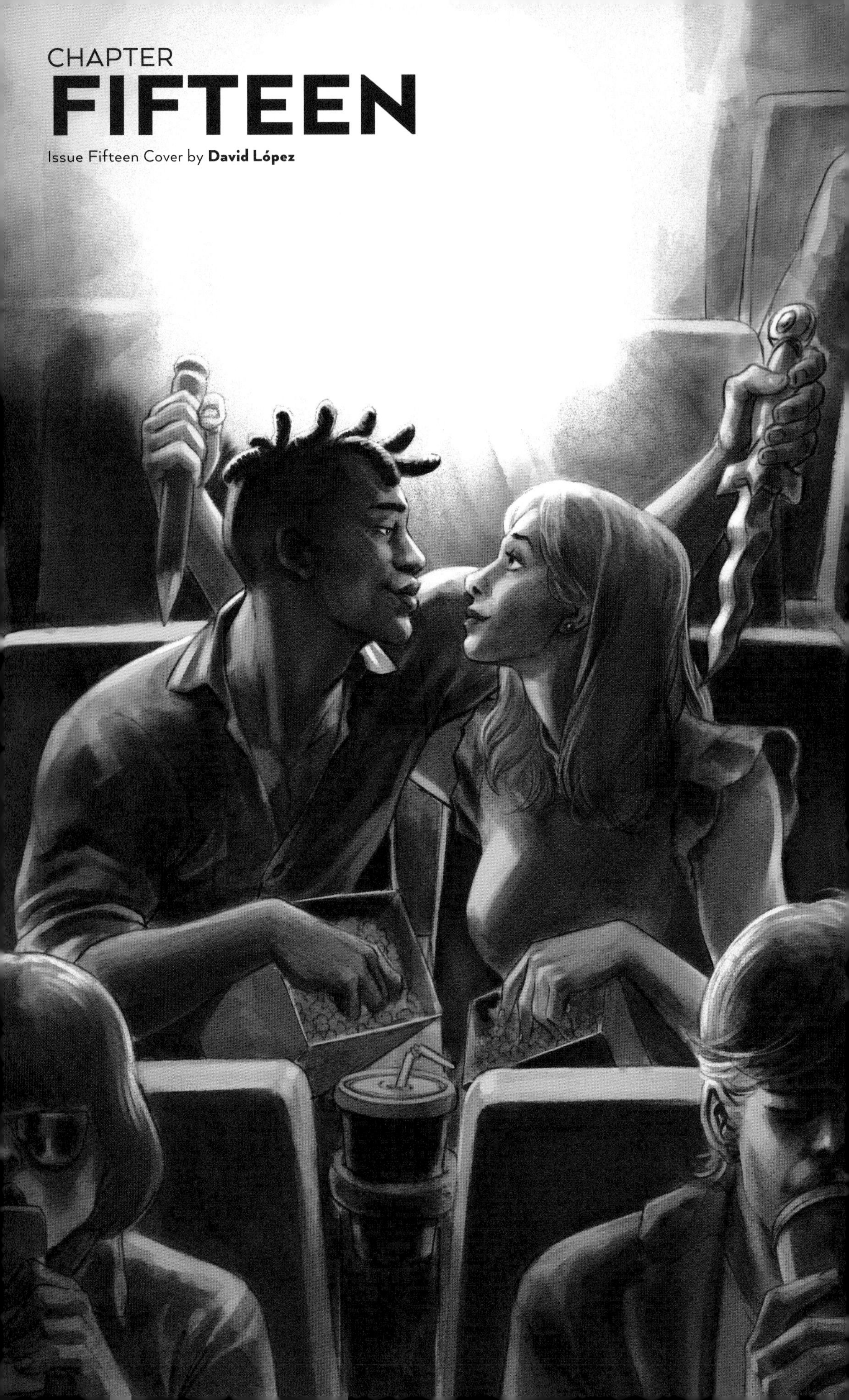

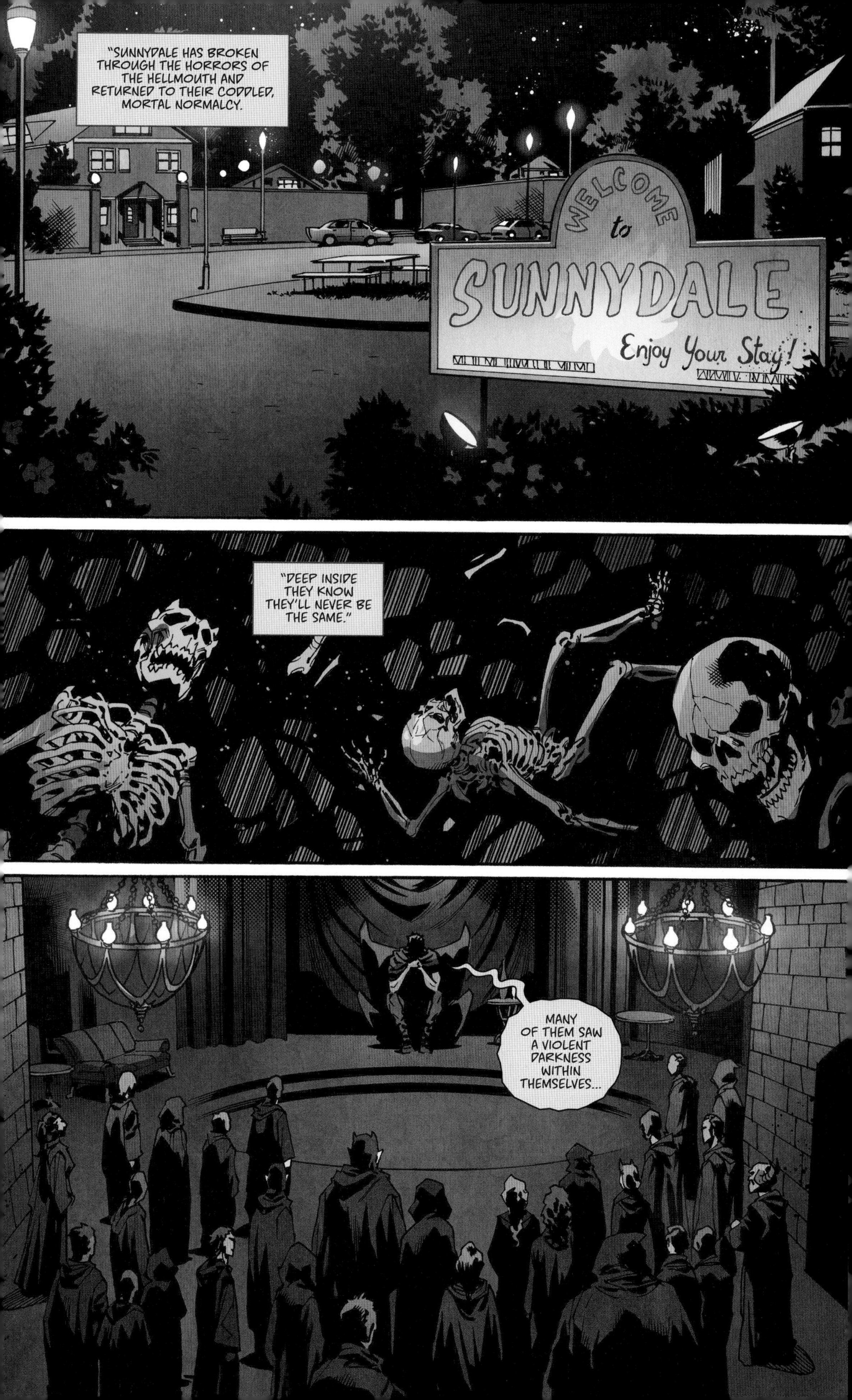
"SUNNYDALE HAS BROKEN THROUGH THE HORRORS OF THE HELLMOUTH AND RETURNED TO THEIR CODDLED, MORTAL NORMALCY.
WELCOME to SUNNYDALE
Enjoy Your Stay!
"DEEP INSIDE THEY KNOW THEY'LL NEVER BE THE SAME."
MANY OF THEM SAW A VIOLENT DARKNESS WITHIN THEMSELVES...

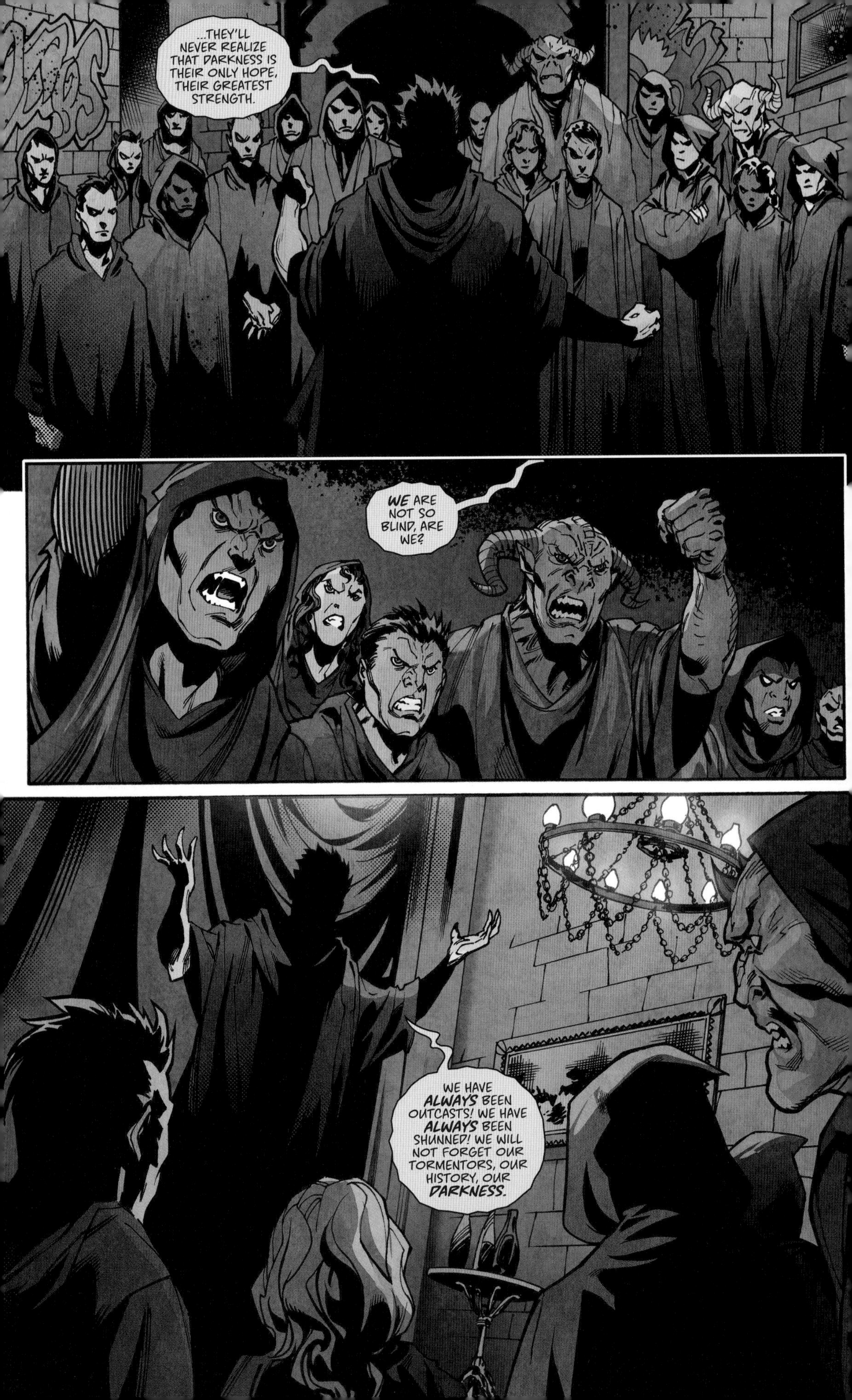
...THEY'LL NEVER REALIZE THAT DARKNESS IS THEIR ONLY HOPE, THEIR GREATEST STRENGTH.
WE ARE NOT SO BLIND, ARE WE?
WE HAVE ALWAYS BEEN OUTCASTS! WE HAVE ALWAYS BEEN SHUNNED! WE WILL NOT FORGET OUR TORMENTORS, OUR HISTORY, OUR DARKNESS.

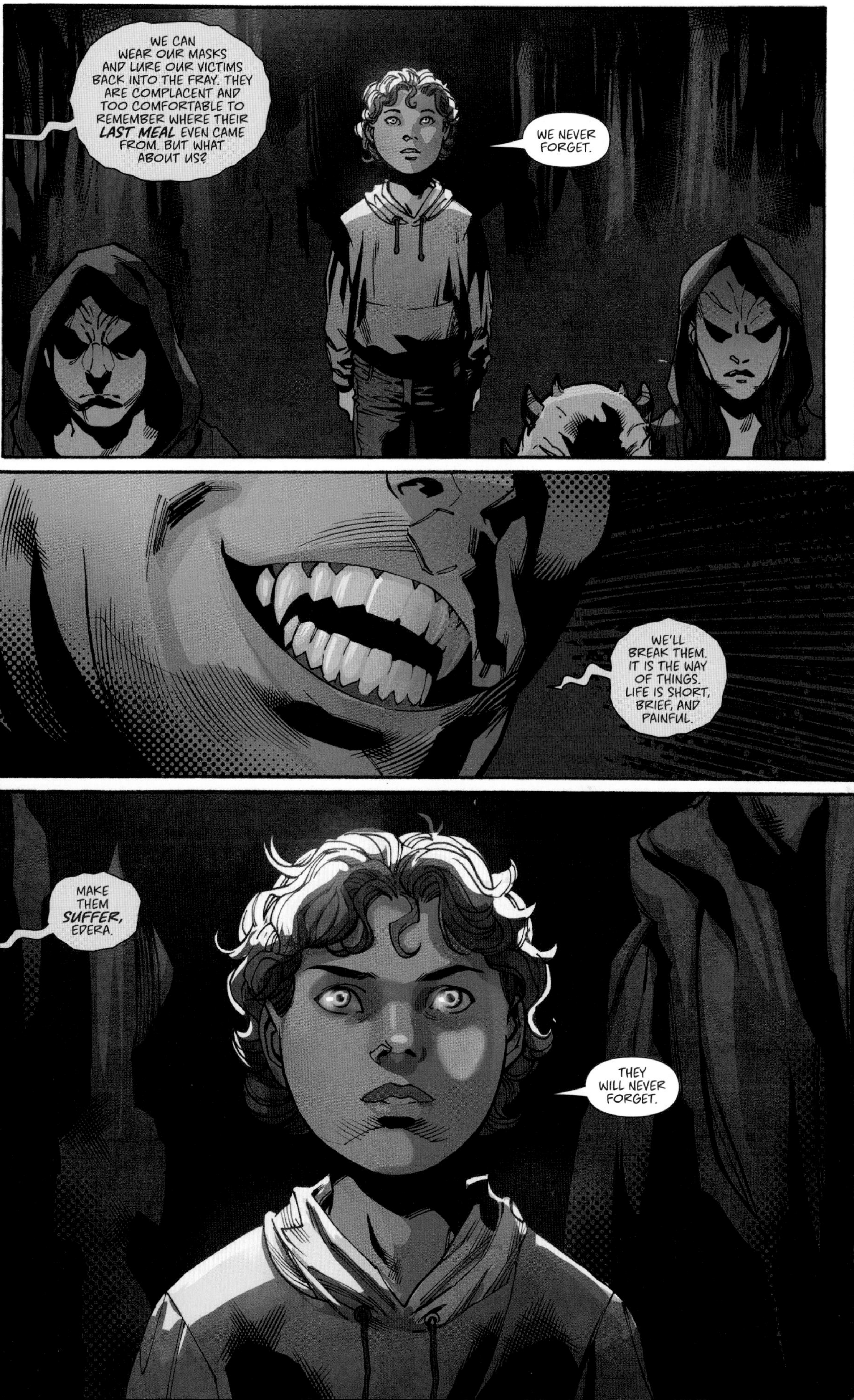
WE CAN WEAR OUR MASKS AND LURE OUR VICTIMS BACK INTO THE FRAY. THEY ARE COMPLACENT AND TOO COMFORTABLE TO REMEMBER WHERE THEIR LAST MEAL EVEN CAME FROM. BUT WHAT ABOUT US?
WE NEVER FORGET.
WE'LL BREAK THEM. IT IS THE WAY OF THINGS. LIFE IS SHORT, BRIEF, AND PAINFUL.
MAKE THEM SUFFER, EDERA.
THEY WILL NEVER FORGET.

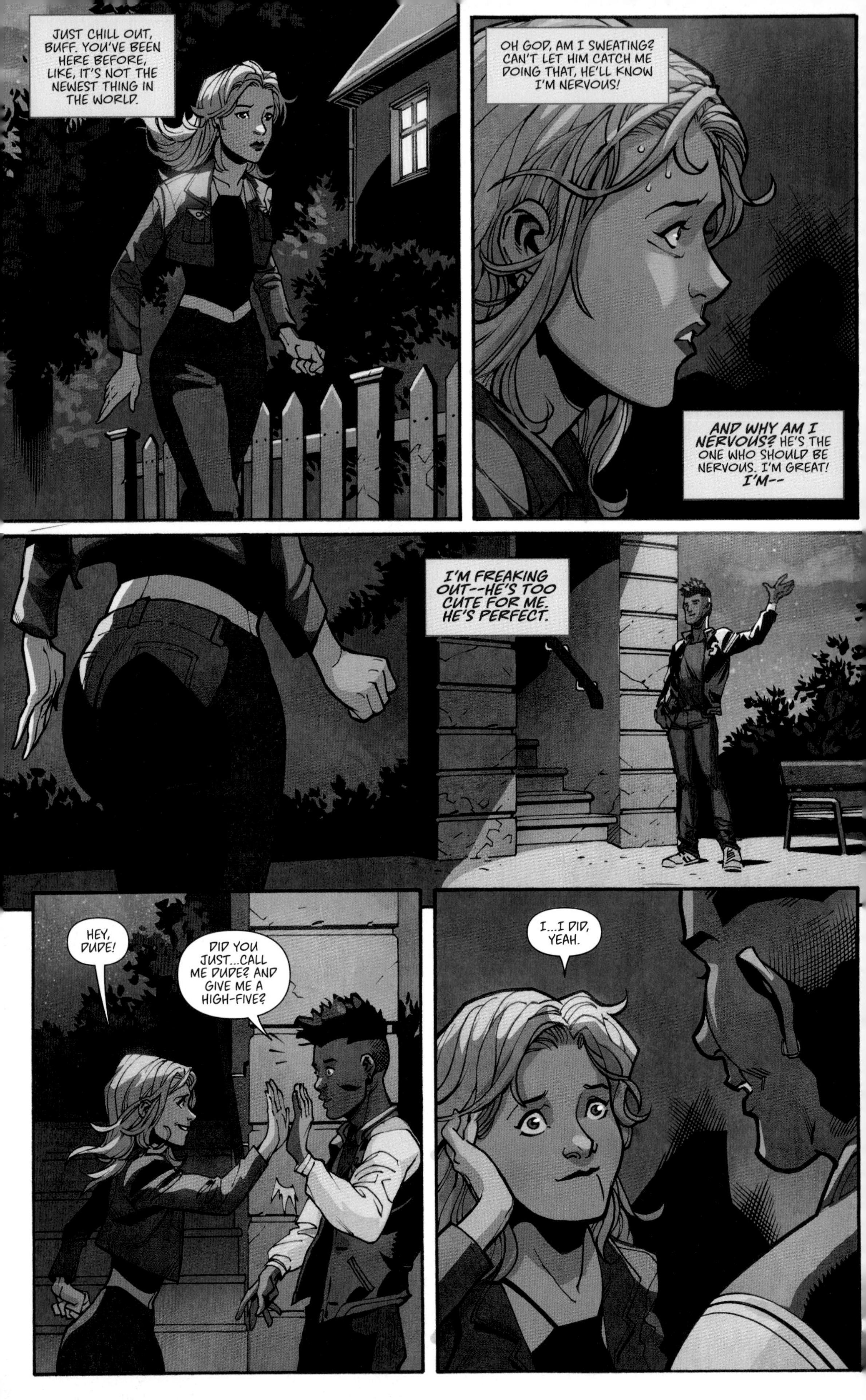
JUST CHILL OUT, BUFF. YOU'VE BEEN HERE BEFORE, LIKE, IT'S NOT THE NEWEST THING IN THE WORLD.
OH GOD, AM I SWEATING? CAN'T LET HIM CATCH ME DOING THAT, HE'LL KNOW I'M NERVOUS!
AND WHY AM I NERVOUS? HE'S THE ONE WHO SHOULD BE NERVOUS. I'M GREAT! I'M--
I'M FREAKING OUT--HE'S TOO CUTE FOR ME. HE'S PERFECT.
HEY, DUDE!
DID YOU JUST...CALL ME DUDE? AND GIVE ME A HIGH-FIVE?
I...I DID, YEAH.

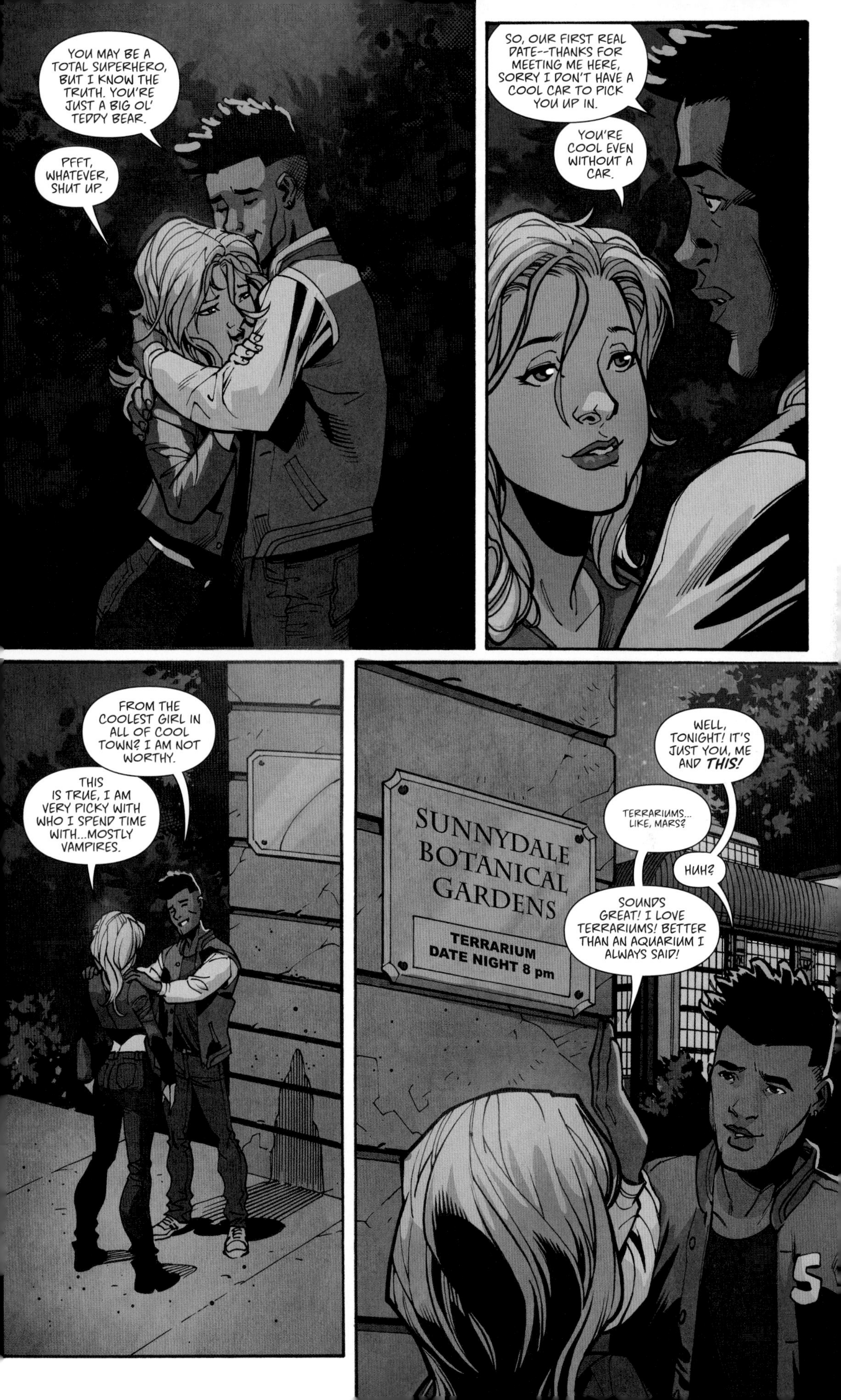
YOU MAY BE A TOTAL SUPERHERO, BUT I KNOW THE TRUTH. YOU'RE JUST A BIG OL' TEDDY BEAR.
PFFT, WHATEVER, SHUT UP.
SO, OUR FIRST REAL DATE--THANKS FOR MEETING ME HERE, SORRY I DON'T HAVE A COOL CAR TO PICK YOU UP IN.
YOU'RE COOL EVEN WITHOUT A CAR.
FROM THE COOLEST GIRL IN ALL OF COOL TOWN? I AM NOT WORTHY.
THIS IS TRUE, I AM VERY PICKY WITH WHO I SPEND TIME WITH...MOSTLY VAMPIRES.
SUNNYDALE BOTANICAL GARDENS
TERRARIUM DATE NIGHT 8 pm
WELL, TONIGHT! IT'S JUST YOU, ME AND **THIS!**
TERRARIUMS... LIKE, MARS?
HUH?
SOUNDS GREAT! I LOVE TERRARIUMS! BETTER THAN AN AQUARIUM I ALWAYS SAID!
5

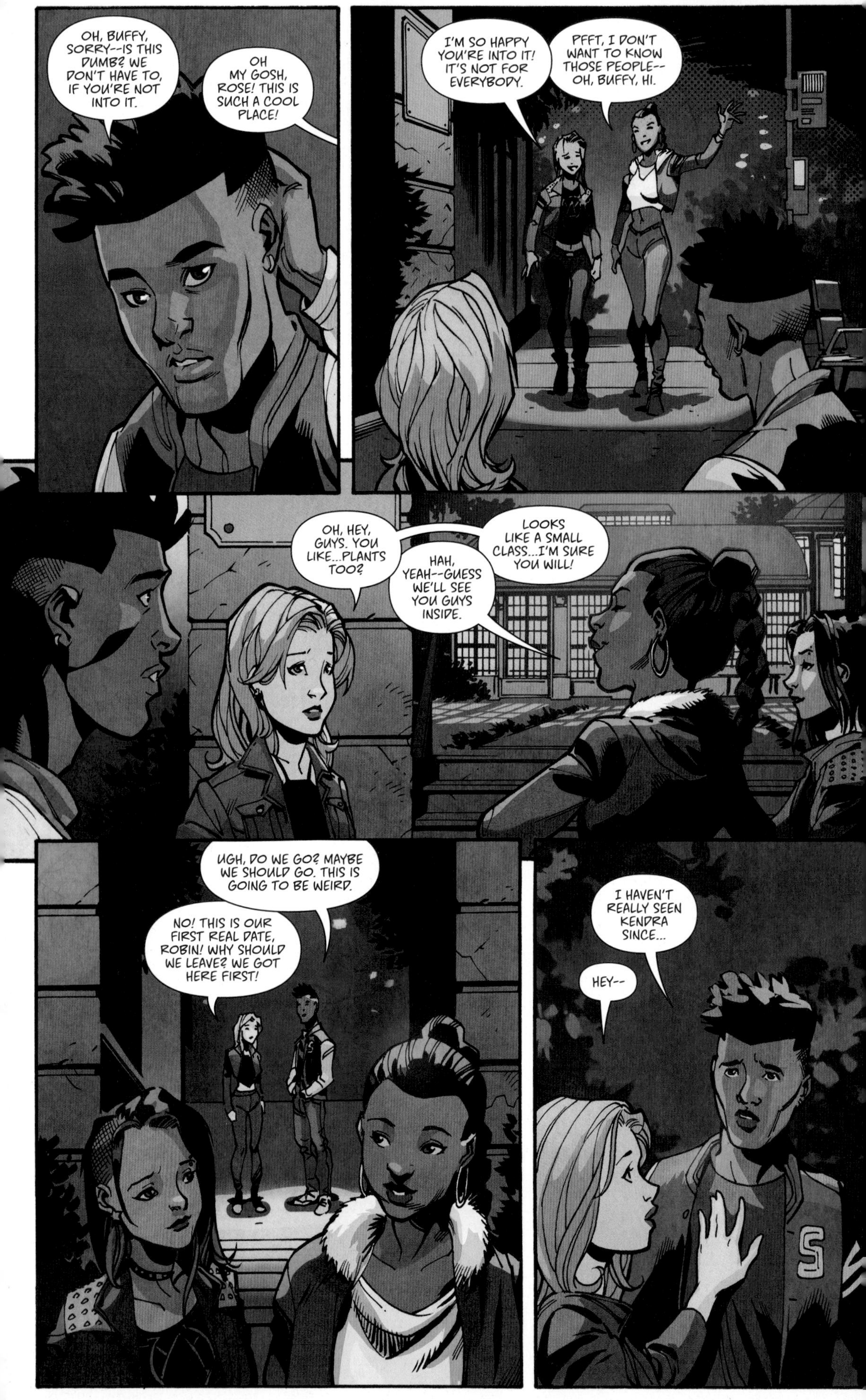
OH, BUFFY, SORRY--IS THIS DUMB? WE DON'T HAVE TO, IF YOU'RE NOT INTO IT.
OH MY GOSH, ROSE! THIS IS SUCH A COOL PLACE!
I'M SO HAPPY YOU'RE INTO IT! IT'S NOT FOR EVERYBODY.
PFFT, I DON'T WANT TO KNOW THOSE PEOPLE-- OH, BUFFY, HI.
OH, HEY, GUYS. YOU LIKE...PLANTS TOO?
LOOKS LIKE A SMALL CLASS...I'M SURE YOU WILL!
HAH, YEAH--GUESS WE'LL SEE YOU GUYS INSIDE.
UGH, DO WE GO? MAYBE WE SHOULD GO. THIS IS GOING TO BE WEIRD.
NO! THIS IS OUR FIRST REAL DATE, ROBIN! WHY SHOULD WE LEAVE? WE GOT HERE FIRST!
I HAVEN'T REALLY SEEN KENDRA SINCE...
HEY--

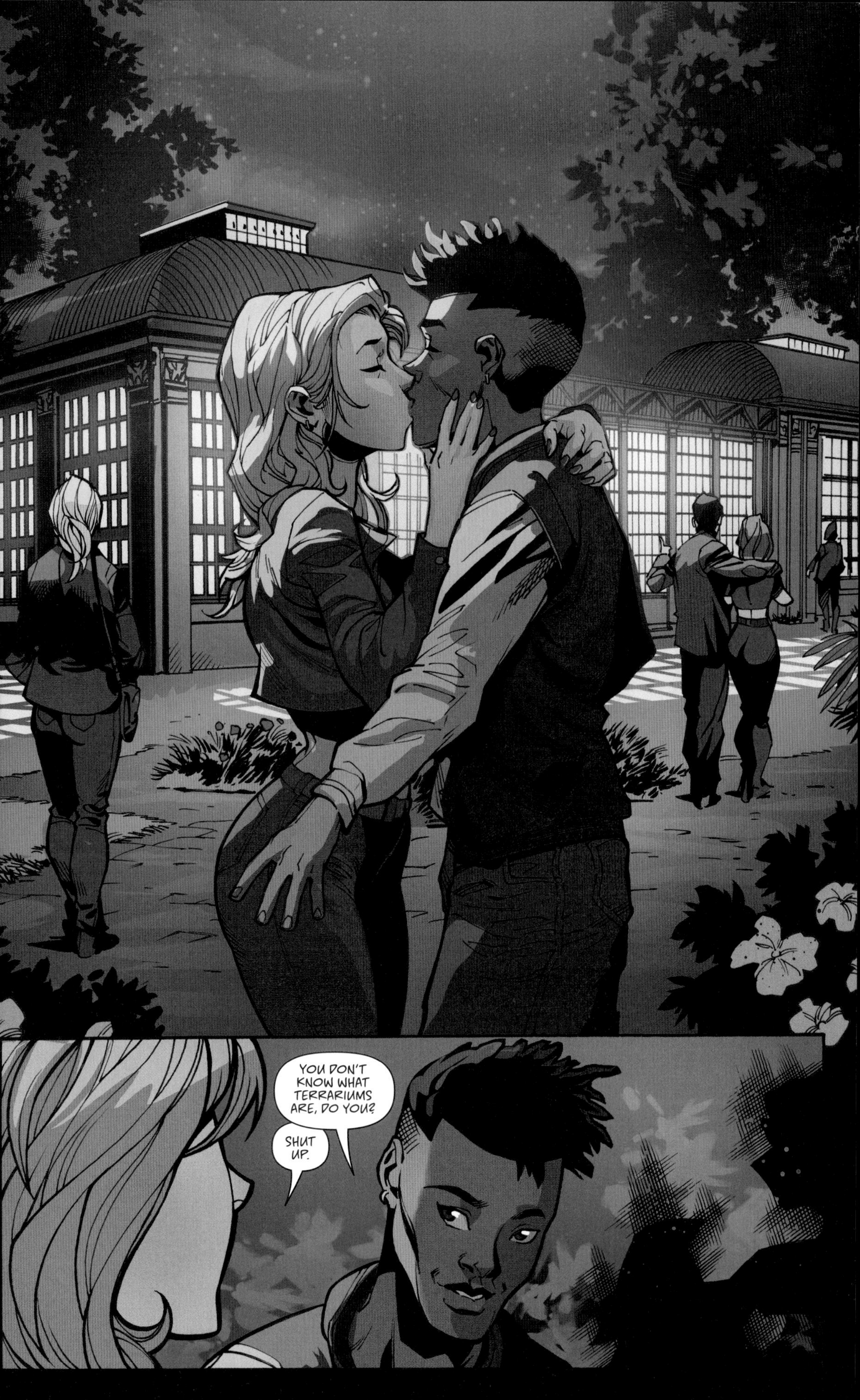
YOU DON'T KNOW WHAT TERRARIUMS ARE, DO YOU?
SHUT UP.

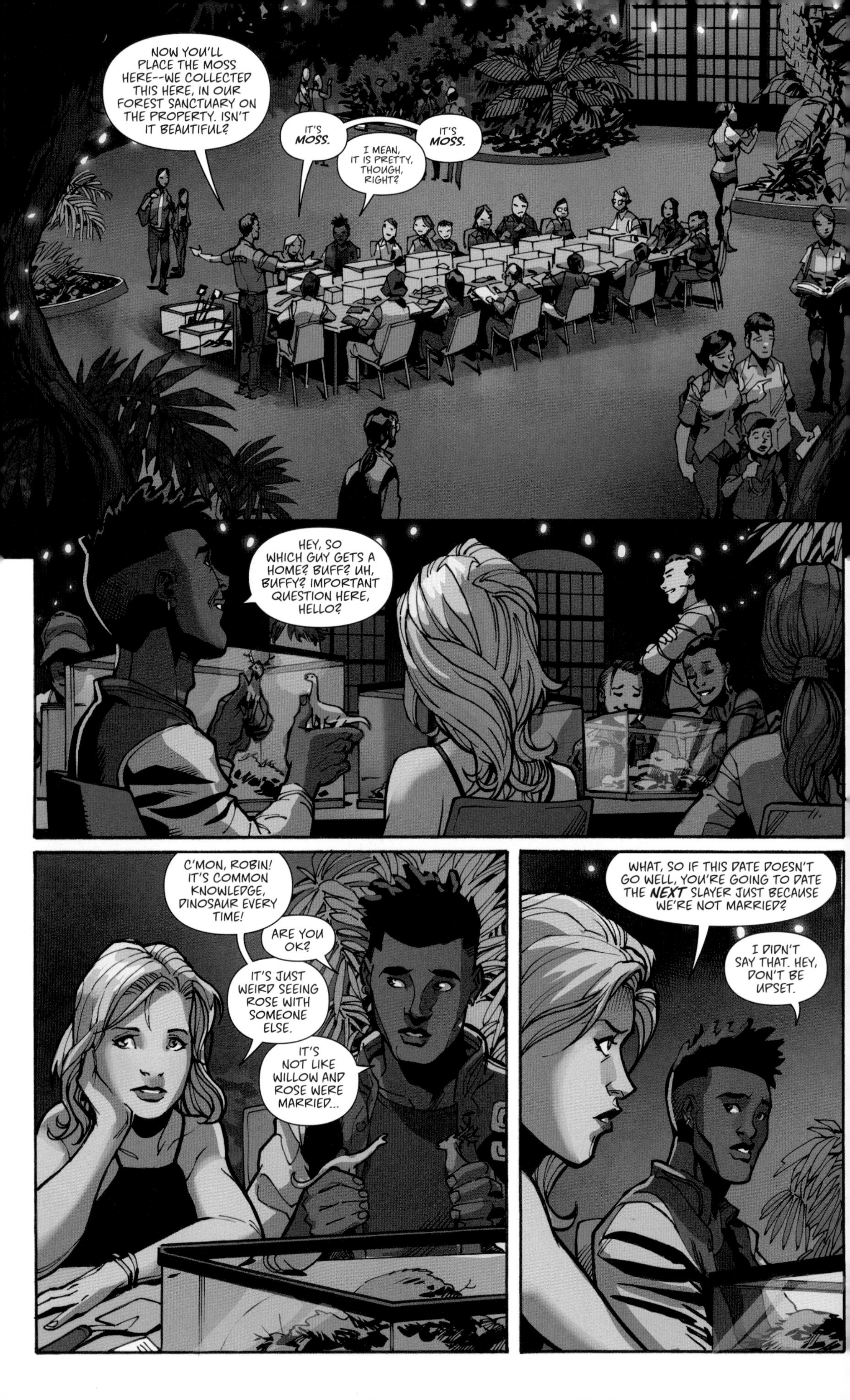
NOW YOU'LL PLACE THE MOSS HERE--WE COLLECTED THIS HERE, IN OUR FOREST SANCTUARY ON THE PROPERTY. ISN'T IT BEAUTIFUL?
IT'S *MOSS.*
IT'S *MOSS.*
I MEAN, IT IS PRETTY, THOUGH, RIGHT?
HEY, SO WHICH GUY GETS A HOME? BUFF? UH, BUFFY? IMPORTANT QUESTION HERE, HELLO?
C'MON, ROBIN! IT'S COMMON KNOWLEDGE, DINOSAUR EVERY TIME!
ARE YOU OK?
IT'S JUST WEIRD SEEING ROSE WITH SOMEONE ELSE.
IT'S NOT LIKE WILLOW AND ROSE WERE MARRIED...
WHAT, SO IF THIS DATE DOESN'T GO WELL, YOU'RE GOING TO DATE THE ***NEXT*** SLAYER JUST BECAUSE WE'RE NOT MARRIED?
I DIDN'T SAY THAT. HEY, DON'T BE UPSET.

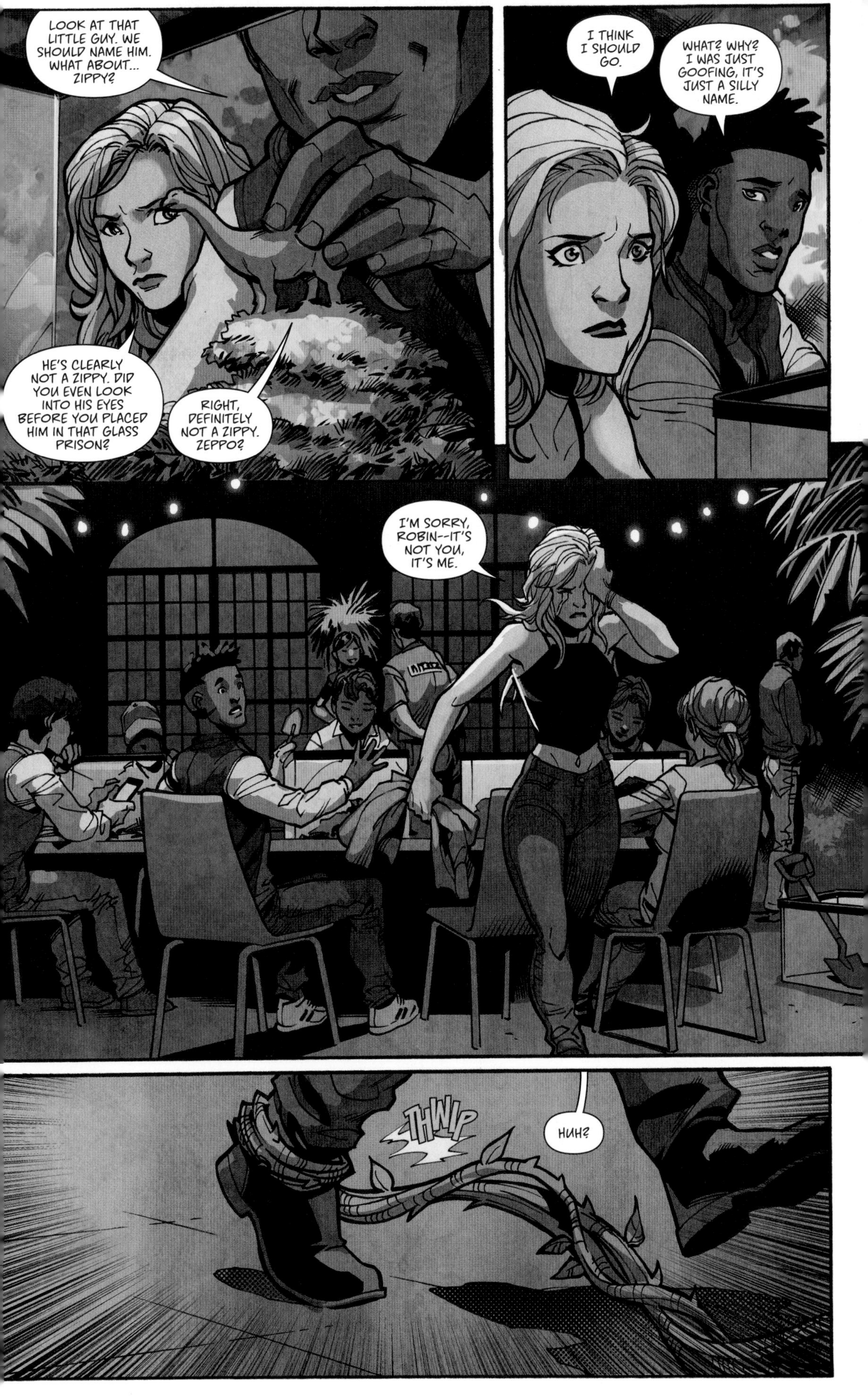
LOOK AT THAT LITTLE GUY. WE SHOULD NAME HIM. WHAT ABOUT... ZIPPY?
HE'S CLEARLY NOT A ZIPPY. DID YOU EVEN LOOK INTO HIS EYES BEFORE YOU PLACED HIM IN THAT GLASS PRISON?
RIGHT, DEFINITELY NOT A ZIPPY. ZEPPO?
I THINK I SHOULD GO.
WHAT? WHY? I WAS JUST GOOFING, IT'S JUST A SILLY NAME.
I'M SORRY, ROBIN--IT'S NOT YOU, IT'S ME.
THWIP
HUH?

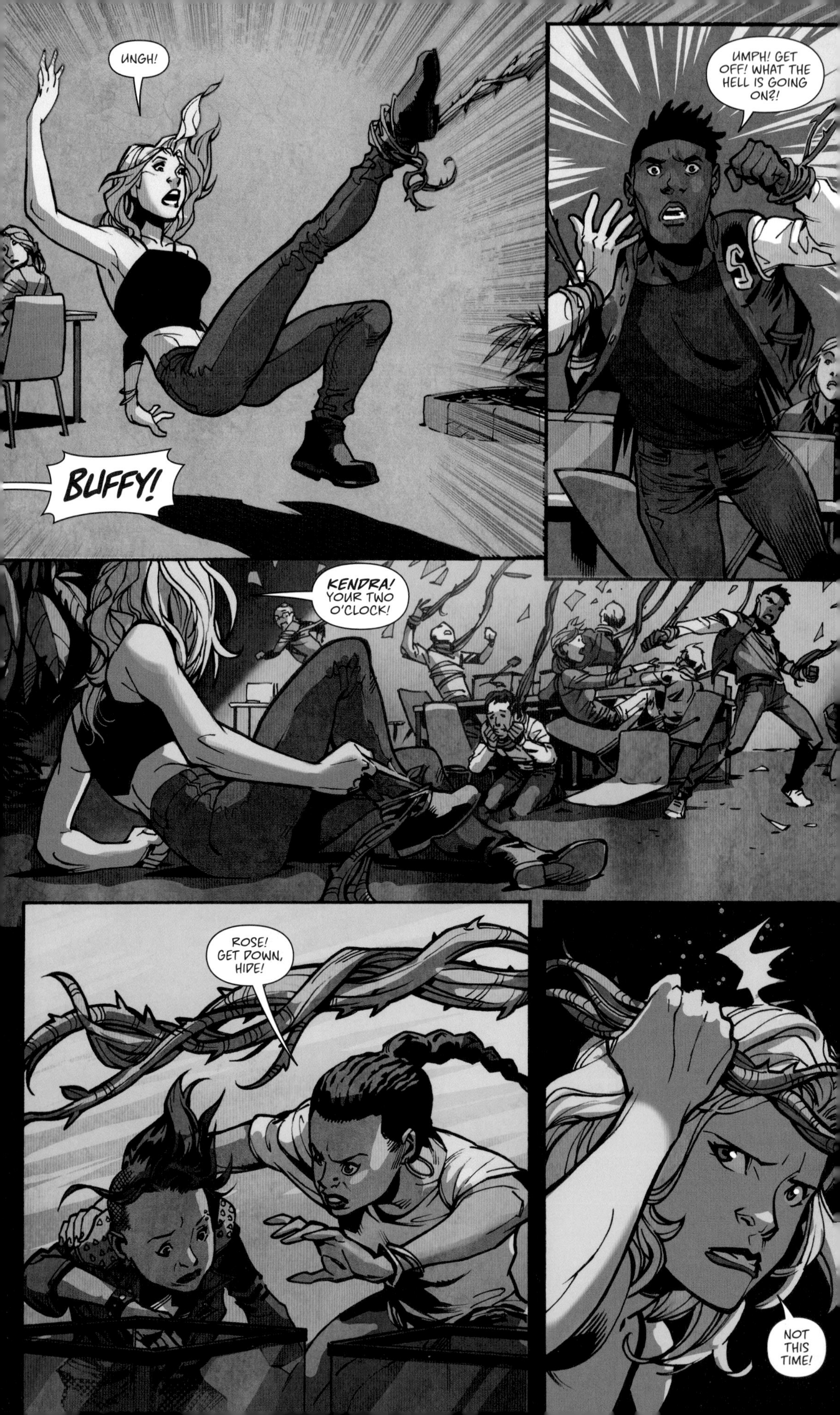
UNGH!
BUFFY!
UMPH! GET OFF! WHAT THE HELL IS GOING ON?!
KENDRA! YOUR TWO O'CLOCK!
ROSE! GET DOWN, HIDE!
NOT THIS TIME!

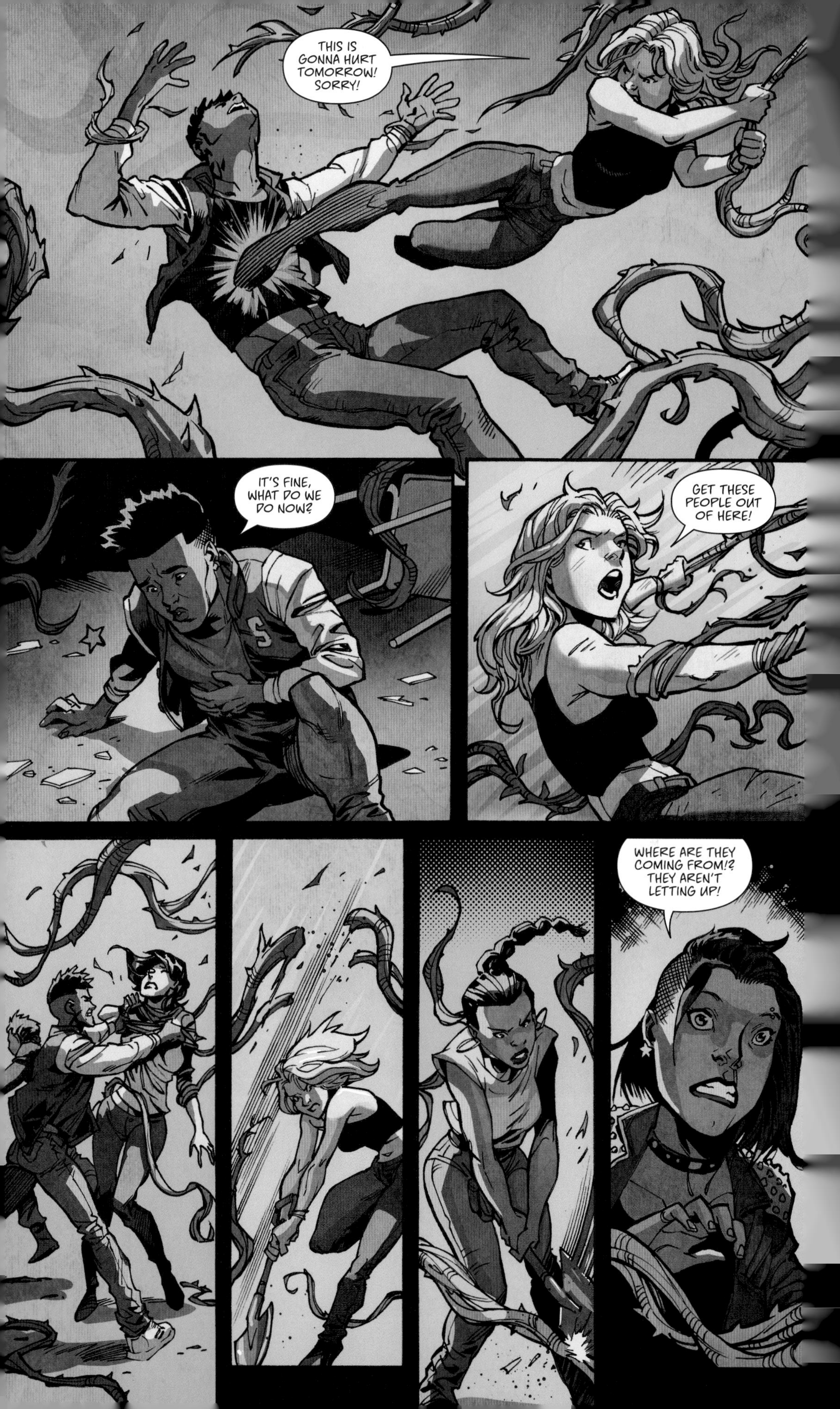

THIS IS GONNA HURT TOMORROW! SORRY!
IT'S FINE, WHAT DO WE DO NOW?
GET THESE PEOPLE OUT OF HERE!
WHERE ARE THEY COMING FROM!? THEY AREN'T LETTING UP!

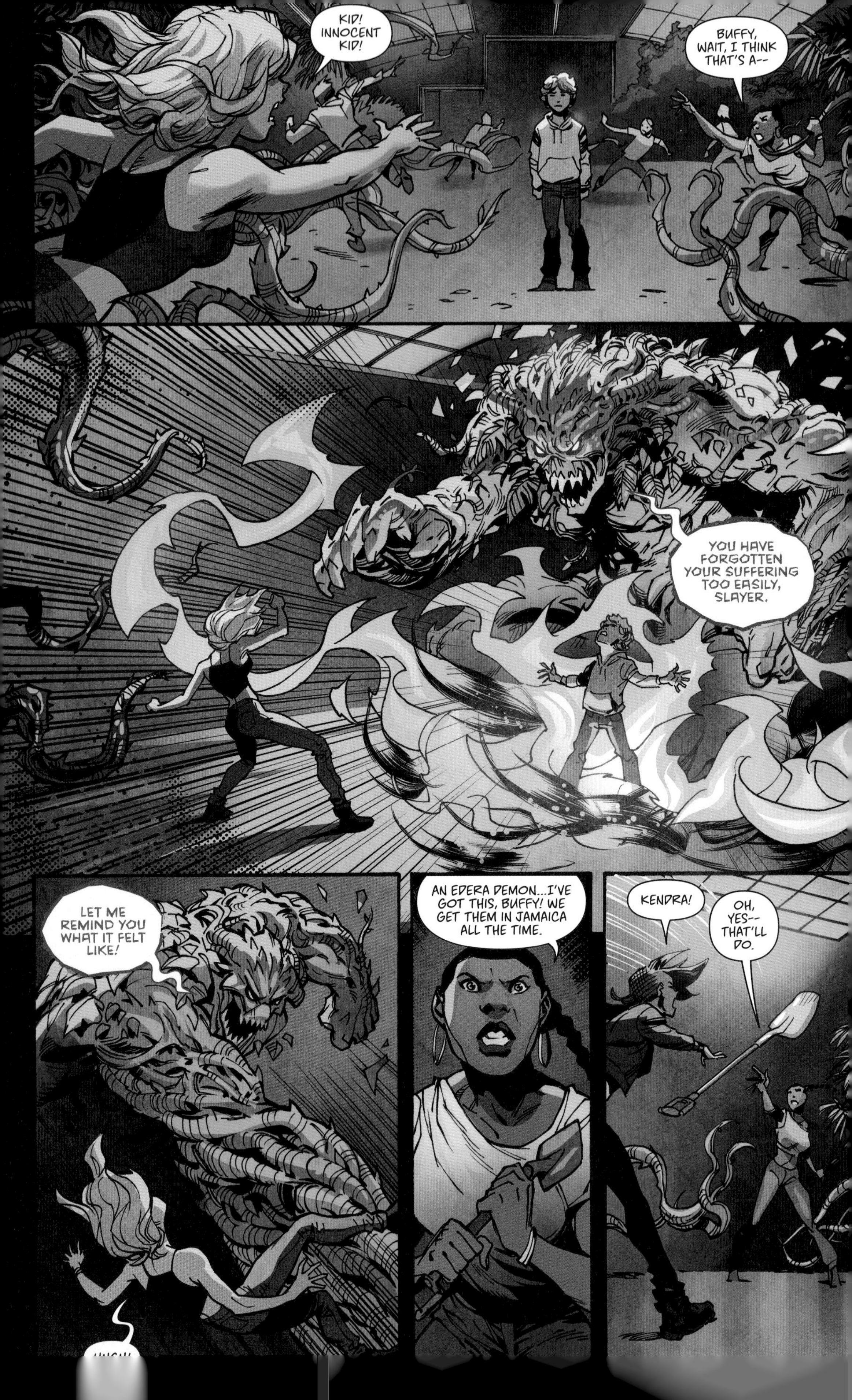
KID! INNOCENT KID!
BUFFY, WAIT, I THINK THAT'S A--
YOU HAVE FORGOTTEN YOUR SUFFERING TOO EASILY, SLAYER.
LET ME REMIND YOU WHAT IT FELT LIKE!
AN EDERA DEMON...I'VE GOT THIS, BUFFY! WE GET THEM IN JAMAICA ALL THE TIME.
KENDRA!
OH, YES-- THAT'LL DO.

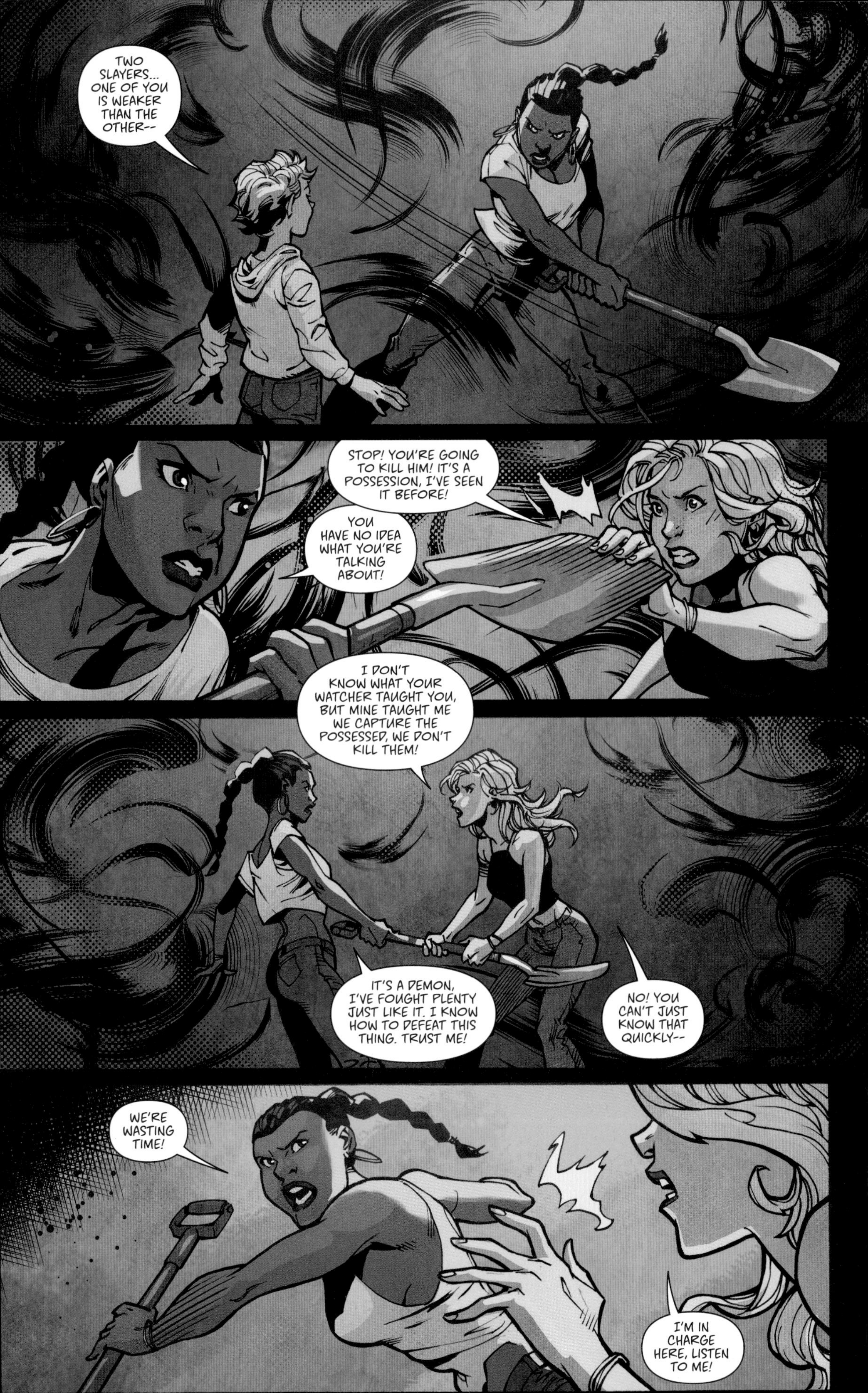

TWO SLAYERS... ONE OF YOU IS WEAKER THAN THE OTHER--
STOP! YOU'RE GOING TO KILL HIM! IT'S A POSSESSION, I'VE SEEN IT BEFORE!
YOU HAVE NO IDEA WHAT YOU'RE TALKING ABOUT!
I DON'T KNOW WHAT YOUR WATCHER TAUGHT YOU, BUT MINE TAUGHT ME WE CAPTURE THE POSSESSED, WE DON'T KILL THEM!
IT'S A DEMON, I'VE FOUGHT PLENTY JUST LIKE IT. I KNOW HOW TO DEFEAT THIS THING. TRUST ME!
NO! YOU CAN'T JUST KNOW THAT QUICKLY--
WE'RE WASTING TIME!
I'M IN CHARGE HERE, LISTEN TO ME!

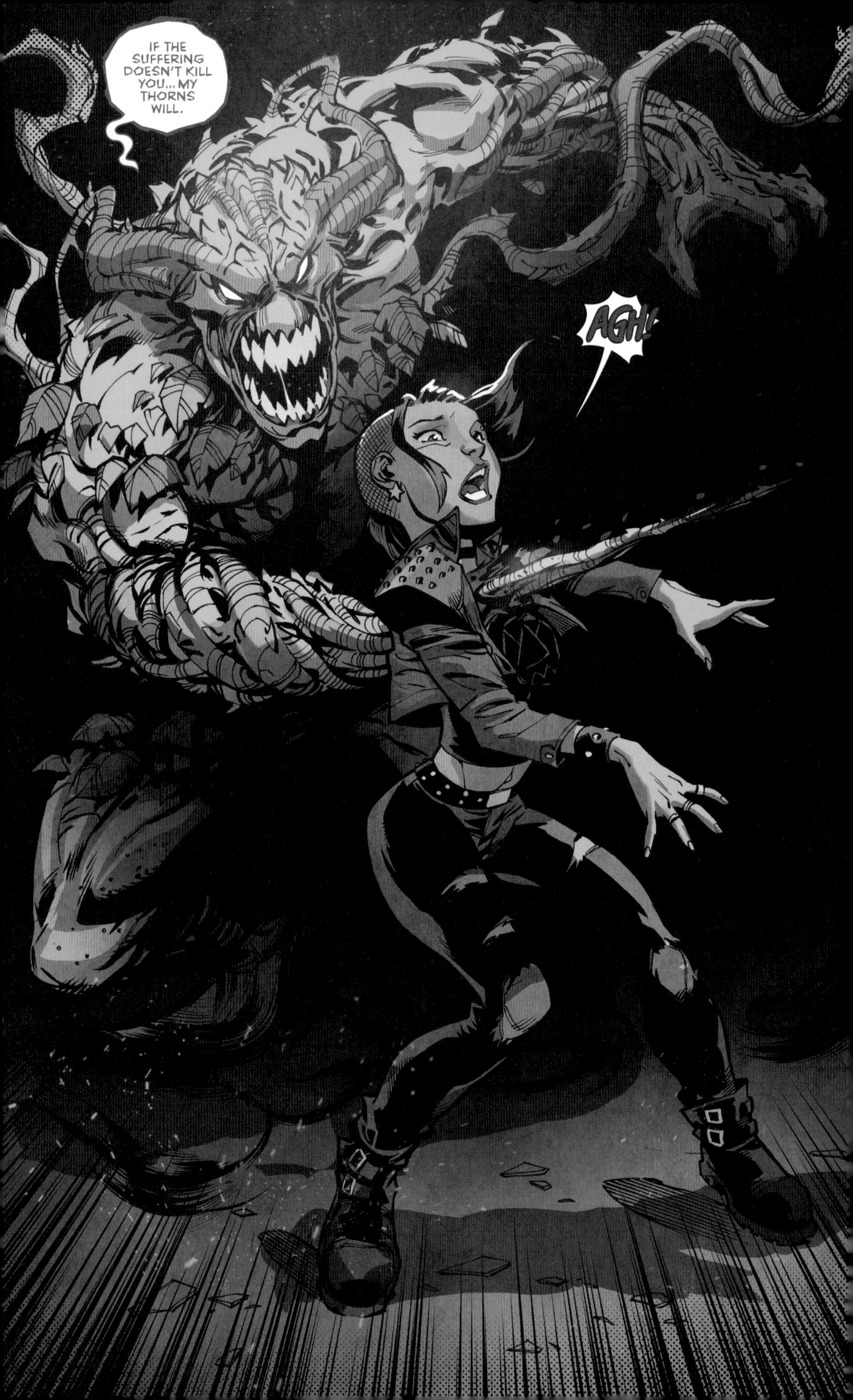
IF THE SUFFERING DOESN'T KILL YOU... MY THORNS WILL.
AGH!

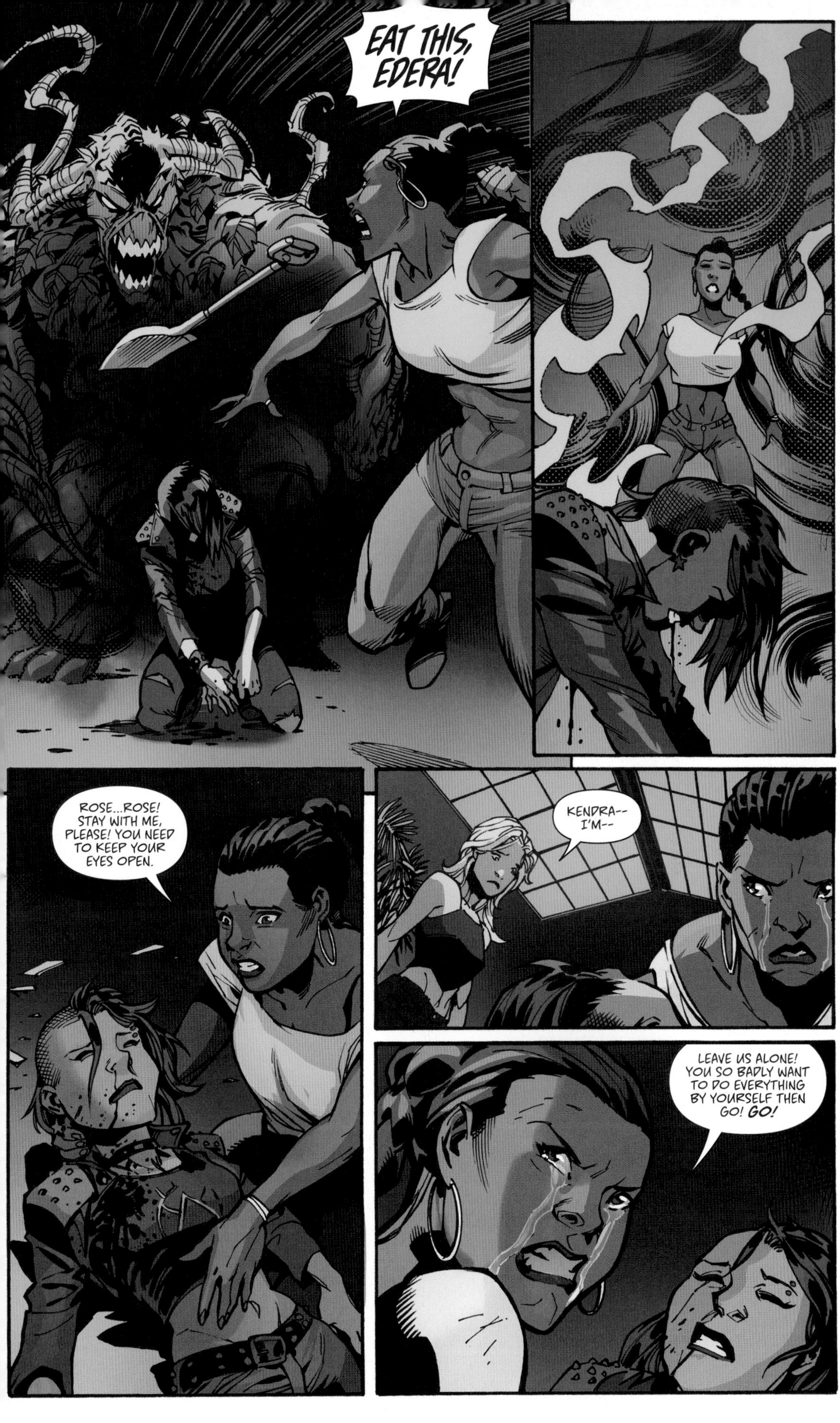
EAT THIS, EDERA!
ROSE...ROSE! STAY WITH ME, PLEASE! YOU NEED TO KEEP YOUR EYES OPEN.
KENDRA-- I'M--
LEAVE US ALONE! YOU SO BADLY WANT TO DO EVERYTHING BY YOURSELF THEN GO! GO!

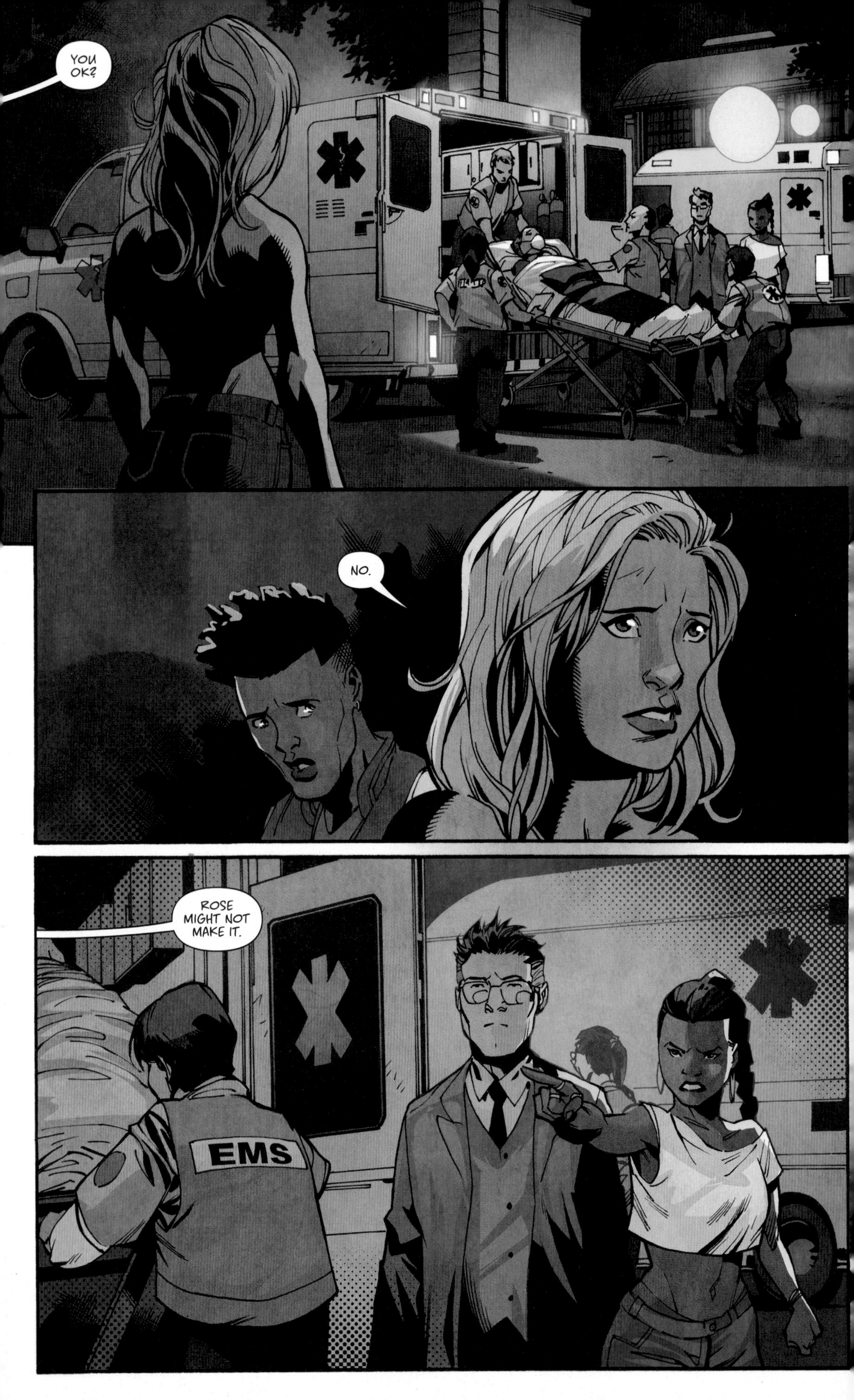
YOU OK?
NO.
ROSE MIGHT NOT MAKE IT.
EMS

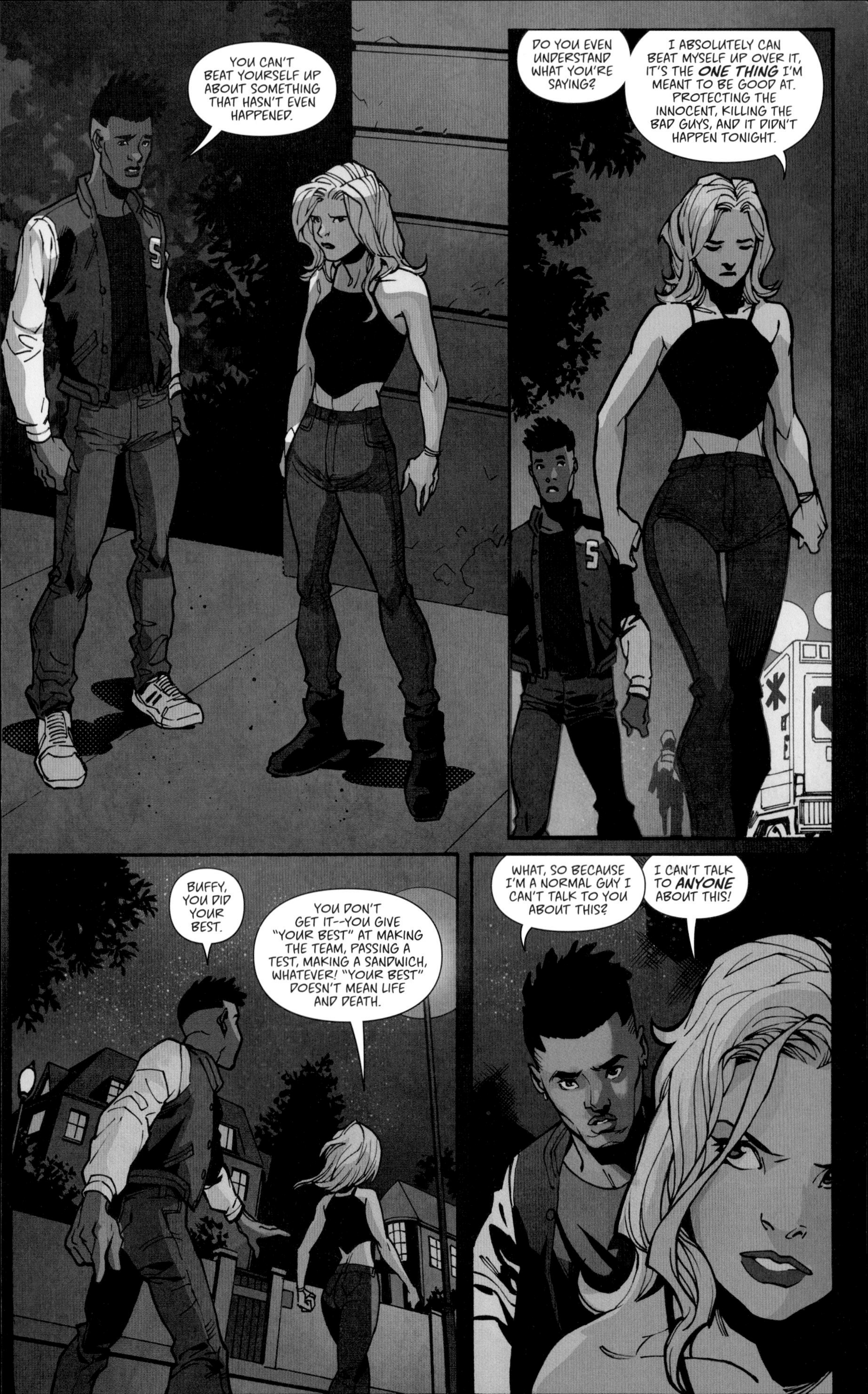
YOU CAN'T BEAT YOURSELF UP ABOUT SOMETHING THAT HASN'T EVEN HAPPENED.
DO YOU EVEN UNDERSTAND WHAT YOU'RE SAYING?
I ABSOLUTELY CAN BEAT MYSELF UP OVER IT, IT'S THE **ONE THING** I'M MEANT TO BE GOOD AT. PROTECTING THE INNOCENT, KILLING THE BAD GUYS, AND IT DIDN'T HAPPEN TONIGHT.
BUFFY, YOU DID YOUR BEST.
YOU DON'T GET IT--YOU GIVE "YOUR BEST" AT MAKING THE TEAM, PASSING A TEST, MAKING A SANDWICH, WHATEVER! "YOUR BEST" DOESN'T MEAN LIFE AND DEATH.
WHAT, SO BECAUSE I'M A NORMAL GUY I CAN'T TALK TO YOU ABOUT THIS?
I CAN'T TALK TO **ANYONE** ABOUT THIS!

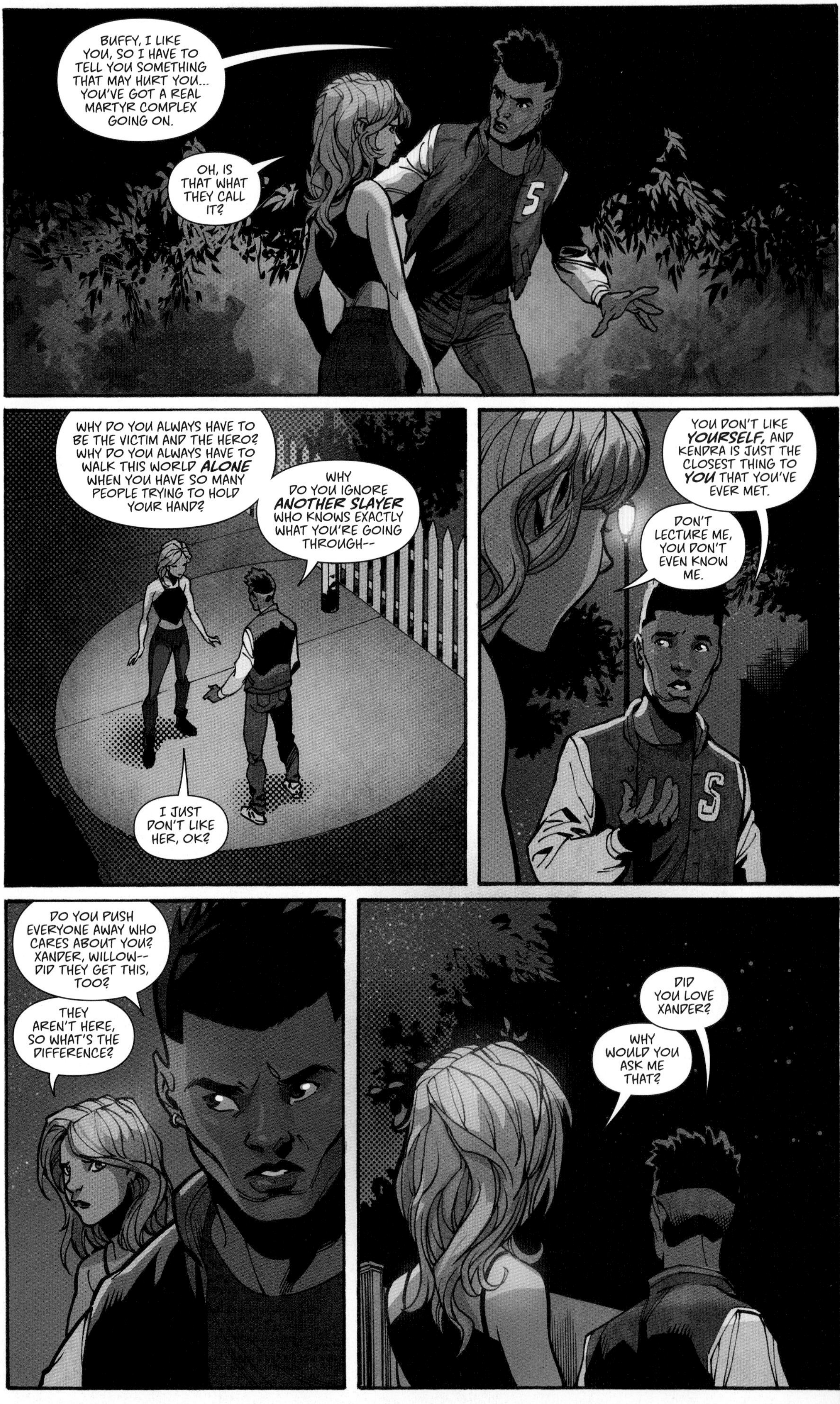

BUFFY, I LIKE YOU, SO I HAVE TO TELL YOU SOMETHING THAT MAY HURT YOU... YOU'VE GOT A REAL MARTYR COMPLEX GOING ON.
OH, IS THAT WHAT THEY CALL IT?
WHY DO YOU ALWAYS HAVE TO BE THE VICTIM AND THE HERO? WHY DO YOU ALWAYS HAVE TO WALK THIS WORLD ALONE WHEN YOU HAVE SO MANY PEOPLE TRYING TO HOLD YOUR HAND?
WHY DO YOU IGNORE ANOTHER SLAYER WHO KNOWS EXACTLY WHAT YOU'RE GOING THROUGH--
I JUST DON'T LIKE HER, OK?
YOU DON'T LIKE YOURSELF, AND KENDRA IS JUST THE CLOSEST THING TO YOU THAT YOU'VE EVER MET.
DON'T LECTURE ME, YOU DON'T EVEN KNOW ME.
DO YOU PUSH EVERYONE AWAY WHO CARES ABOUT YOU? XANDER, WILLOW-- DID THEY GET THIS, TOO?
THEY AREN'T HERE, SO WHAT'S THE DIFFERENCE?
DID YOU LOVE XANDER?
WHY WOULD YOU ASK ME THAT?

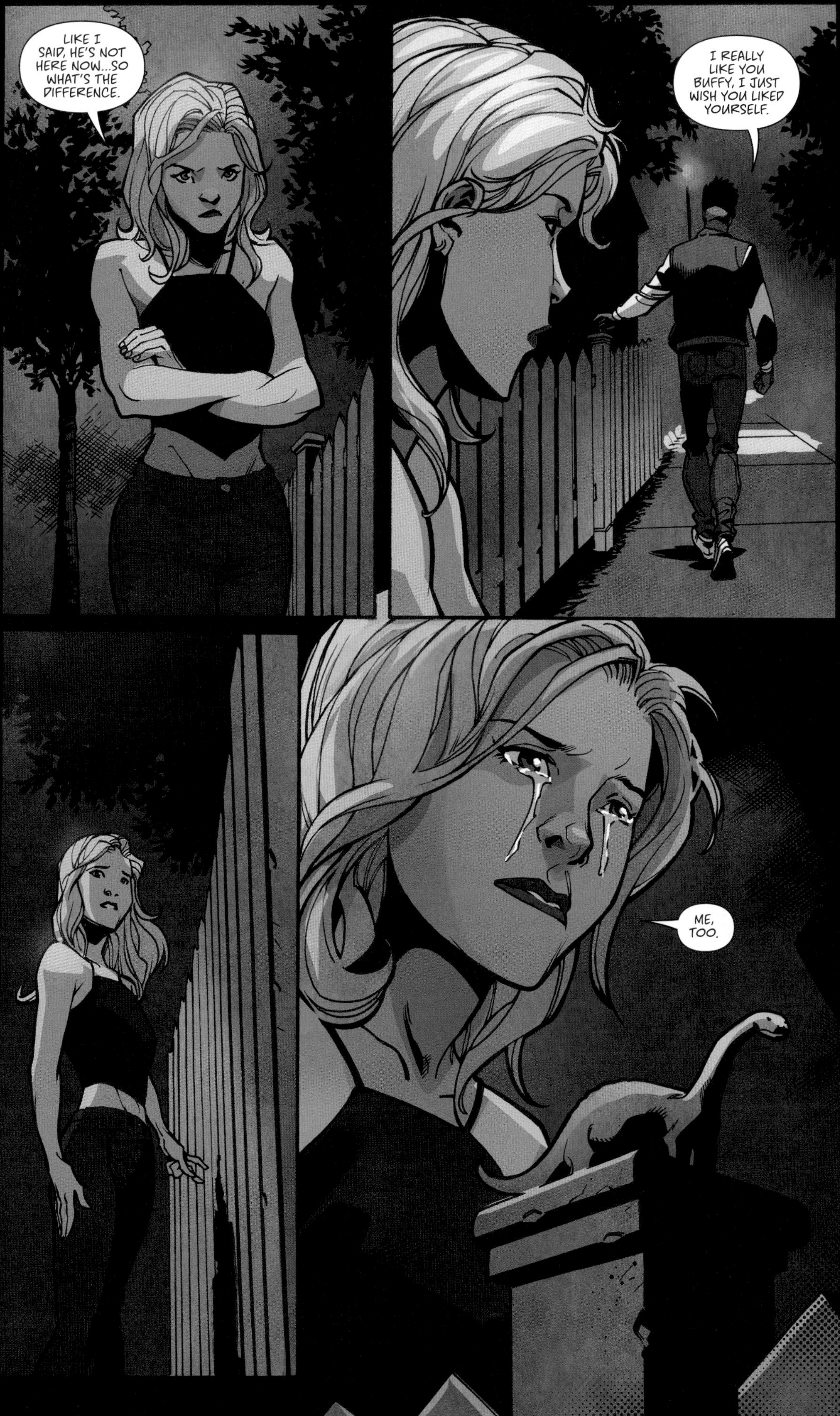
LIKE I SAID, HE'S NOT HERE NOW...SO WHAT'S THE DIFFERENCE.
I REALLY LIKE YOU BUFFY, I JUST WISH YOU LIKED YOURSELF.
ME, TOO.

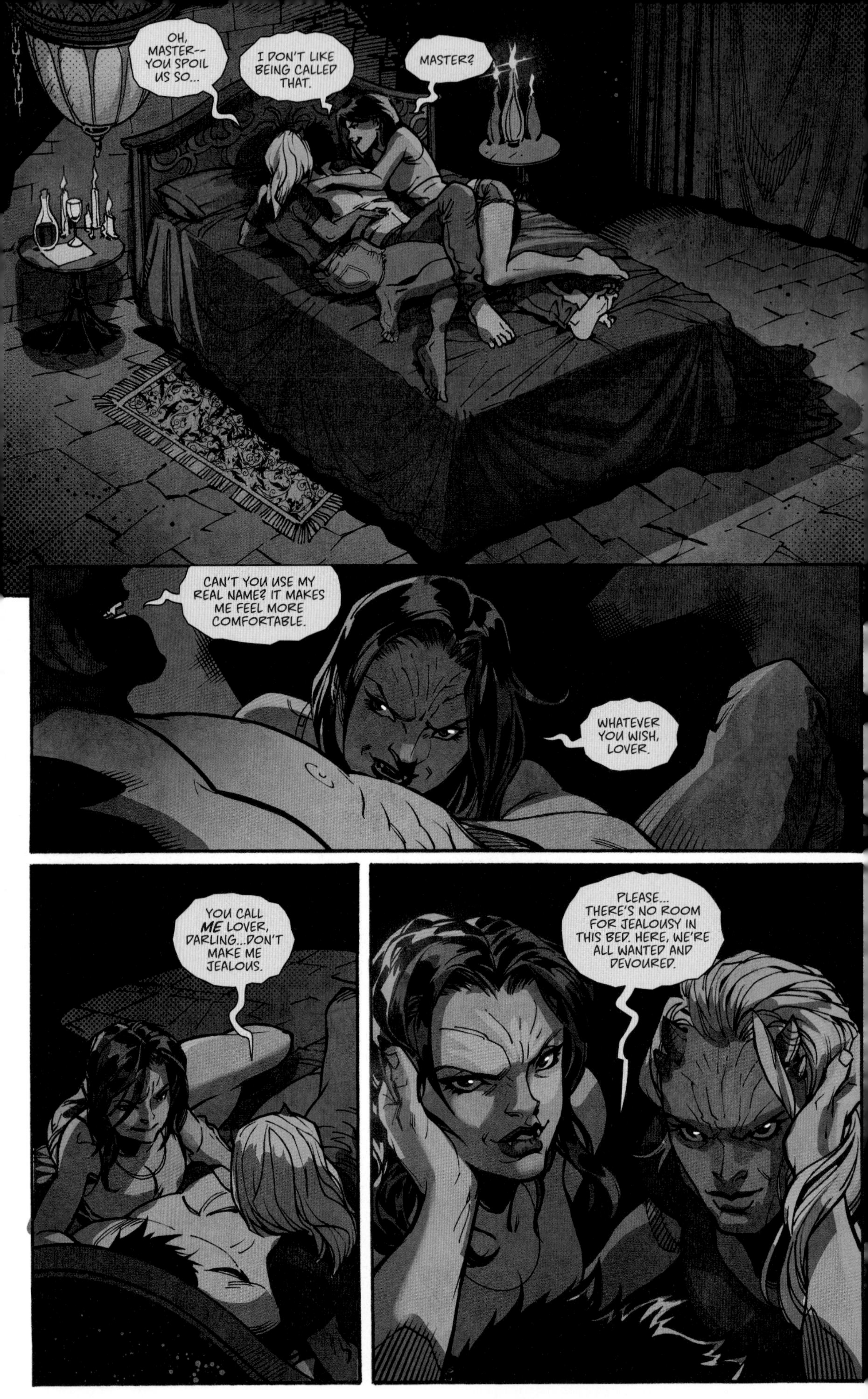
OH, MASTER-- YOU SPOIL US SO...
I DON'T LIKE BEING CALLED THAT.
MASTER?
CAN'T YOU USE MY REAL NAME? IT MAKES ME FEEL MORE COMFORTABLE.
WHATEVER YOU WISH, LOVER.
YOU CALL ME LOVER, DARLING...DON'T MAKE ME JEALOUS.
PLEASE... THERE'S NO ROOM FOR JEALOUSY IN THIS BED. HERE, WE'RE ALL WANTED AND DEVOURED.

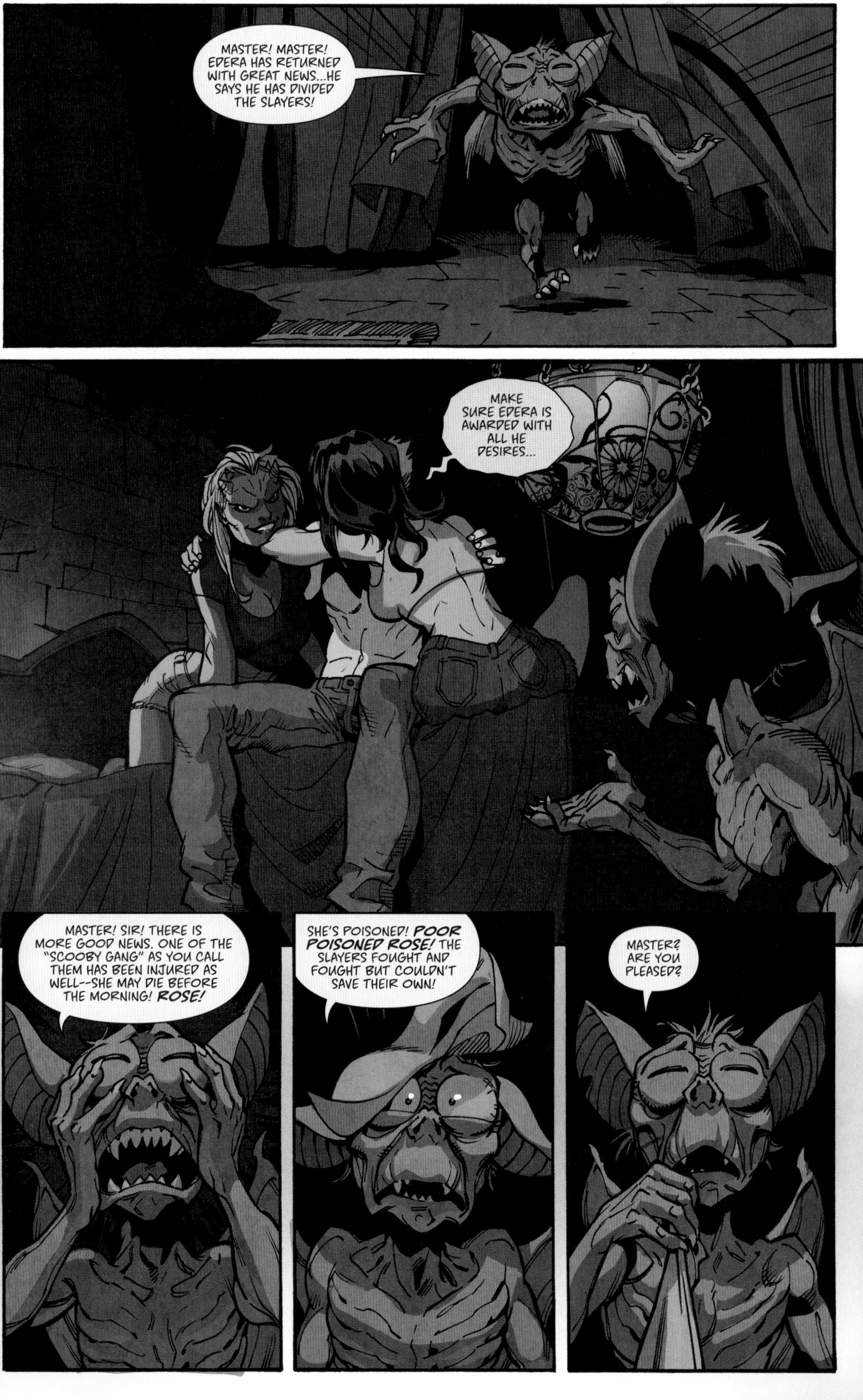
MASTER! MASTER! EDERA HAS RETURNED WITH GREAT NEWS...HE SAYS HE HAS DIVIDED THE SLAYERS!
MAKE SURE EDERA IS AWARDED WITH ALL HE DESIRES...
MASTER! SIR! THERE IS MORE GOOD NEWS. ONE OF THE "SCOOBY GANG" AS YOU CALL THEM HAS BEEN INJURED AS WELL--SHE MAY DIE BEFORE THE MORNING! ROSE!
SHE'S POISONED! POOR POISONED ROSE! THE SLAYERS FOUGHT AND FOUGHT BUT COULDN'T SAVE THEIR OWN!
MASTER? ARE YOU PLEASED?

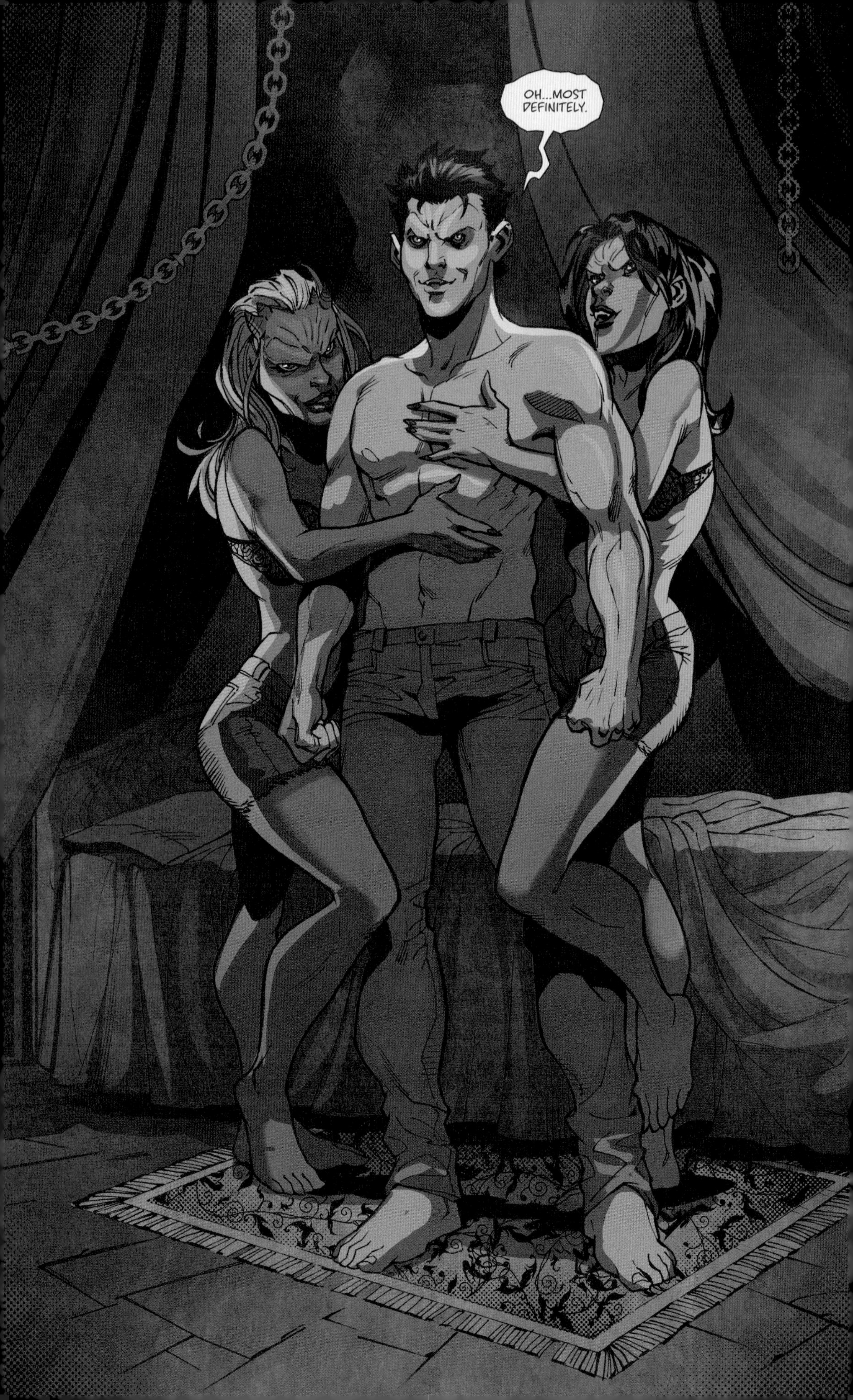
OH...MOST DEFINITELY.

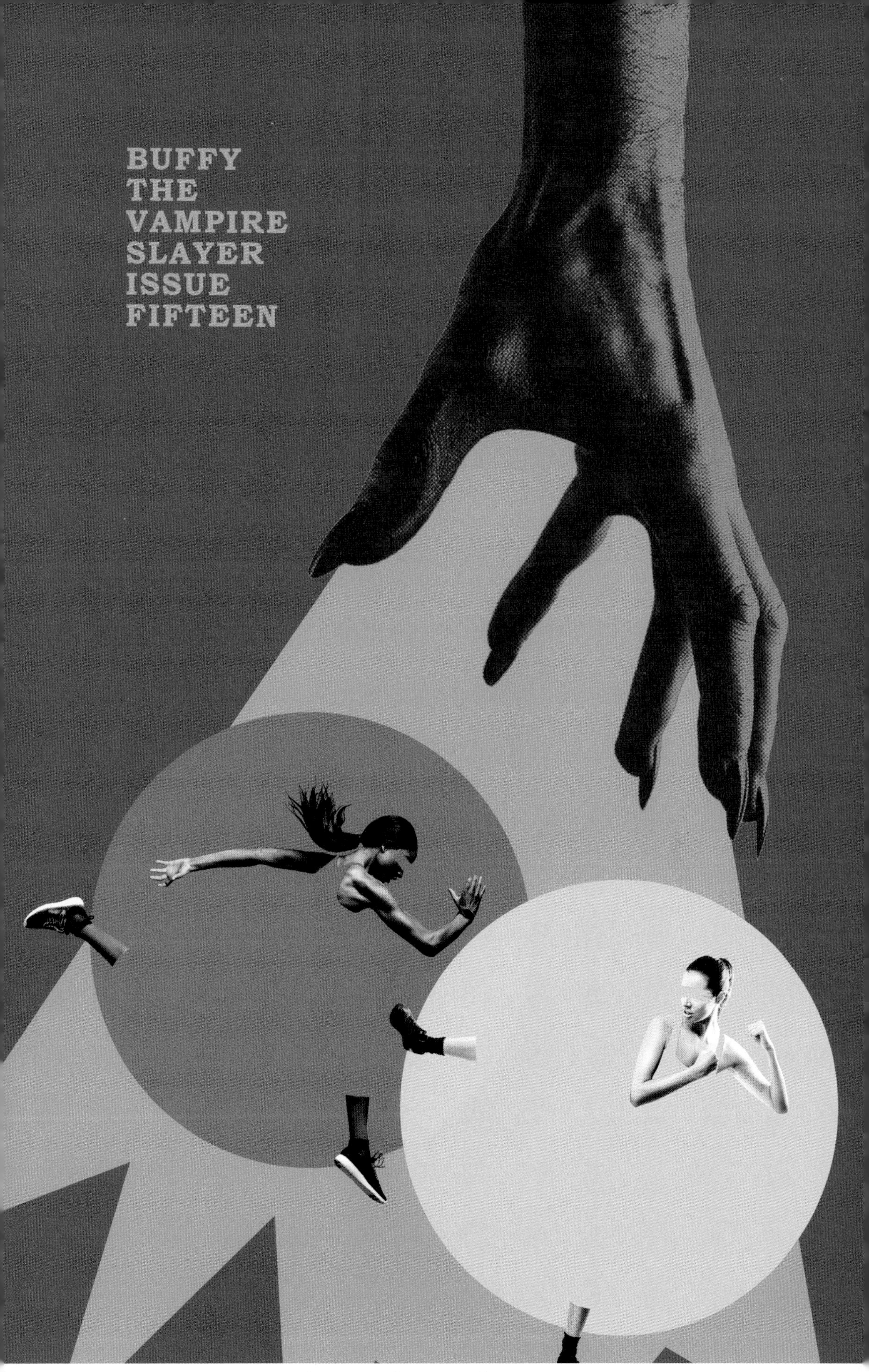
BUFFY
THE
VAMPIRE
SLAYER
ISSUE
FIFTEEN

Issue Fifteen Ring of Fire Cover by **Becca Carey**

CHAPTER
SIXTEEN

Issue Sixteen Cover by **David López**

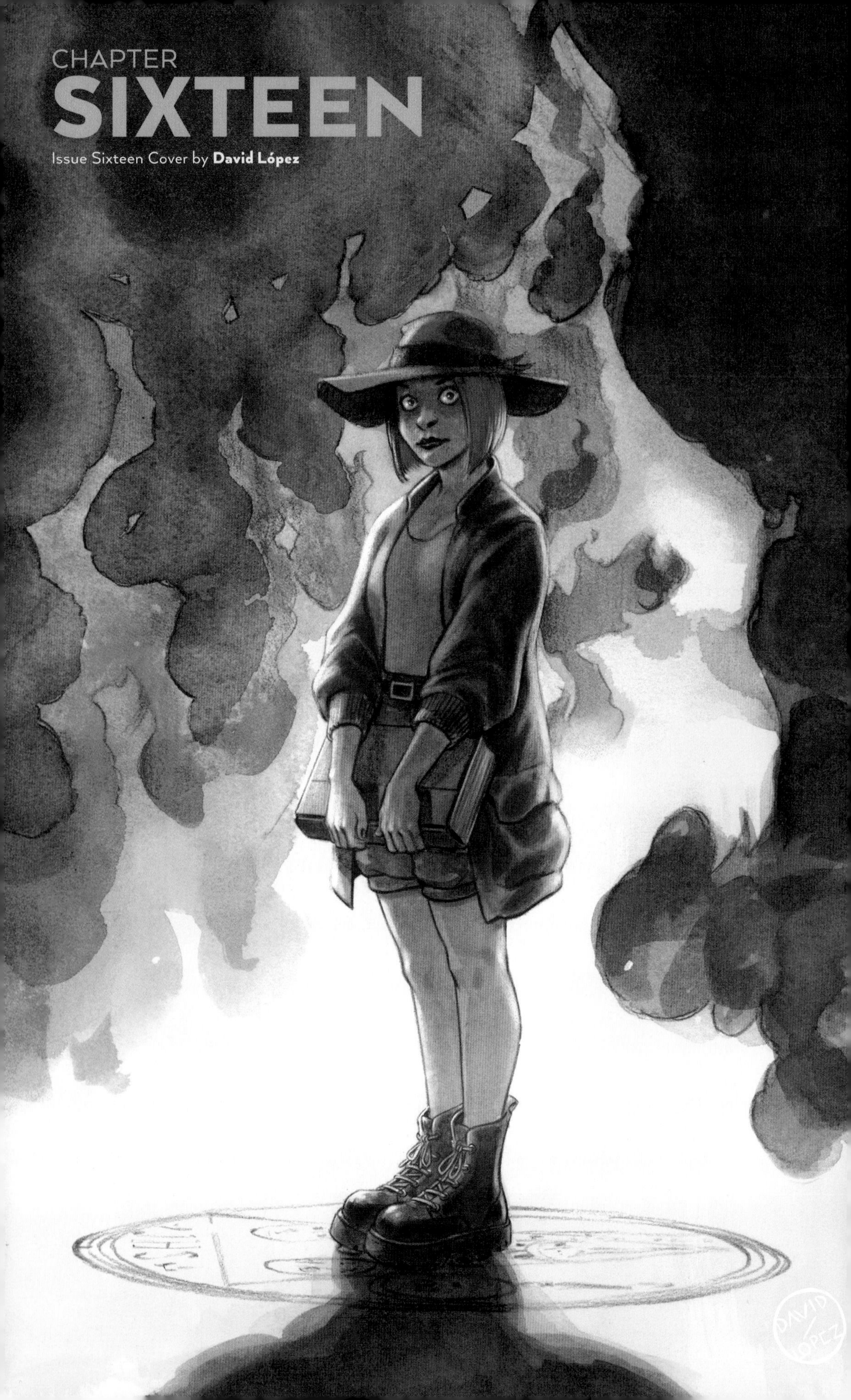
DAVID
LOPEZ

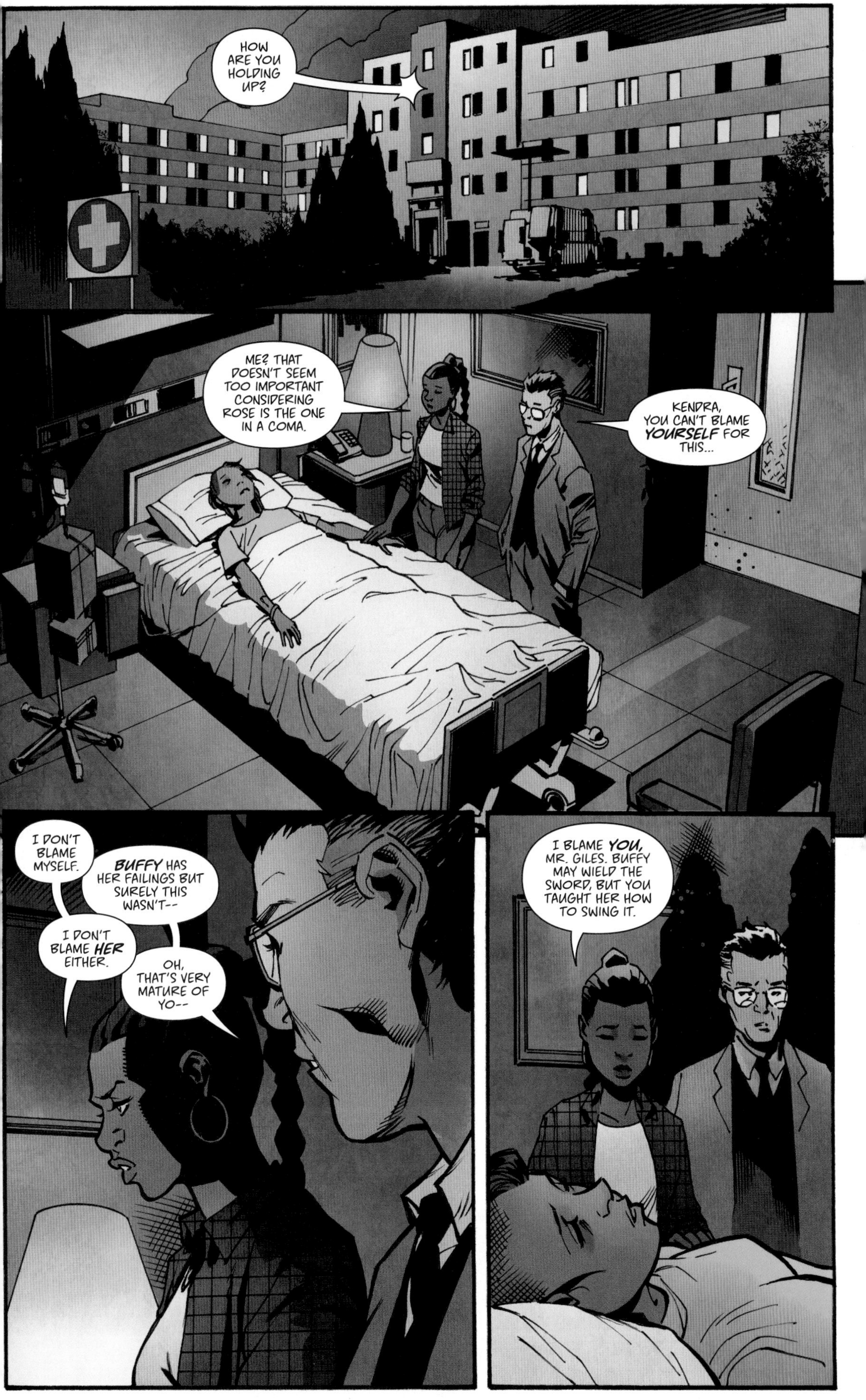
HOW ARE YOU HOLDING UP?
ME? THAT DOESN'T SEEM TOO IMPORTANT CONSIDERING ROSE IS THE ONE IN A COMA.
KENDRA, YOU CAN'T BLAME YOURSELF FOR THIS...
I DON'T BLAME MYSELF.
BUFFY HAS HER FAILINGS BUT SURELY THIS WASN'T--
I DON'T BLAME HER EITHER.
OH, THAT'S VERY MATURE OF YO--
I BLAME YOU, MR. GILES. BUFFY MAY WIELD THE SWORD, BUT YOU TAUGHT HER HOW TO SWING IT.

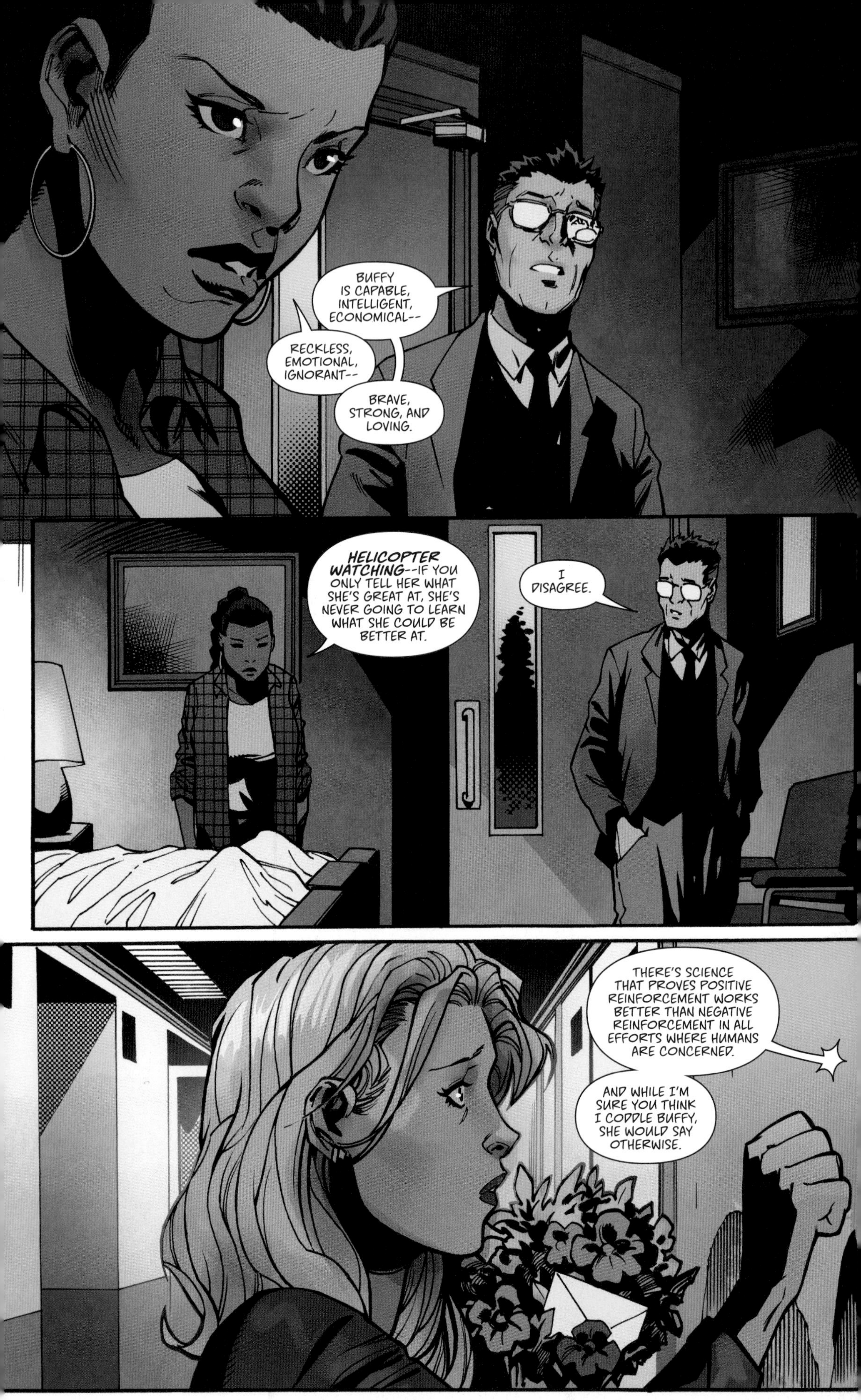
BUFFY IS CAPABLE, INTELLIGENT, ECONOMICAL--
RECKLESS, EMOTIONAL, IGNORANT--
BRAVE, STRONG, AND LOVING.
HELICOPTER WATCHING--IF YOU ONLY TELL HER WHAT SHE'S GREAT AT, SHE'S NEVER GOING TO LEARN WHAT SHE COULD BE BETTER AT.
I DISAGREE.
THERE'S SCIENCE THAT PROVES POSITIVE REINFORCEMENT WORKS BETTER THAN NEGATIVE REINFORCEMENT IN ALL EFFORTS WHERE HUMANS ARE CONCERNED.
AND WHILE I'M SURE YOU THINK I CODDLE BUFFY, SHE WOULD SAY OTHERWISE.

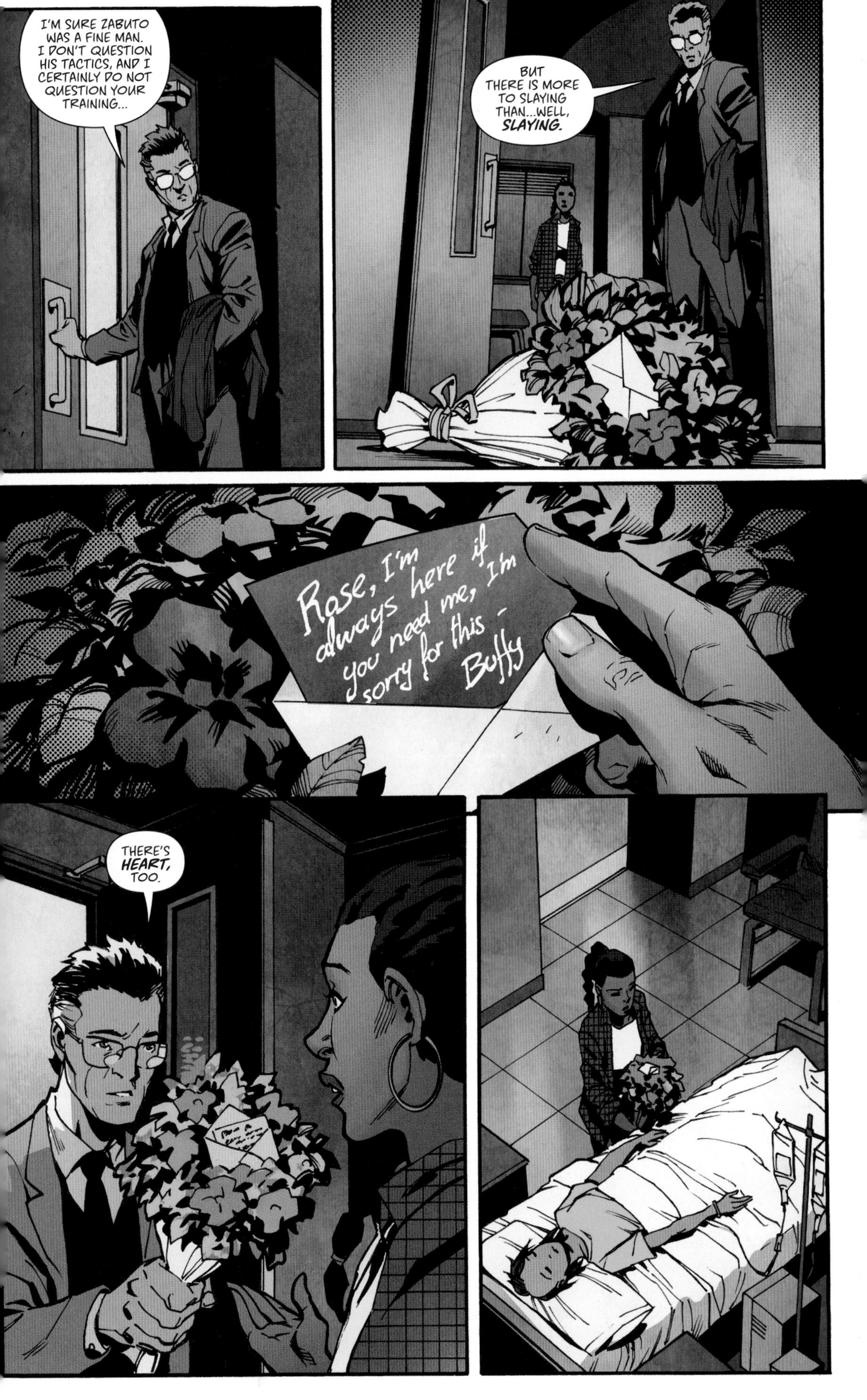
I'M SURE ZABUTO WAS A FINE MAN. I DON'T QUESTION HIS TACTICS, AND I CERTAINLY DO NOT QUESTION YOUR TRAINING...
BUT THERE IS MORE TO SLAYING THAN...WELL, SLAYING.
Rose, I'm always here if you need me, I'm sorry for this - Buffy
THERE'S HEART, TOO.

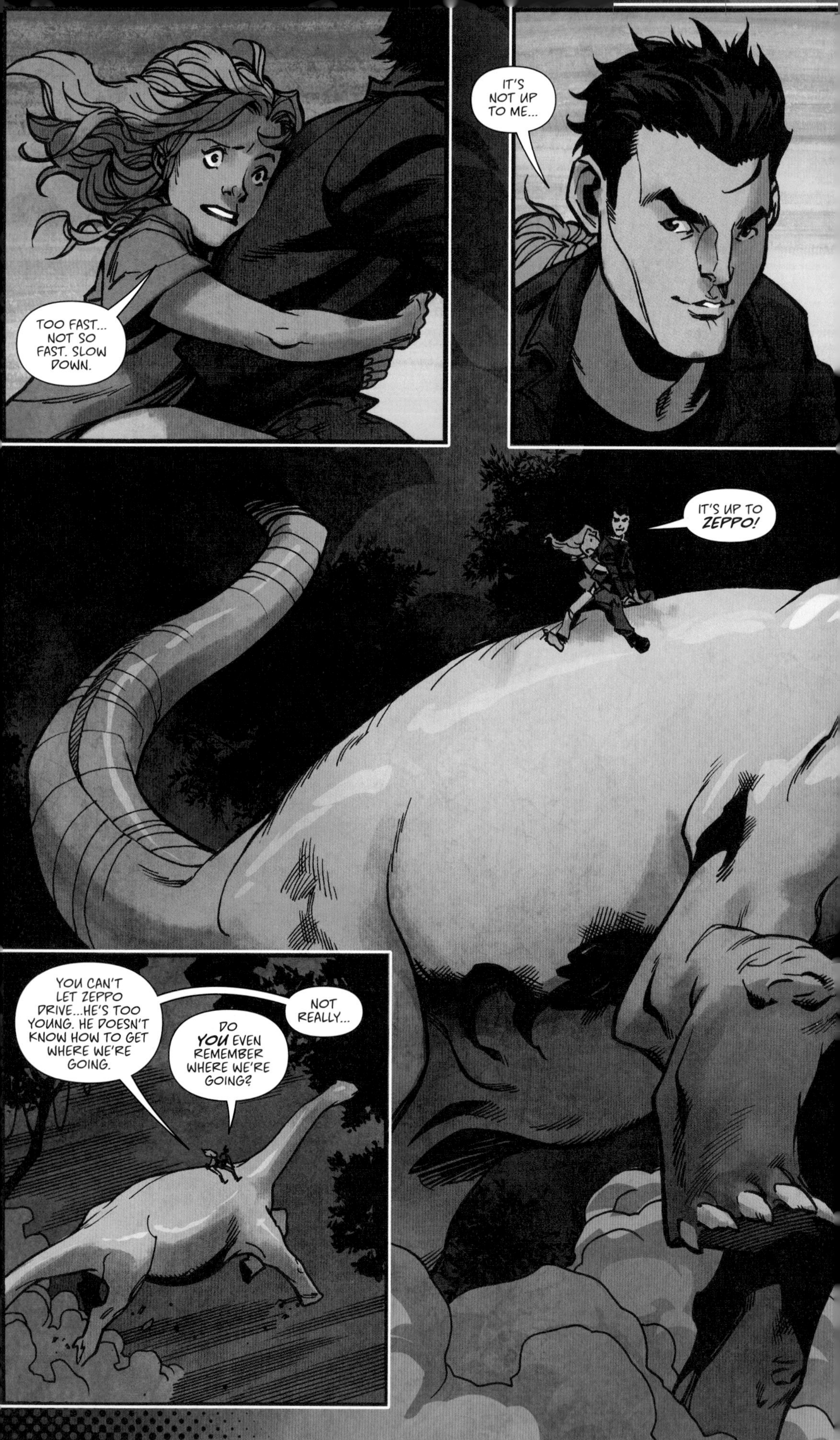
TOO FAST... NOT SO FAST. SLOW DOWN.
IT'S NOT UP TO ME...
IT'S UP TO ZEPPO!
YOU CAN'T LET ZEPPO DRIVE...HE'S TOO YOUNG. HE DOESN'T KNOW HOW TO GET WHERE WE'RE GOING.
NOT REALLY...
DO YOU EVEN REMEMBER WHERE WE'RE GOING?

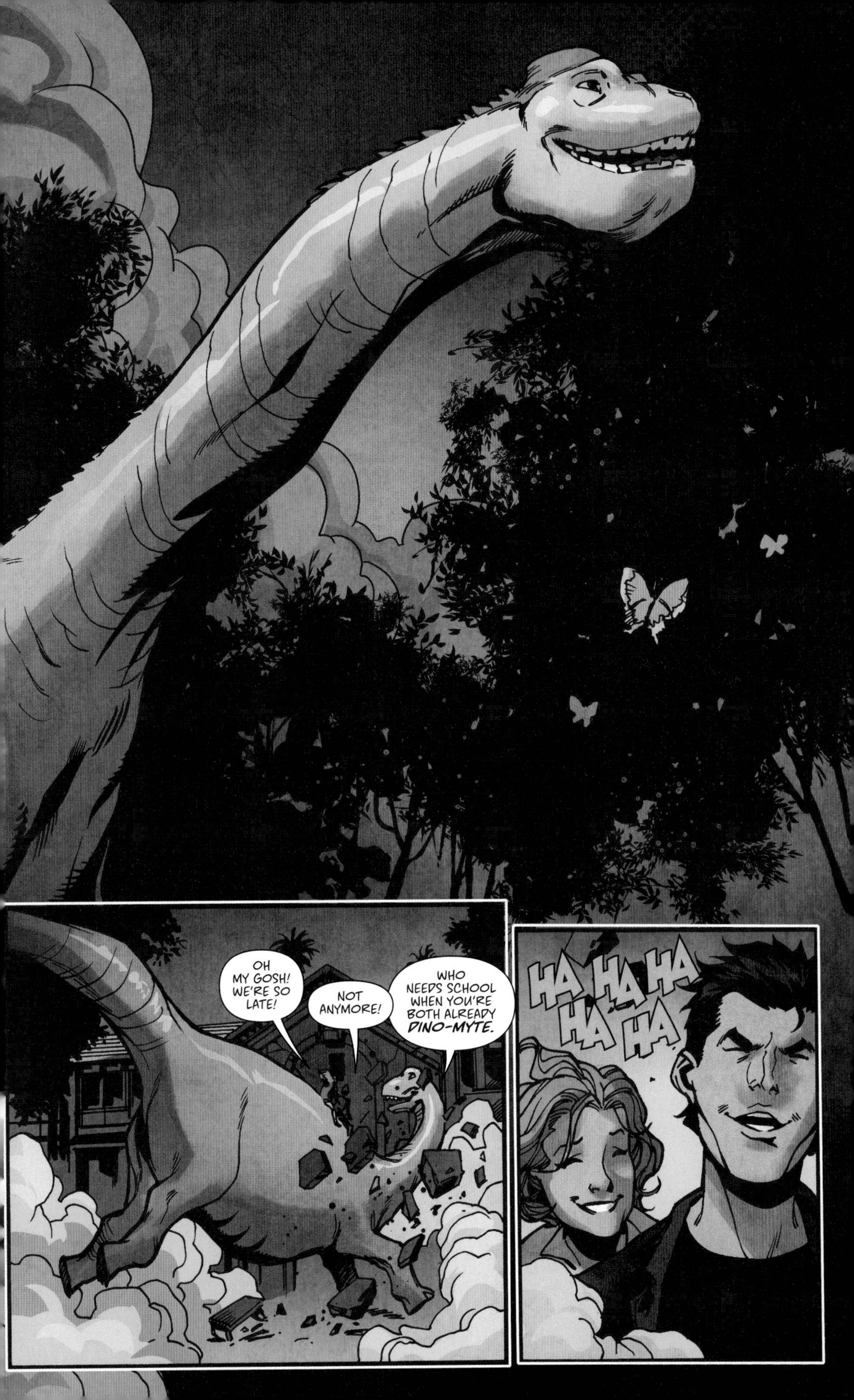
OH MY GOSH! WE'RE SO LATE!
NOT ANYMORE!
WHO NEEDS SCHOOL WHEN YOU'RE BOTH ALREADY *DINO-MYTE*.
HA HA HA HA HA

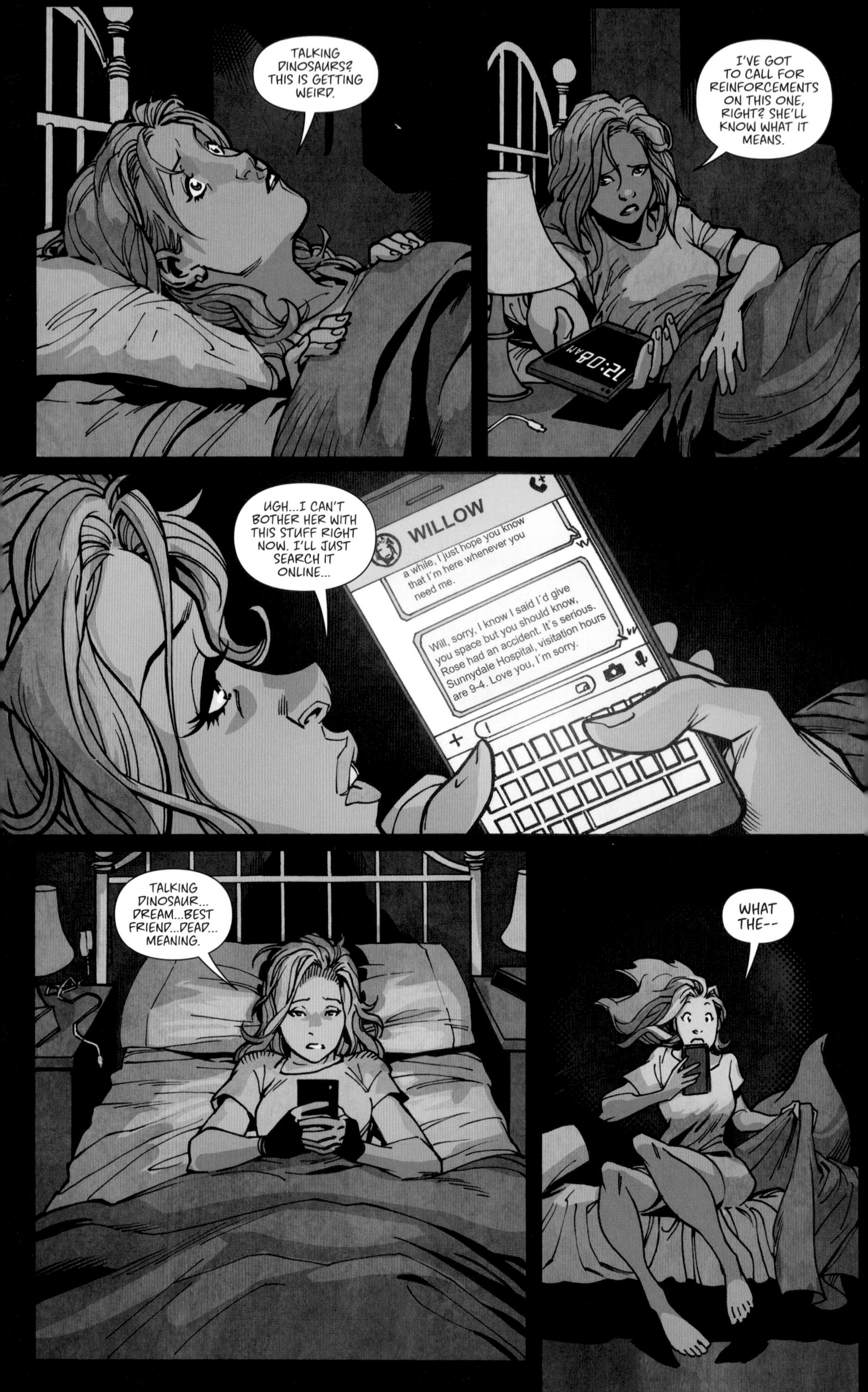
TALKING DINOSAURS? THIS IS GETTING WEIRD.
I'VE GOT TO CALL FOR REINFORCEMENTS ON THIS ONE, RIGHT? SHE'LL KNOW WHAT IT MEANS.
12:08 AM
UGH...I CAN'T BOTHER HER WITH THIS STUFF RIGHT NOW. I'LL JUST SEARCH IT ONLINE...
WILLOW
a while, I just hope you know that I´m here whenever you need me.
Will, sorry, I know I said I´d give you space but you should know, Rose had an accident. It´s serious. Sunnydale Hospital, visitation hours are 9-4. Love you, I´m sorry.
TALKING DINOSAUR...DREAM...BEST FRIEND...DEAD... MEANING.
WHAT THE--

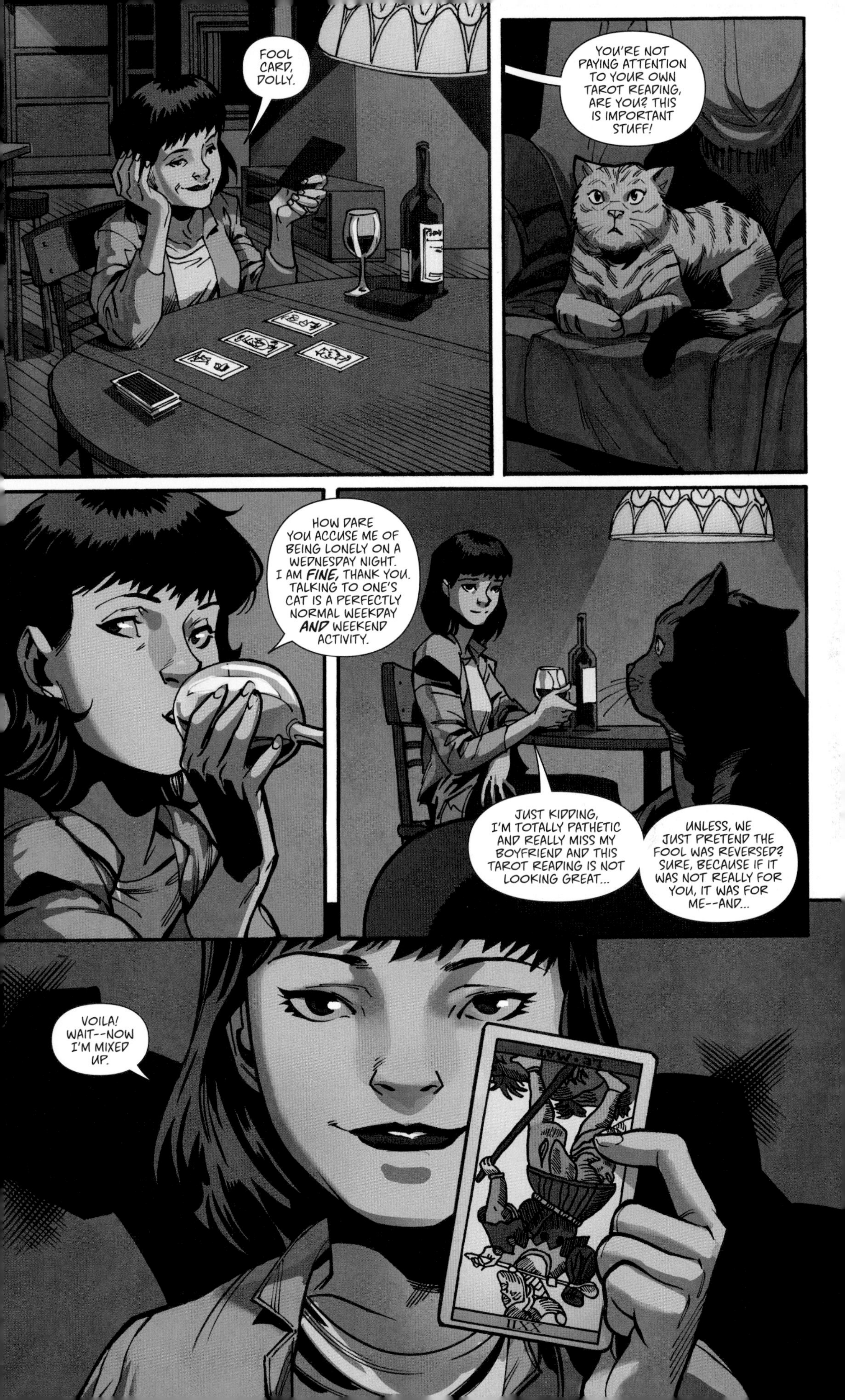
FOOL CARD, DOLLY.
YOU'RE NOT PAYING ATTENTION TO YOUR OWN TAROT READING, ARE YOU? THIS IS IMPORTANT STUFF!
HOW DARE YOU ACCUSE ME OF BEING LONELY ON A WEDNESDAY NIGHT. I AM FINE, THANK YOU. TALKING TO ONE'S CAT IS A PERFECTLY NORMAL WEEKDAY AND WEEKEND ACTIVITY.
JUST KIDDING, I'M TOTALLY PATHETIC AND REALLY MISS MY BOYFRIEND AND THIS TAROT READING IS NOT LOOKING GREAT...
UNLESS, WE JUST PRETEND THE FOOL WAS REVERSED? SURE, BECAUSE IF IT WAS NOT REALLY FOR YOU, IT WAS FOR ME--AND...
VOILA! WAIT--NOW I'M MIXED UP.

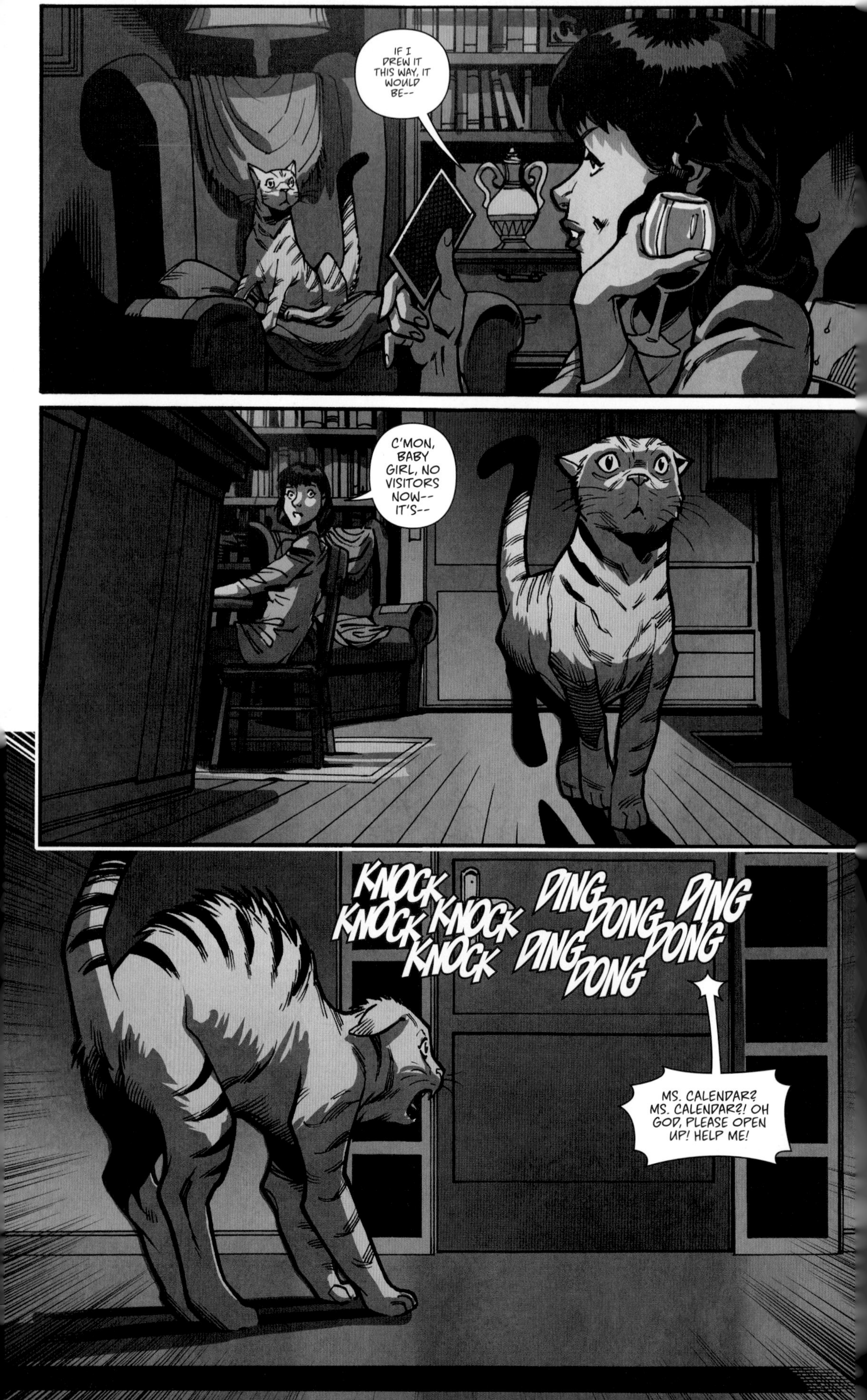
IF I DREW IT THIS WAY, IT WOULD BE--
C'MON, BABY GIRL, NO VISITORS NOW-- IT'S--
KNOCK KNOCK KNOCK KNOCK
DING DONG DING DONG DING DONG
MS. CALENDAR? MS. CALENDAR?! OH GOD, PLEASE OPEN UP! HELP ME!

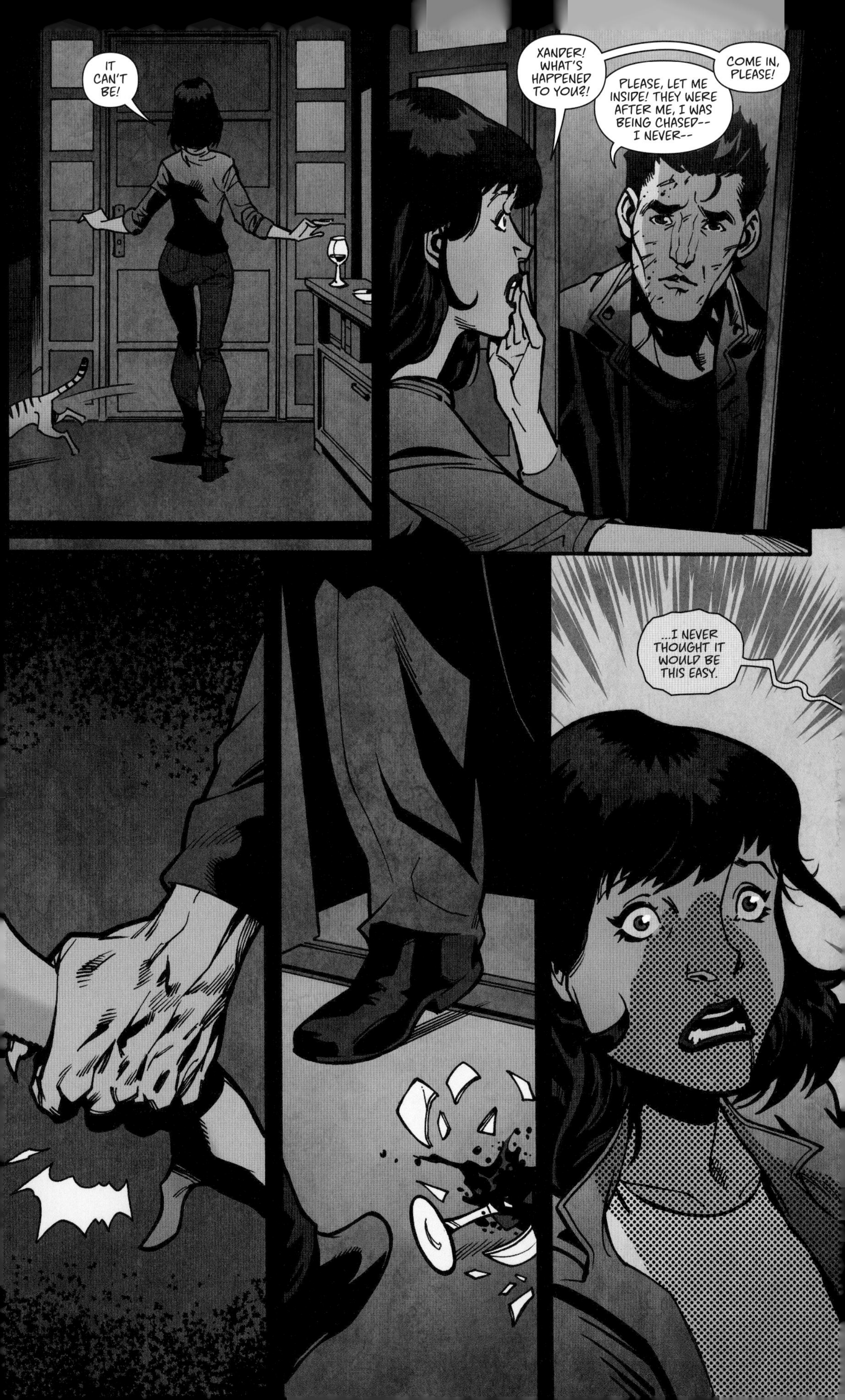
IT CAN'T BE!
XANDER! WHAT'S HAPPENED TO YOU?!
PLEASE, LET ME INSIDE! THEY WERE AFTER ME, I WAS BEING CHASED-- I NEVER--
COME IN, PLEASE!
...I NEVER THOUGHT IT WOULD BE THIS EASY.

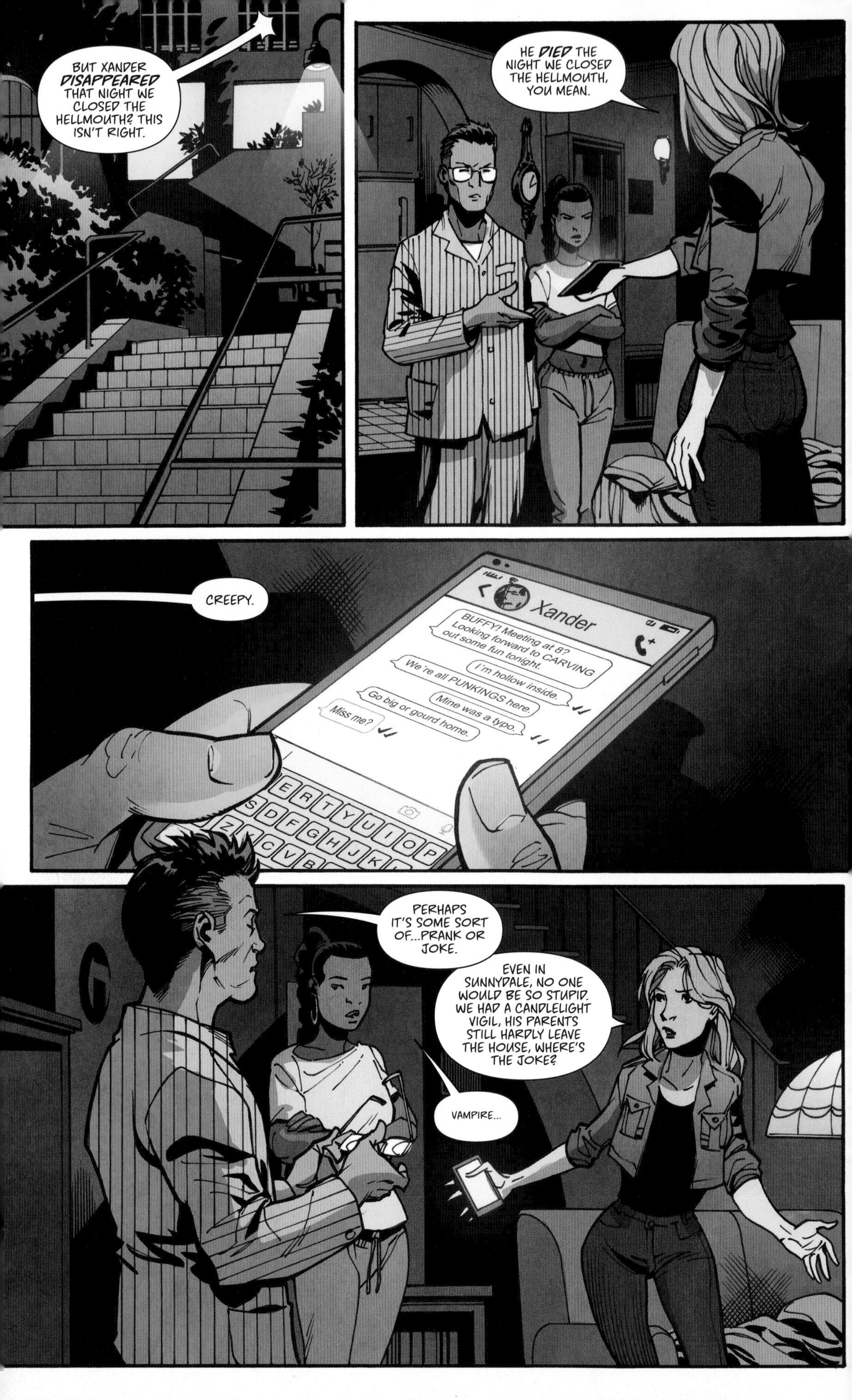
BUT XANDER *DISAPPEARED* THAT NIGHT WE CLOSED THE HELLMOUTH? THIS ISN'T RIGHT.
HE *DIED* THE NIGHT WE CLOSED THE HELLMOUTH, YOU MEAN.
CREEPY.
Xander
BUFFY! Meeting at 8? Looking forward to CARVING out some fun tonight.
I'm hollow inside.
We're all PUNKINGS here.
Mine was a typo.
Go big or gourd home.
Miss me?
PERHAPS IT'S SOME SORT OF...PRANK OR JOKE.
EVEN IN SUNNYDALE, NO ONE WOULD BE SO STUPID. WE HAD A CANDLELIGHT VIGIL, HIS PARENTS STILL HARDLY LEAVE THE HOUSE, WHERE'S THE JOKE?
VAMPIRE...

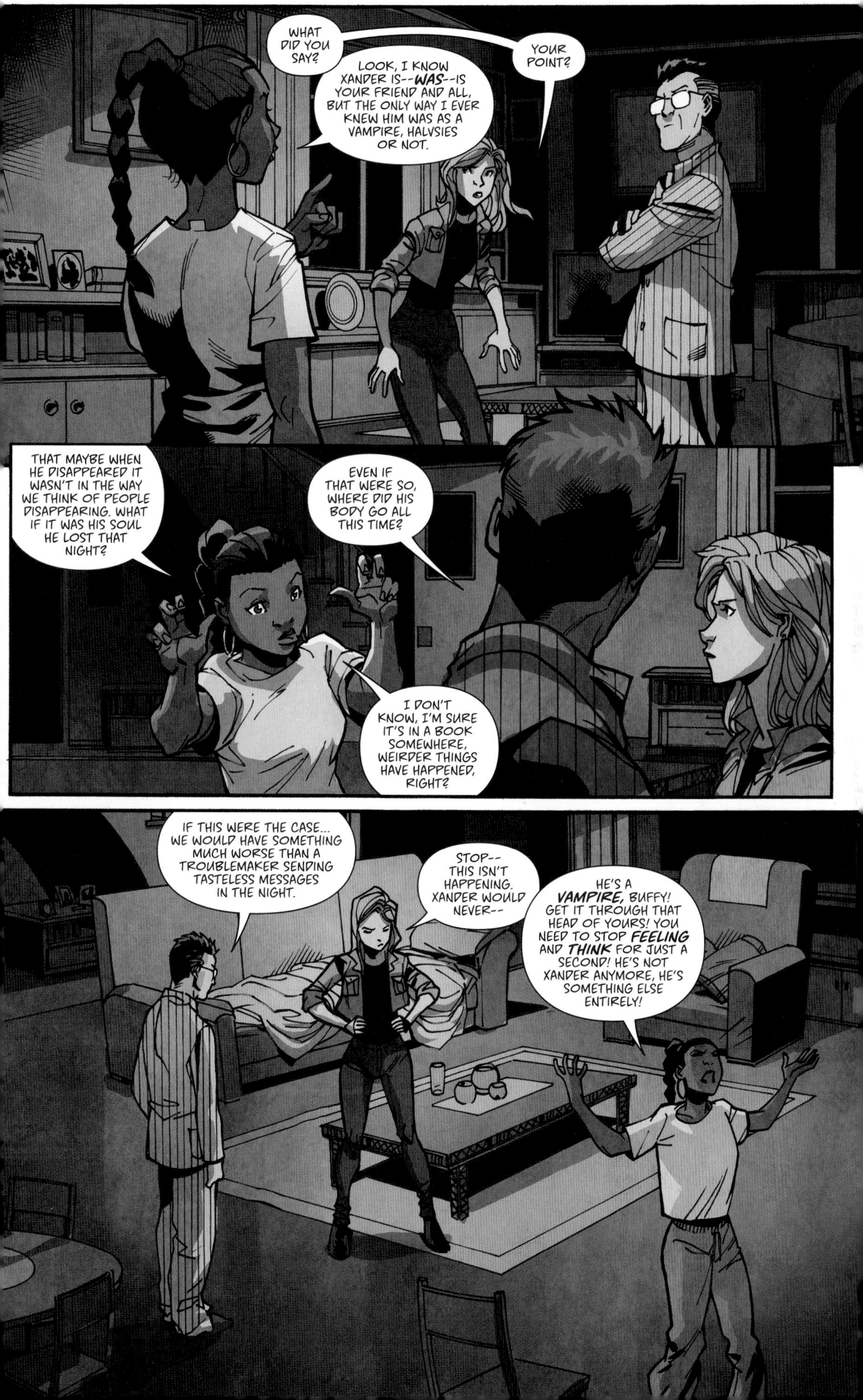
WHAT DID YOU SAY?
LOOK, I KNOW XANDER IS--**WAS**--IS YOUR FRIEND AND ALL, BUT THE ONLY WAY I EVER KNEW HIM WAS AS A VAMPIRE, HALVSIES OR NOT.
YOUR POINT?
THAT MAYBE WHEN HE DISAPPEARED IT WASN'T IN THE WAY WE THINK OF PEOPLE DISAPPEARING. WHAT IF IT WAS HIS SOUL HE LOST THAT NIGHT?
EVEN IF THAT WERE SO, WHERE DID HIS BODY GO ALL THIS TIME?
I DON'T KNOW, I'M SURE IT'S IN A BOOK SOMEWHERE, WEIRDER THINGS HAVE HAPPENED, RIGHT?
IF THIS WERE THE CASE... WE WOULD HAVE SOMETHING MUCH WORSE THAN A TROUBLEMAKER SENDING TASTELESS MESSAGES IN THE NIGHT.
STOP-- THIS ISN'T HAPPENING. XANDER WOULD NEVER--
HE'S A **VAMPIRE,** BUFFY! GET IT THROUGH THAT HEAD OF YOURS! YOU NEED TO STOP **FEELING** AND **THINK** FOR JUST A SECOND! HE'S NOT XANDER ANYMORE, HE'S SOMETHING ELSE ENTIRELY!

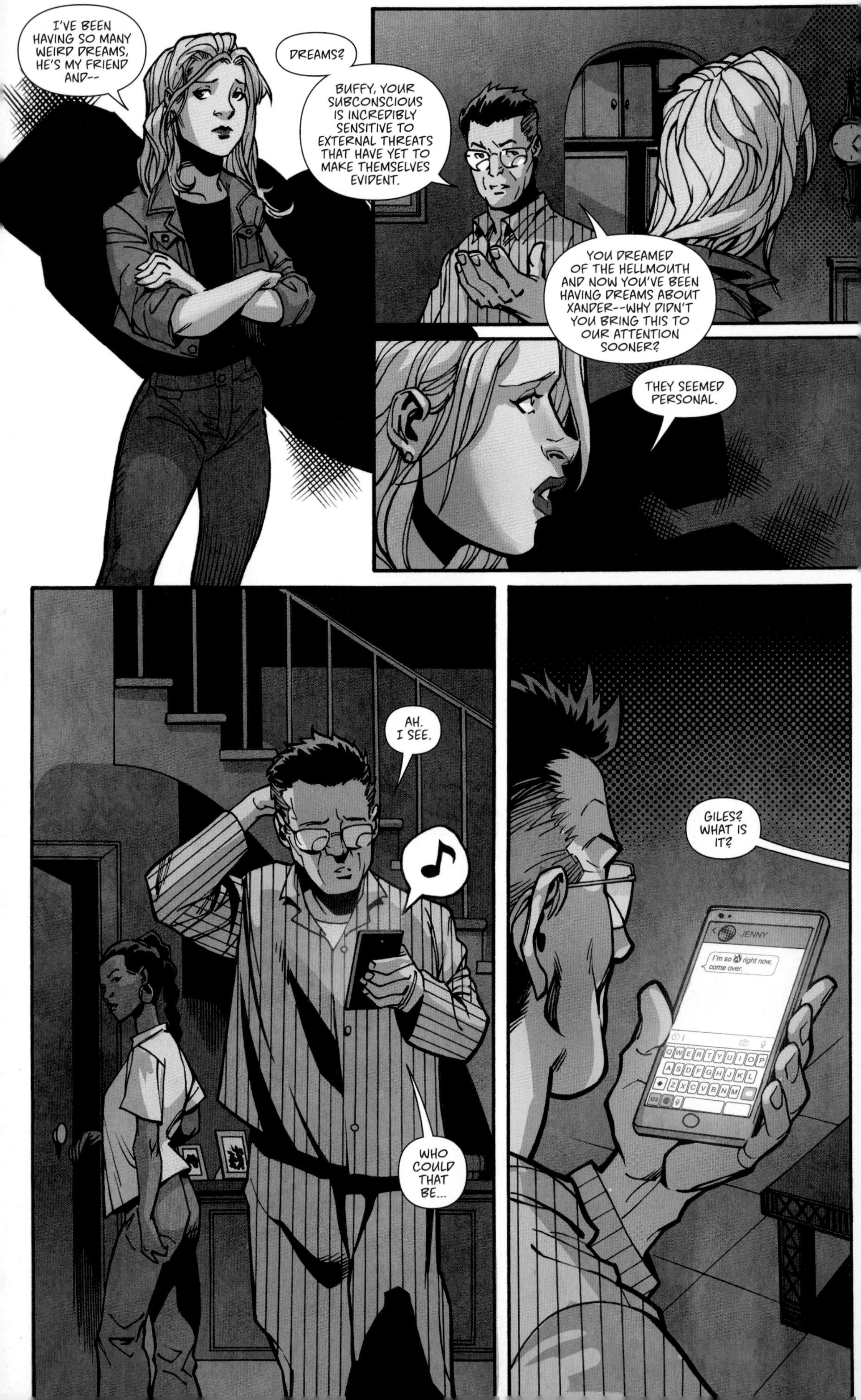
I'VE BEEN HAVING SO MANY WEIRD DREAMS, HE'S MY FRIEND AND--
DREAMS?
BUFFY, YOUR SUBCONSCIOUS IS INCREDIBLY SENSITIVE TO EXTERNAL THREATS THAT HAVE YET TO MAKE THEMSELVES EVIDENT.
YOU DREAMED OF THE HELLMOUTH AND NOW YOU'VE BEEN HAVING DREAMS ABOUT XANDER--WHY DIDN'T YOU BRING THIS TO OUR ATTENTION SOONER?
THEY SEEMED PERSONAL.
AH. I SEE.
♪
WHO COULD THAT BE...
GILES? WHAT IS IT?
JENNY
I'm so right now, come over.

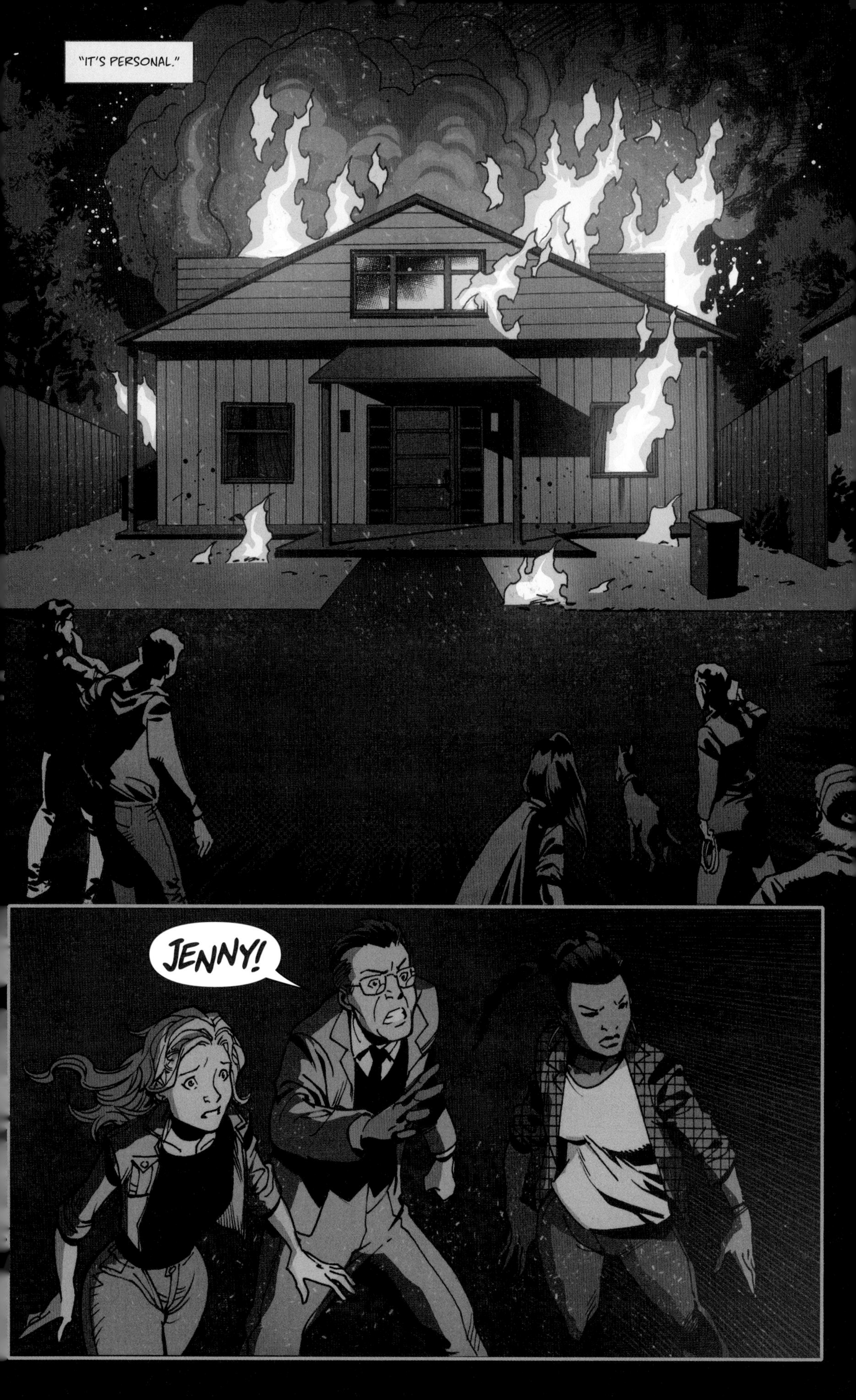
"IT'S PERSONAL."
JENNY!

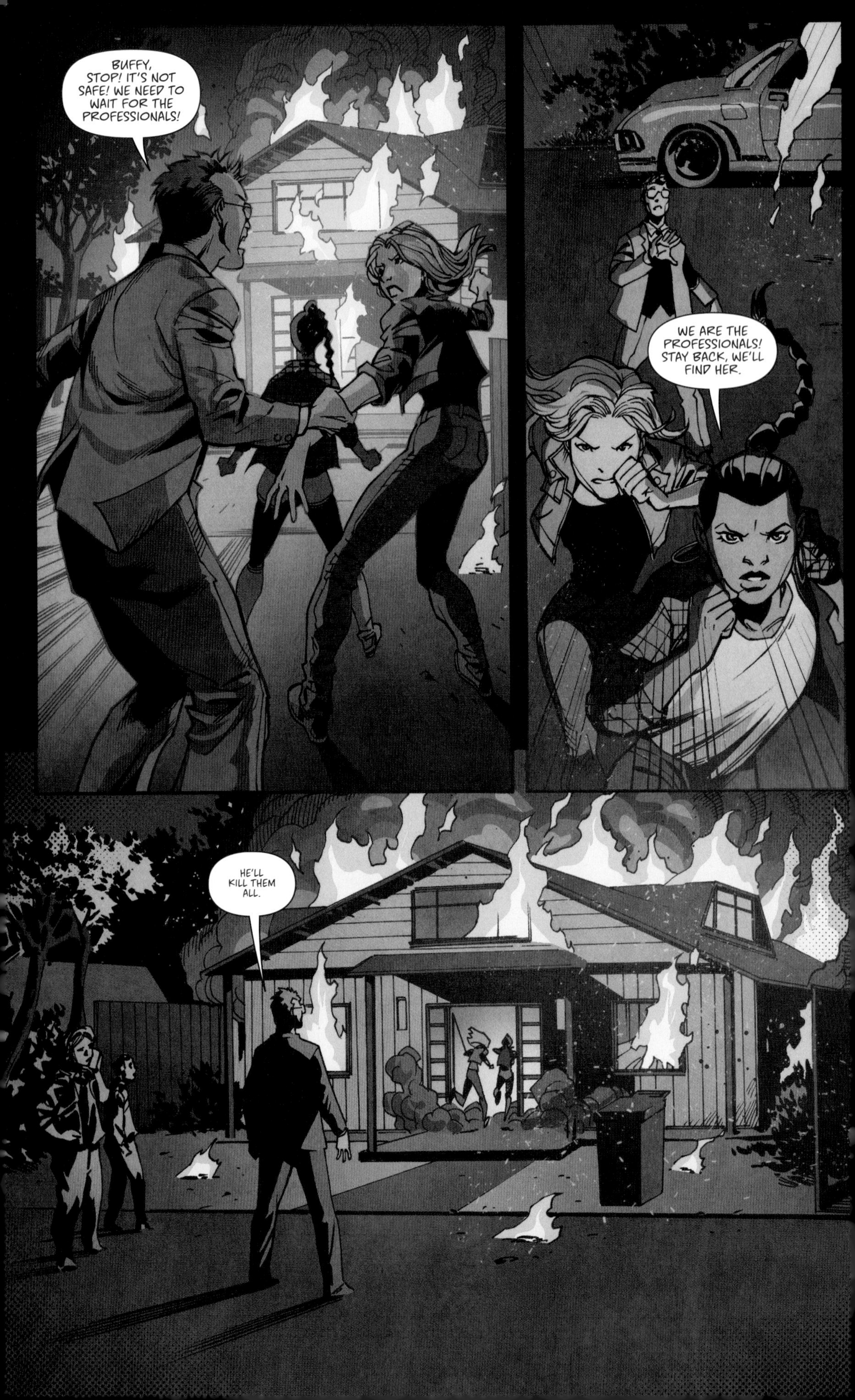
BUFFY, STOP! IT'S NOT SAFE! WE NEED TO WAIT FOR THE PROFESSIONALS!
WE ARE THE PROFESSIONALS! STAY BACK, WE'LL FIND HER.
HE'LL KILL THEM ALL.

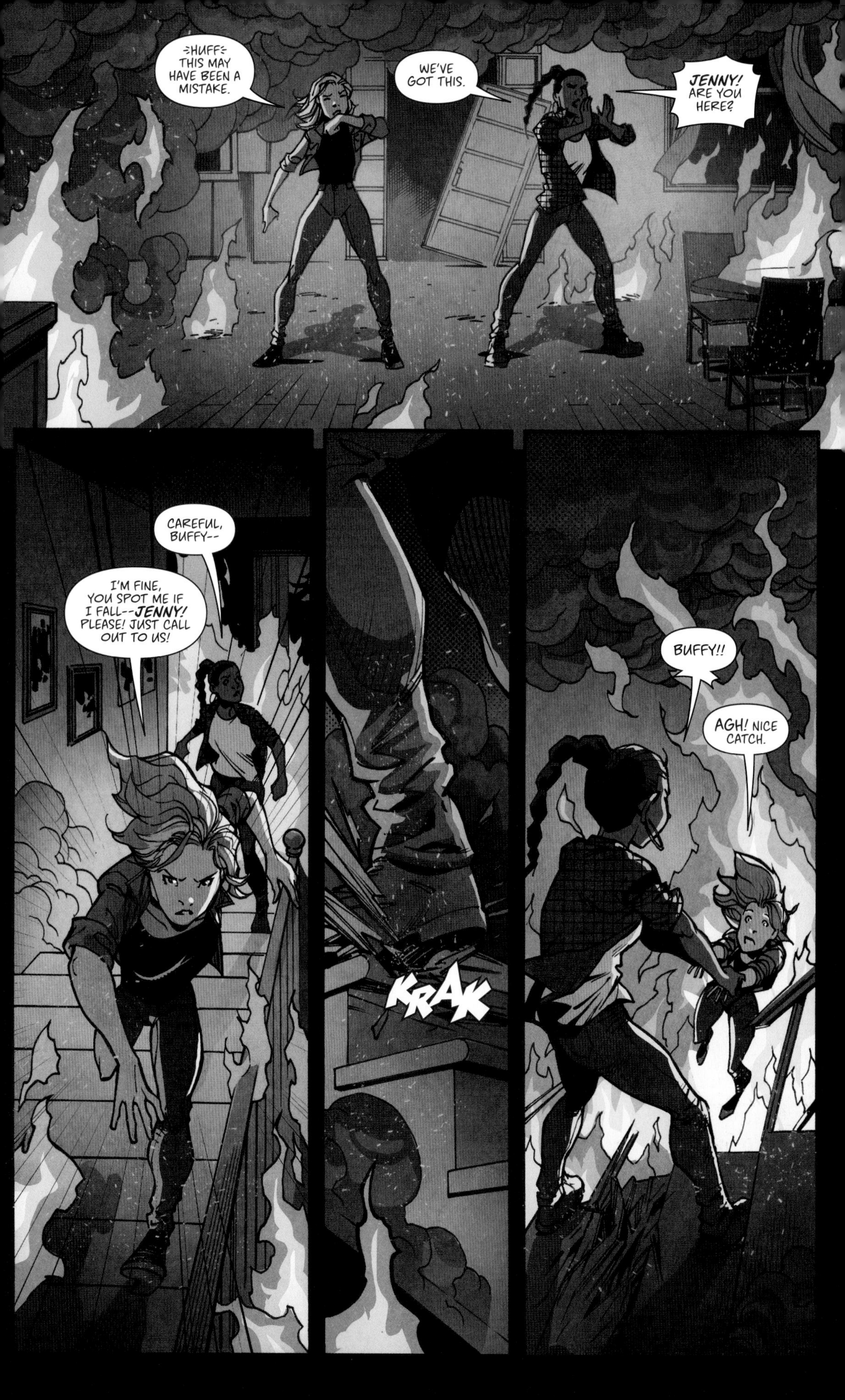

=HUFF= THIS MAY HAVE BEEN A MISTAKE.
WE'VE GOT THIS.
JENNY! ARE YOU HERE?
CAREFUL, BUFFY--
I'M FINE, YOU SPOT ME IF I FALL--JENNY! PLEASE! JUST CALL OUT TO US!
KRAK
BUFFY!!
AGH! NICE CATCH.

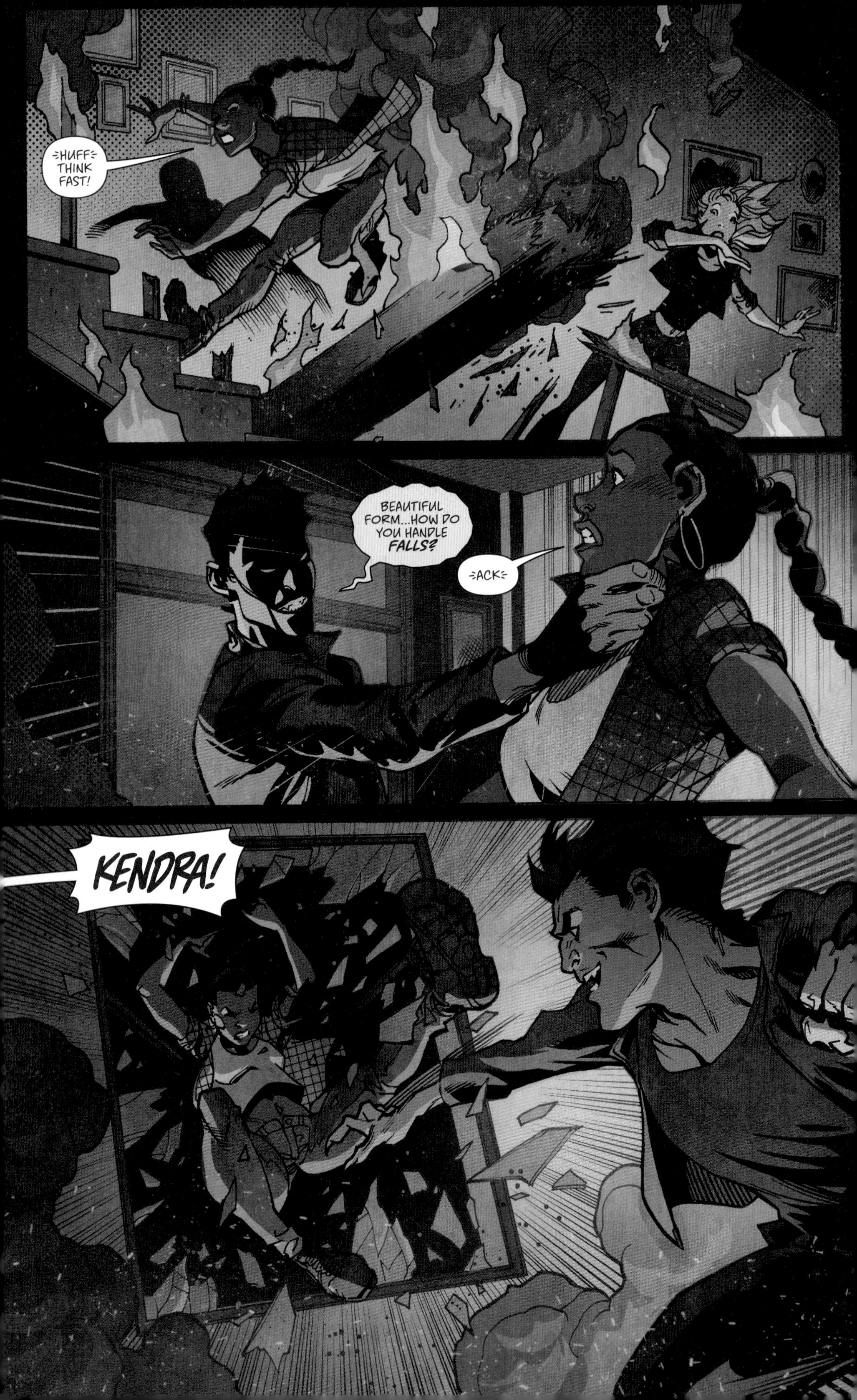

=HUFF= THINK FAST!
BEAUTIFUL FORM...HOW DO YOU HANDLE FALLS?
=ACK=
KENDRA!

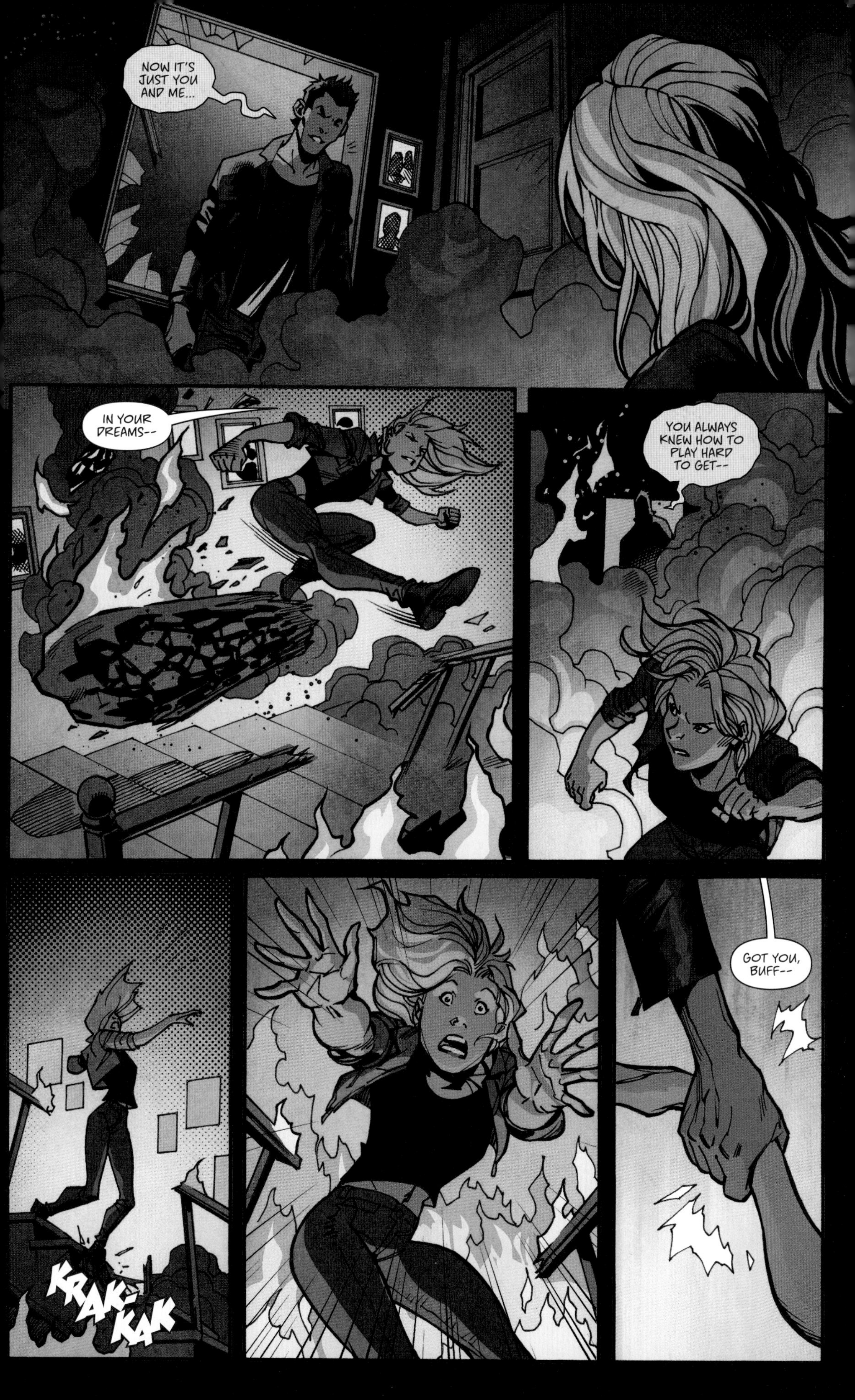
NOW IT'S JUST YOU AND ME...
IN YOUR DREAMS--
YOU ALWAYS KNEW HOW TO PLAY HARD TO GET--
KRAK-KAK
GOT YOU, BUFF--

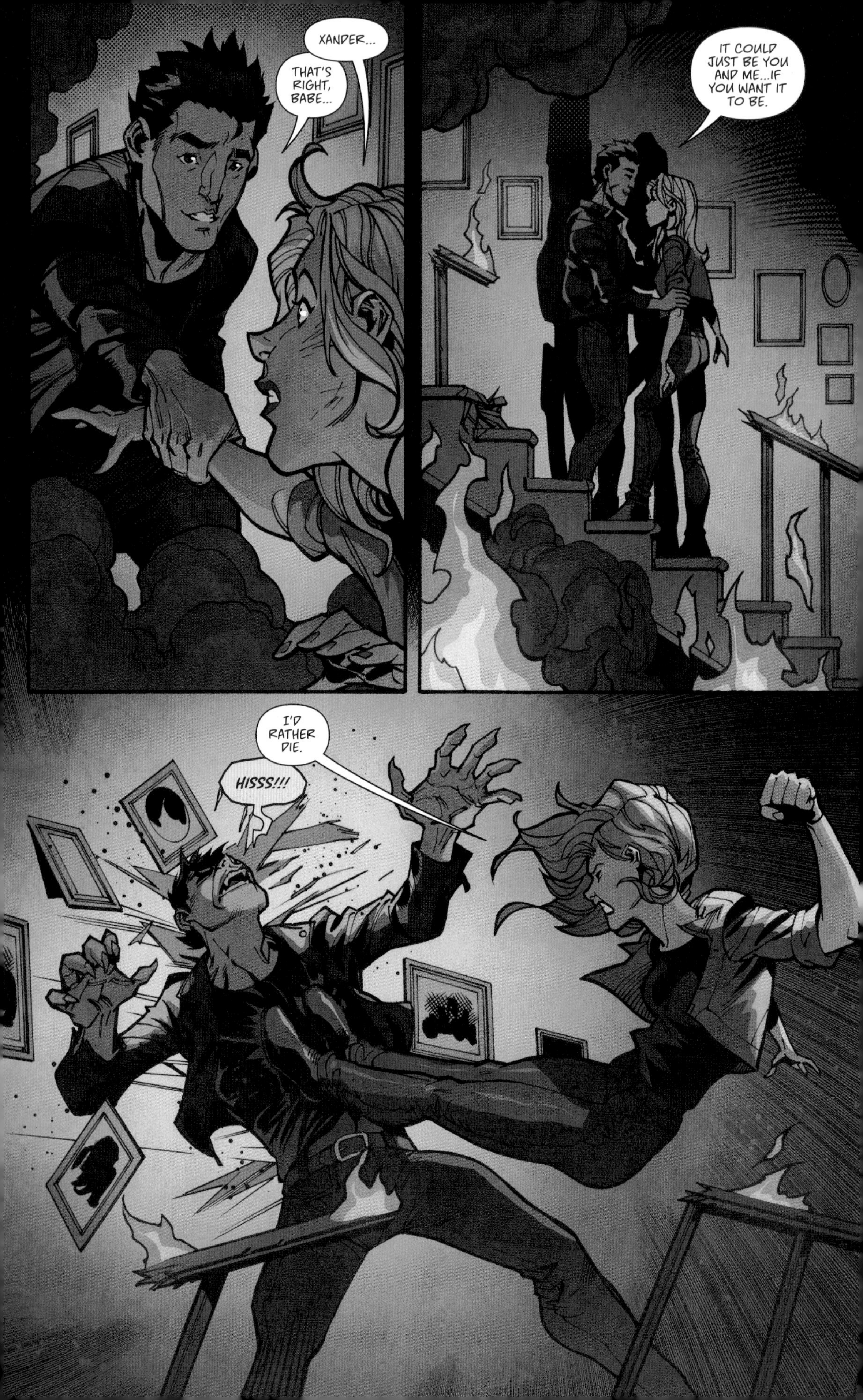
XANDER...
THAT'S RIGHT, BABE...
IT COULD JUST BE YOU AND ME...IF YOU WANT IT TO BE.
HISSS!!!
I'D RATHER DIE.

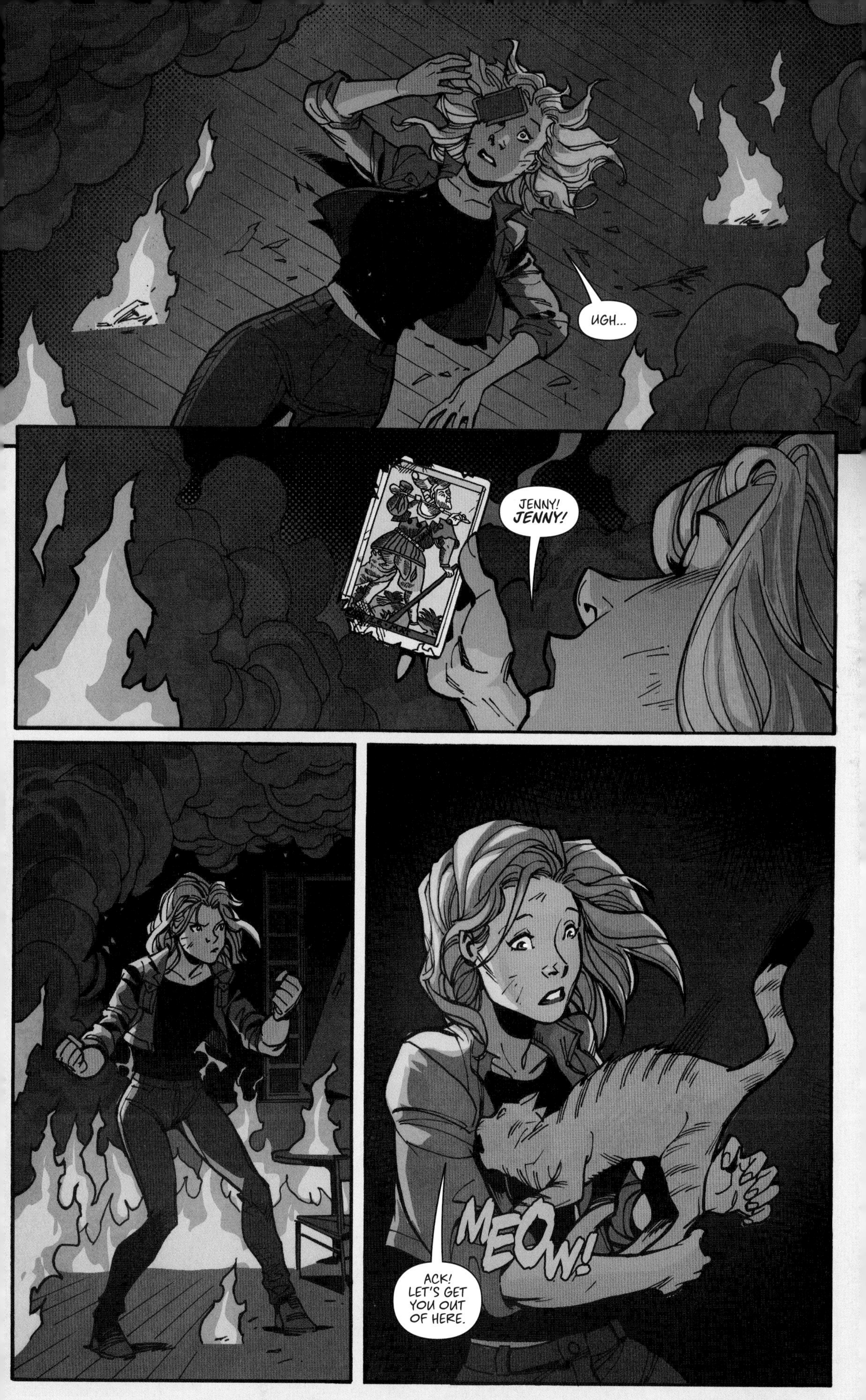
UGH...
JENNY! JENNY!
MEOW!
ACK! LET'S GET YOU OUT OF HERE.

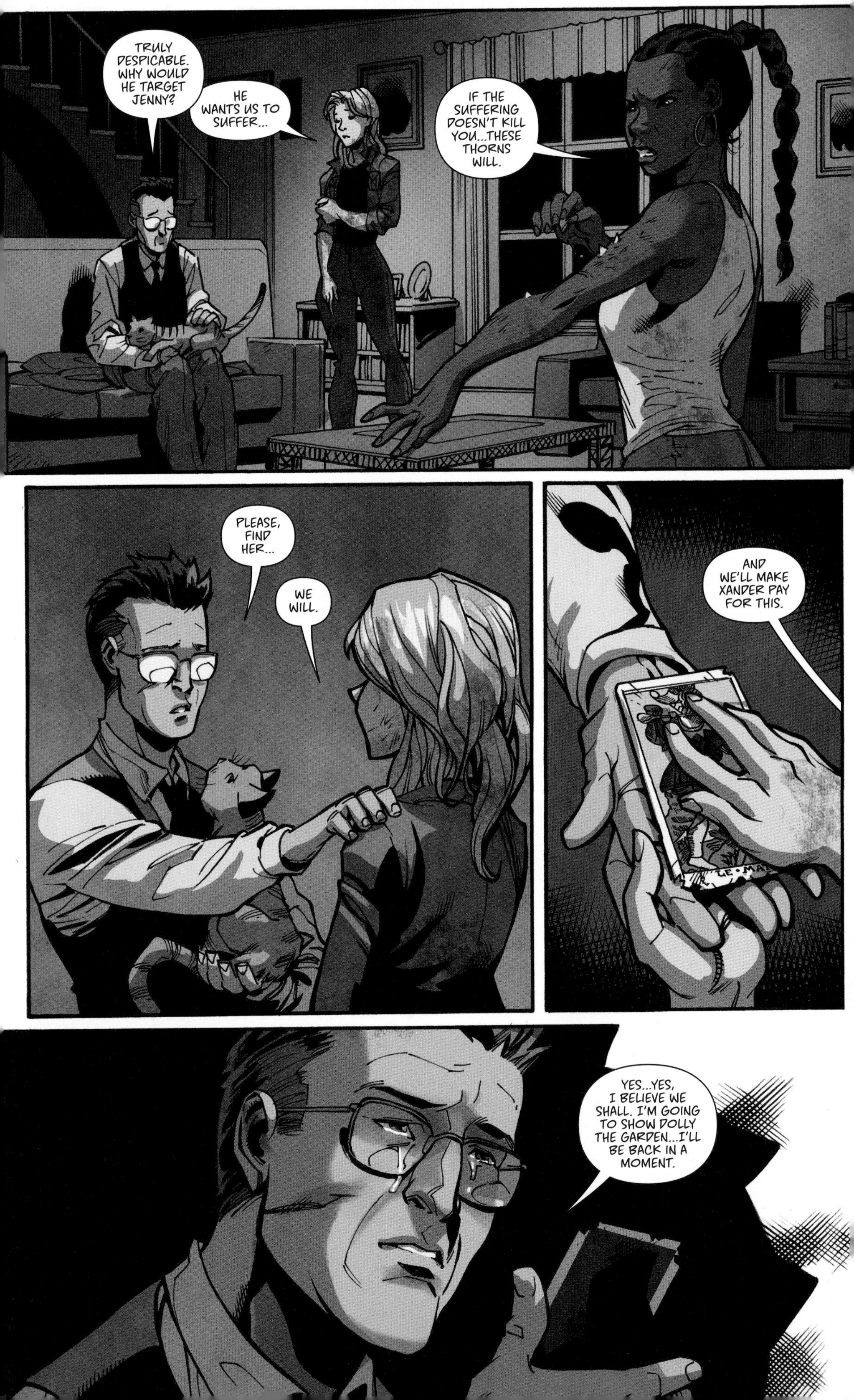

TRULY DESPICABLE. WHY WOULD HE TARGET JENNY?
HE WANTS US TO SUFFER...
IF THE SUFFERING DOESN'T KILL YOU...THESE THORNS WILL.
PLEASE, FIND HER...
WE WILL.
AND WE'LL MAKE XANDER PAY FOR THIS.
YES...YES, I BELIEVE WE SHALL. I'M GOING TO SHOW DOLLY THE GARDEN...I'LL BE BACK IN A MOMENT.

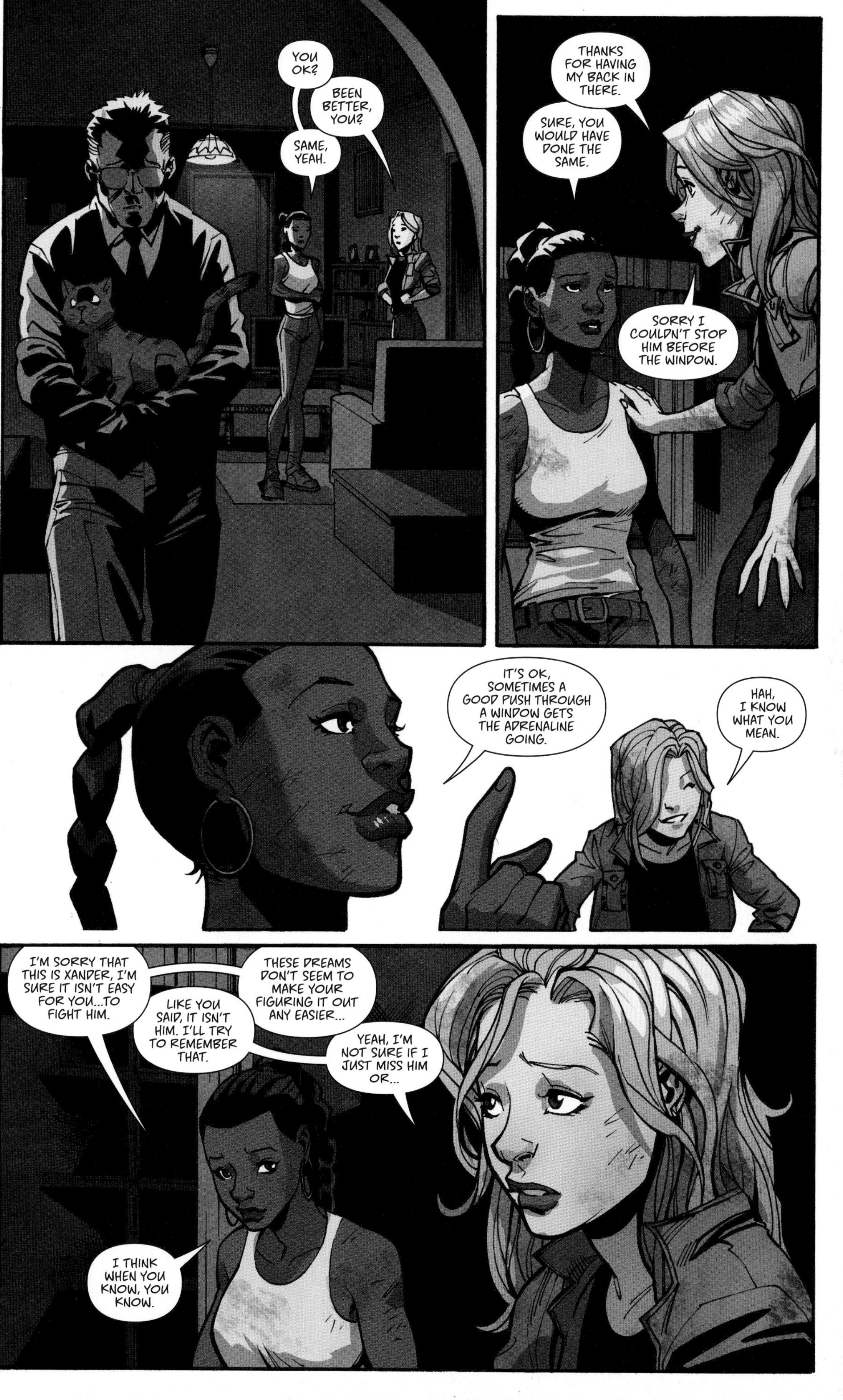
YOU OK?
BEEN BETTER, YOU?
SAME, YEAH.
THANKS FOR HAVING MY BACK IN THERE.
SURE, YOU WOULD HAVE DONE THE SAME.
SORRY I COULDN'T STOP HIM BEFORE THE WINDOW.
IT'S OK, SOMETIMES A GOOD PUSH THROUGH A WINDOW GETS THE ADRENALINE GOING.
HAH, I KNOW WHAT YOU MEAN.
I'M SORRY THAT THIS IS XANDER, I'M SURE IT ISN'T EASY FOR YOU...TO FIGHT HIM.
LIKE YOU SAID, IT ISN'T HIM. I'LL TRY TO REMEMBER THAT.
THESE DREAMS DON'T SEEM TO MAKE YOUR FIGURING IT OUT ANY EASIER...
YEAH, I'M NOT SURE IF I JUST MISS HIM OR...
I THINK WHEN YOU KNOW, YOU KNOW.

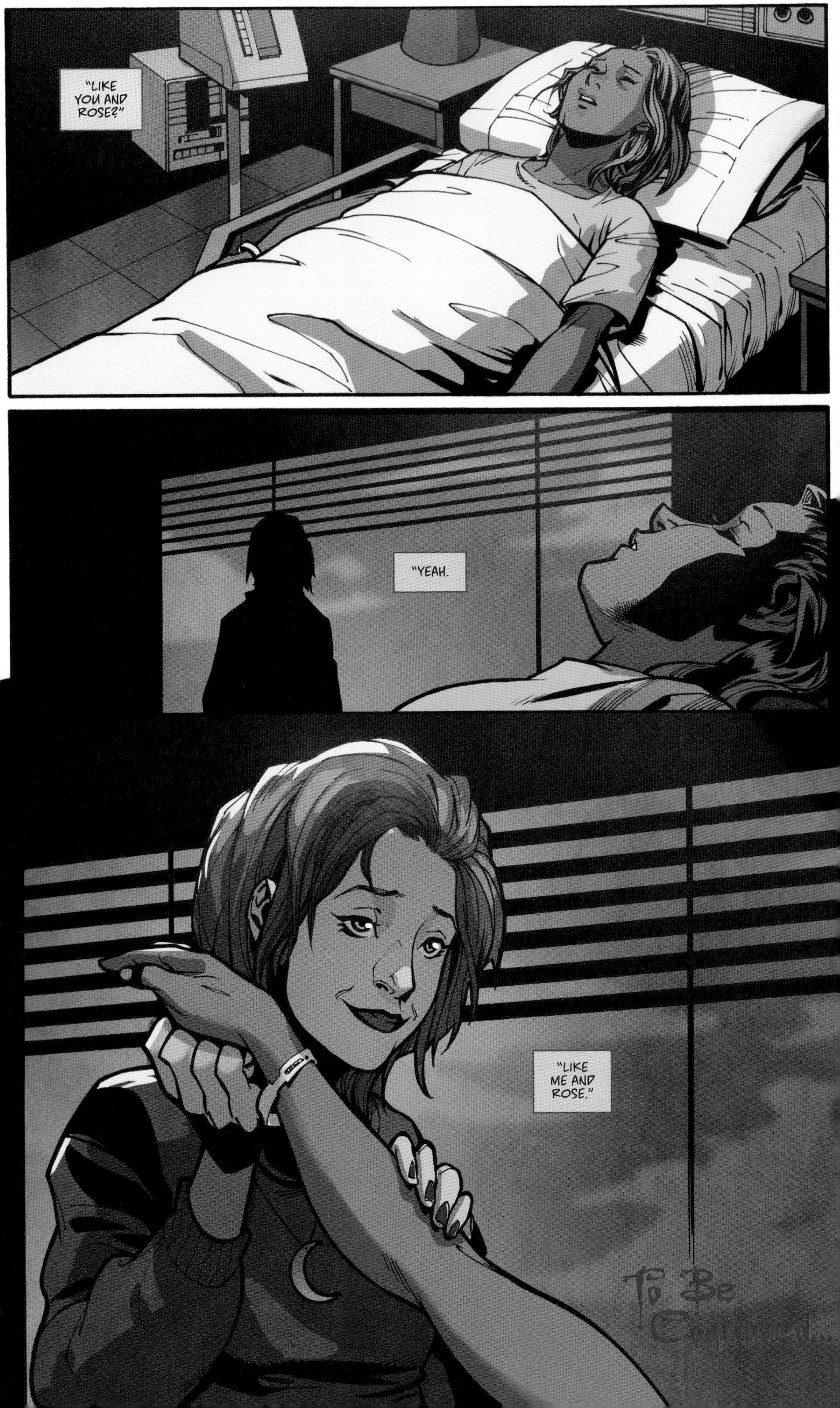
"LIKE YOU AND ROSE?"
"YEAH.
"LIKE ME AND ROSE."
To Be Continued...

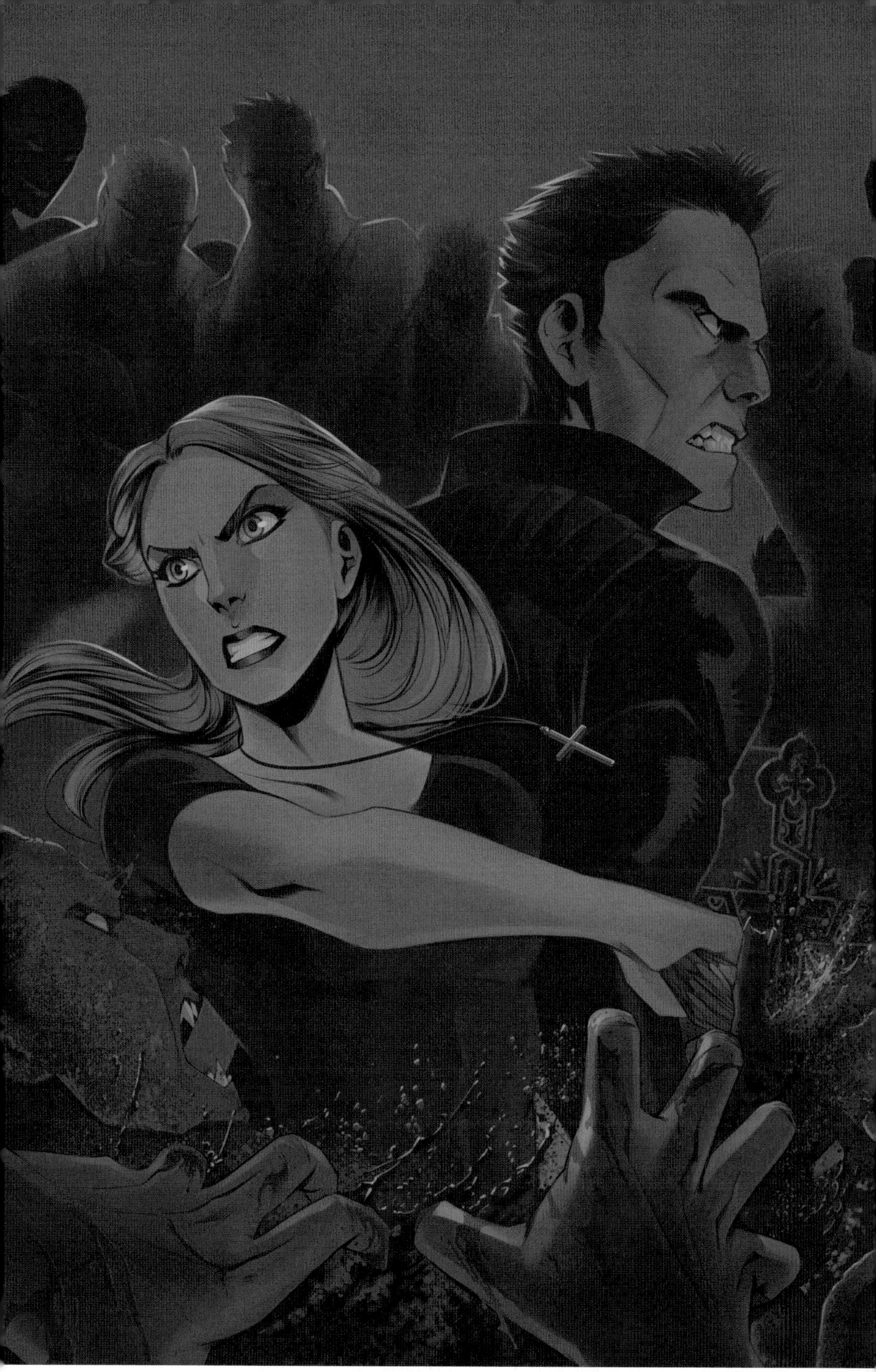

Issue Sixteen Ring of Fire Cover by **Kim**

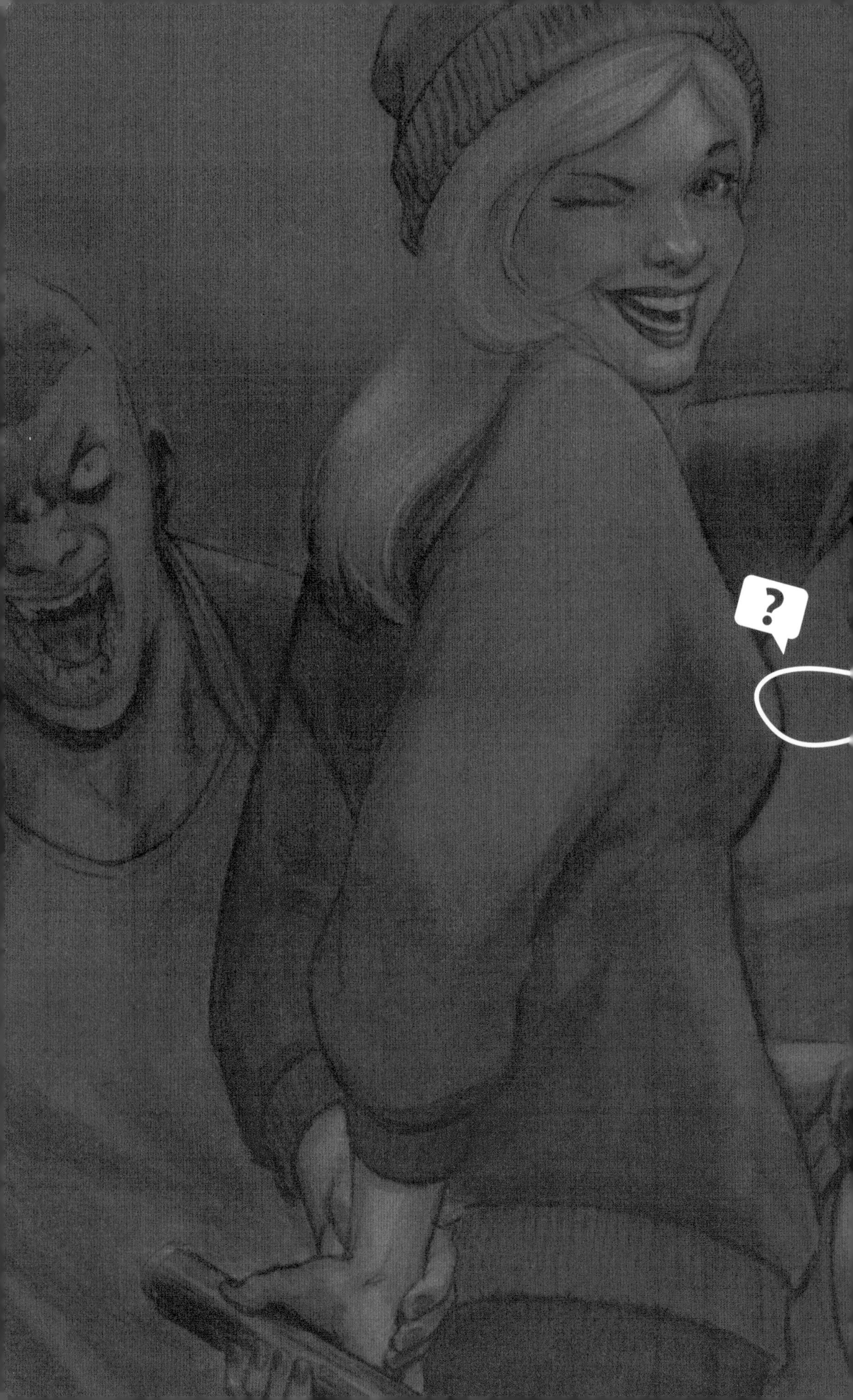
?

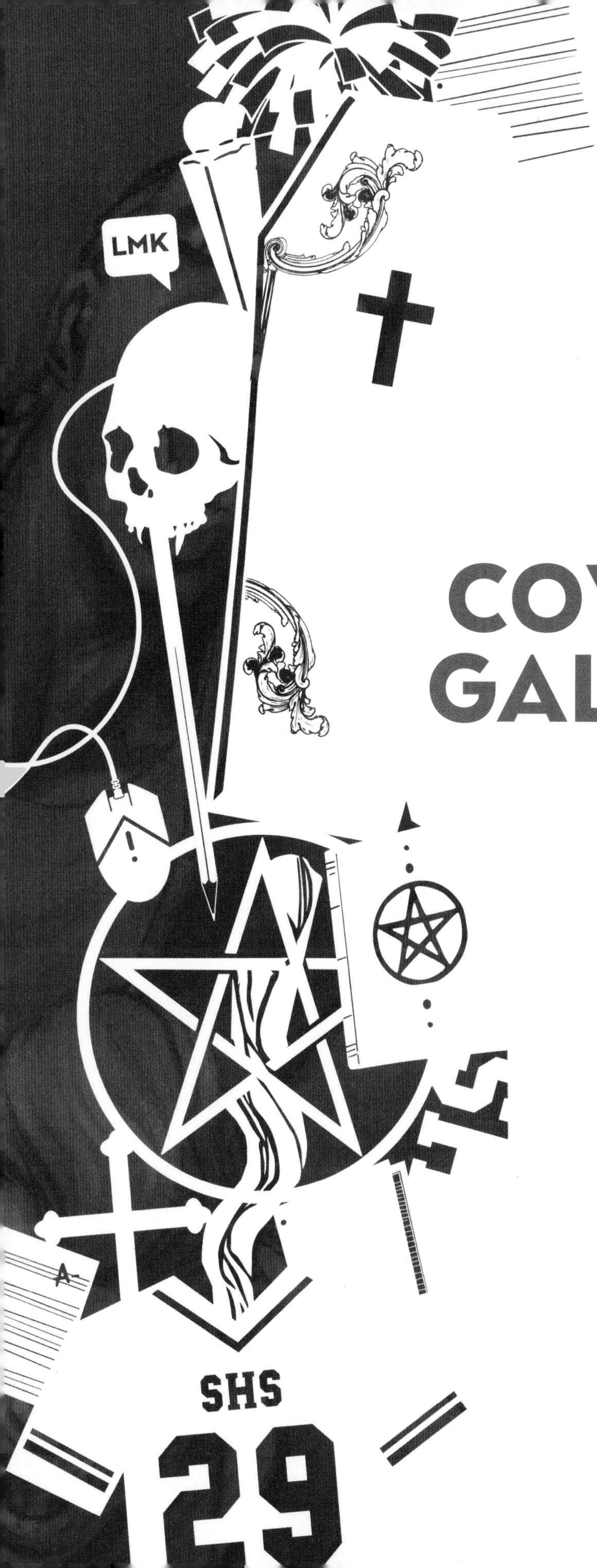
LMK
SHS
29

COVER GALLERY

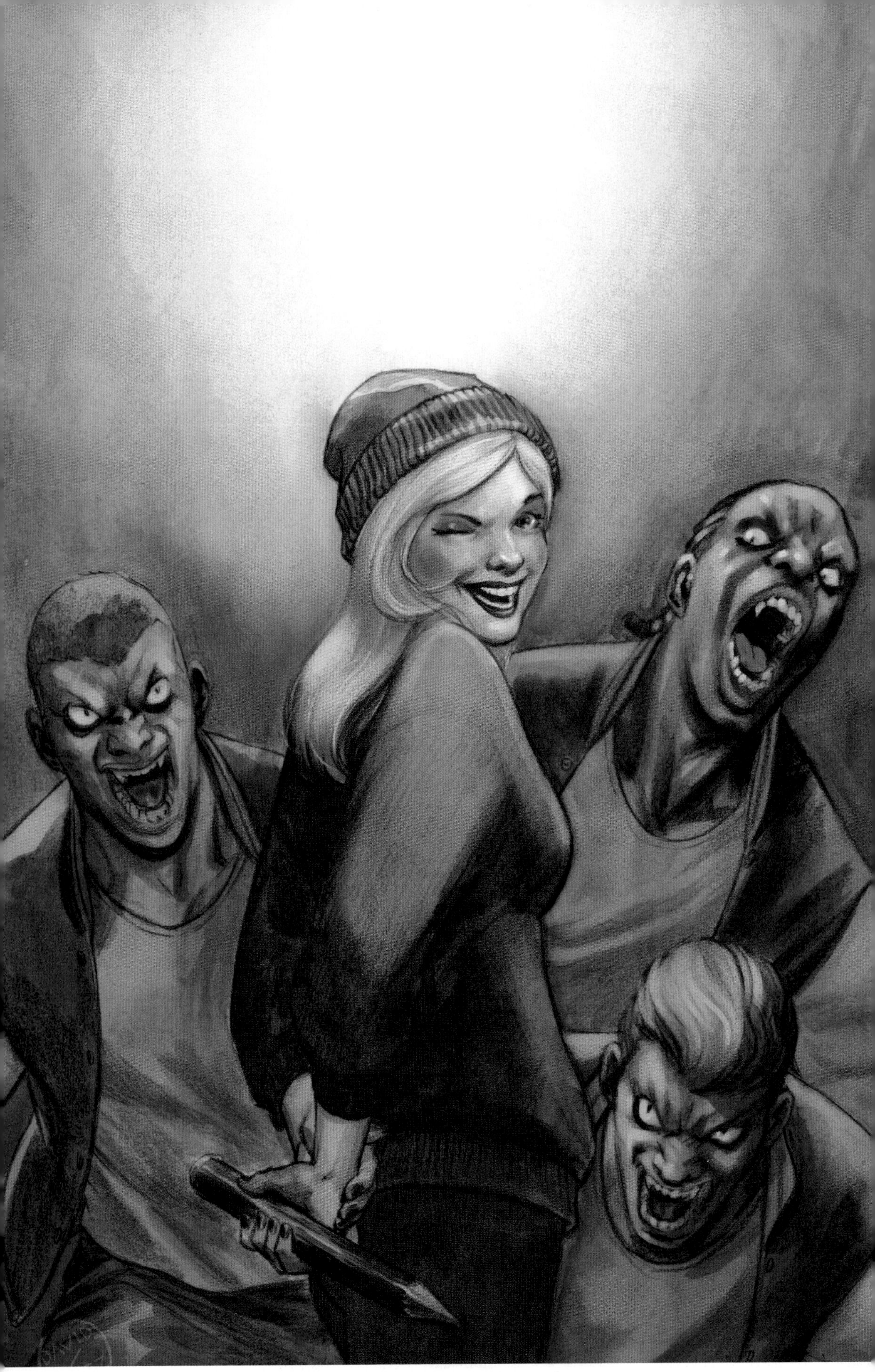

Issue Thirteen Buffy Cover by **David López**

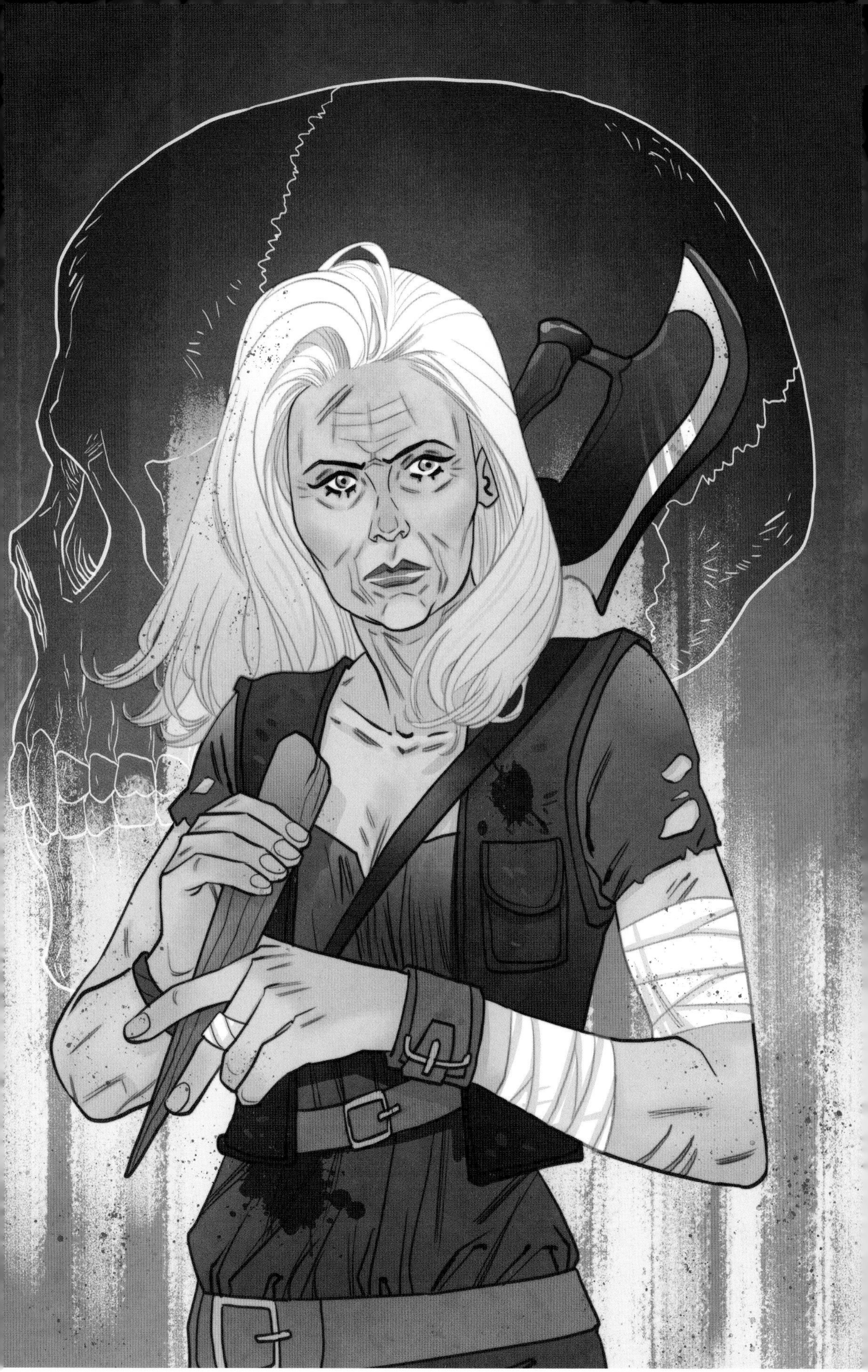

Issue Fourteen Multiverse Cover by **Marguerite Sauvage**

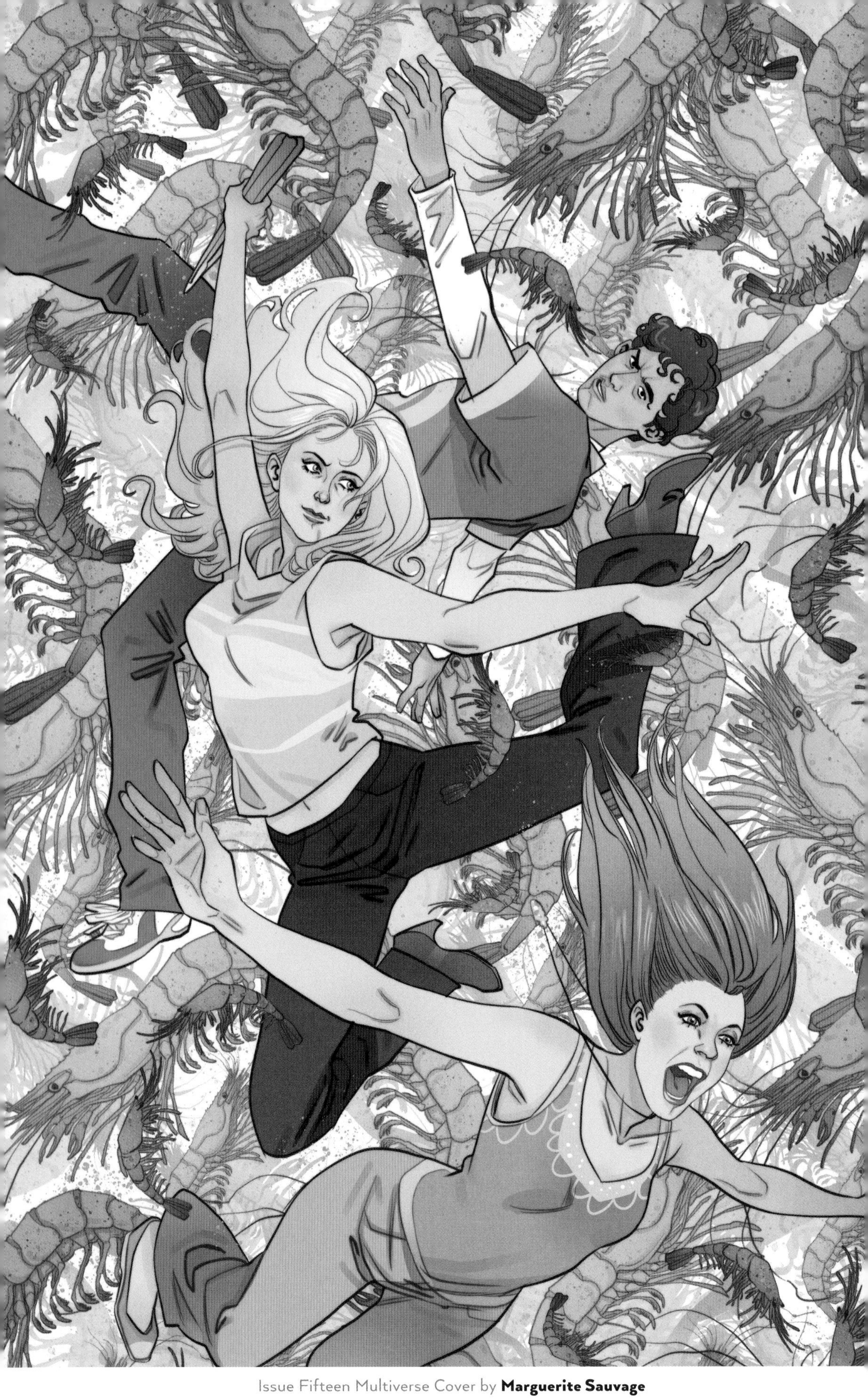

Issue Fifteen Multiverse Cover by **Marguerite Sauvage**

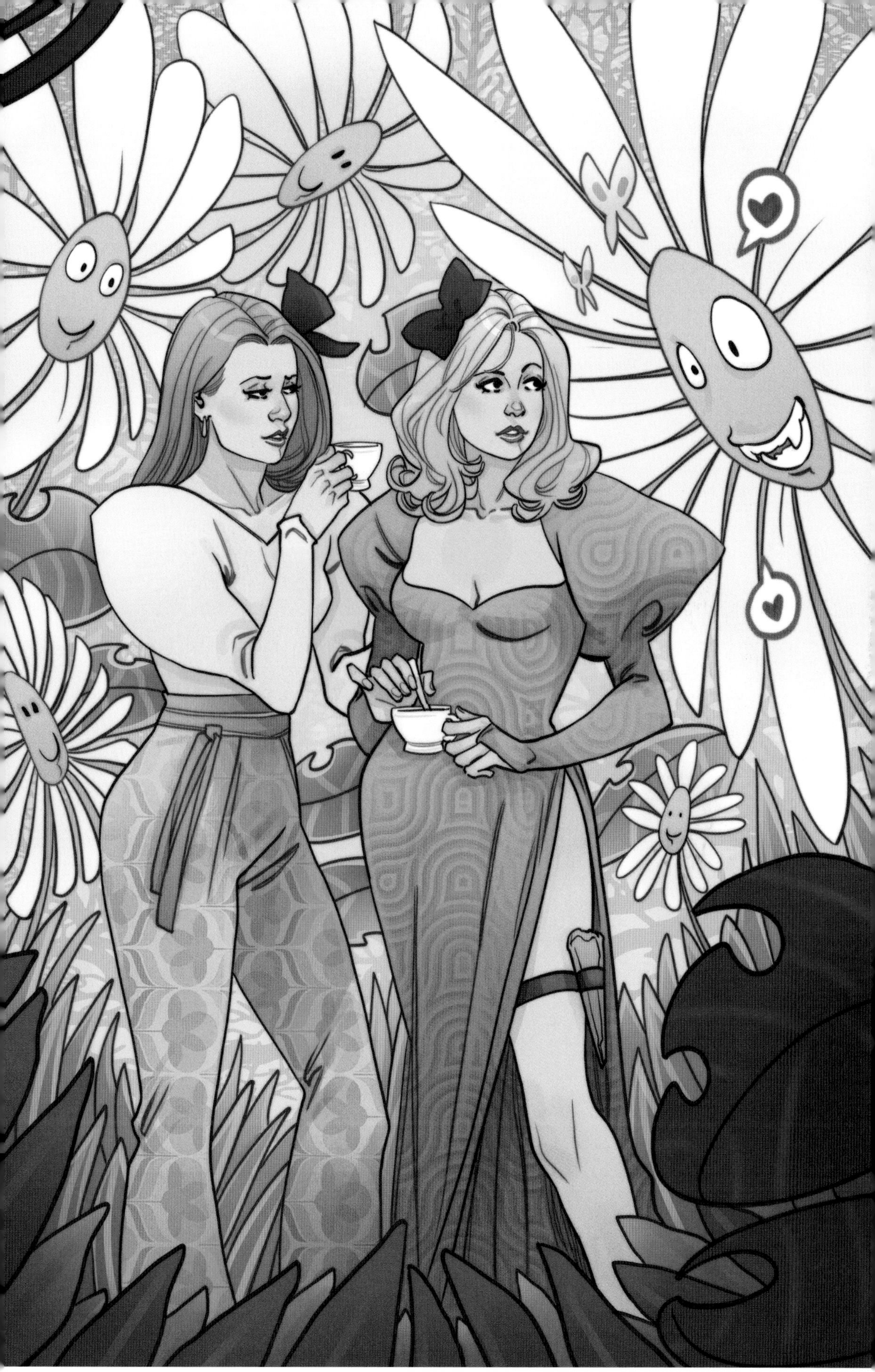

Issue Sixteen Multiverse Cover by **Marguerite Sauvage**

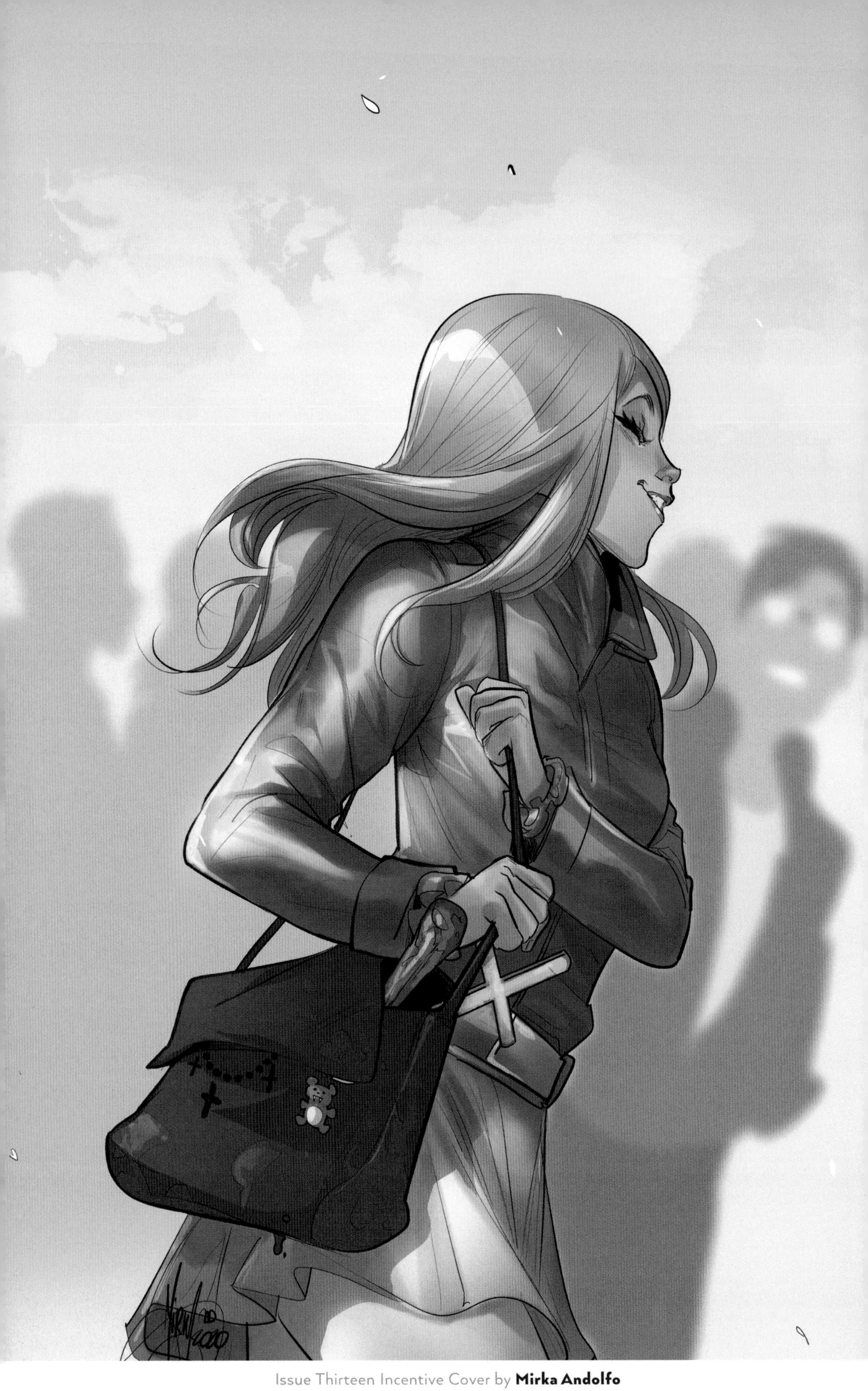

Issue Thirteen Incentive Cover by **Mirka Andolfo**

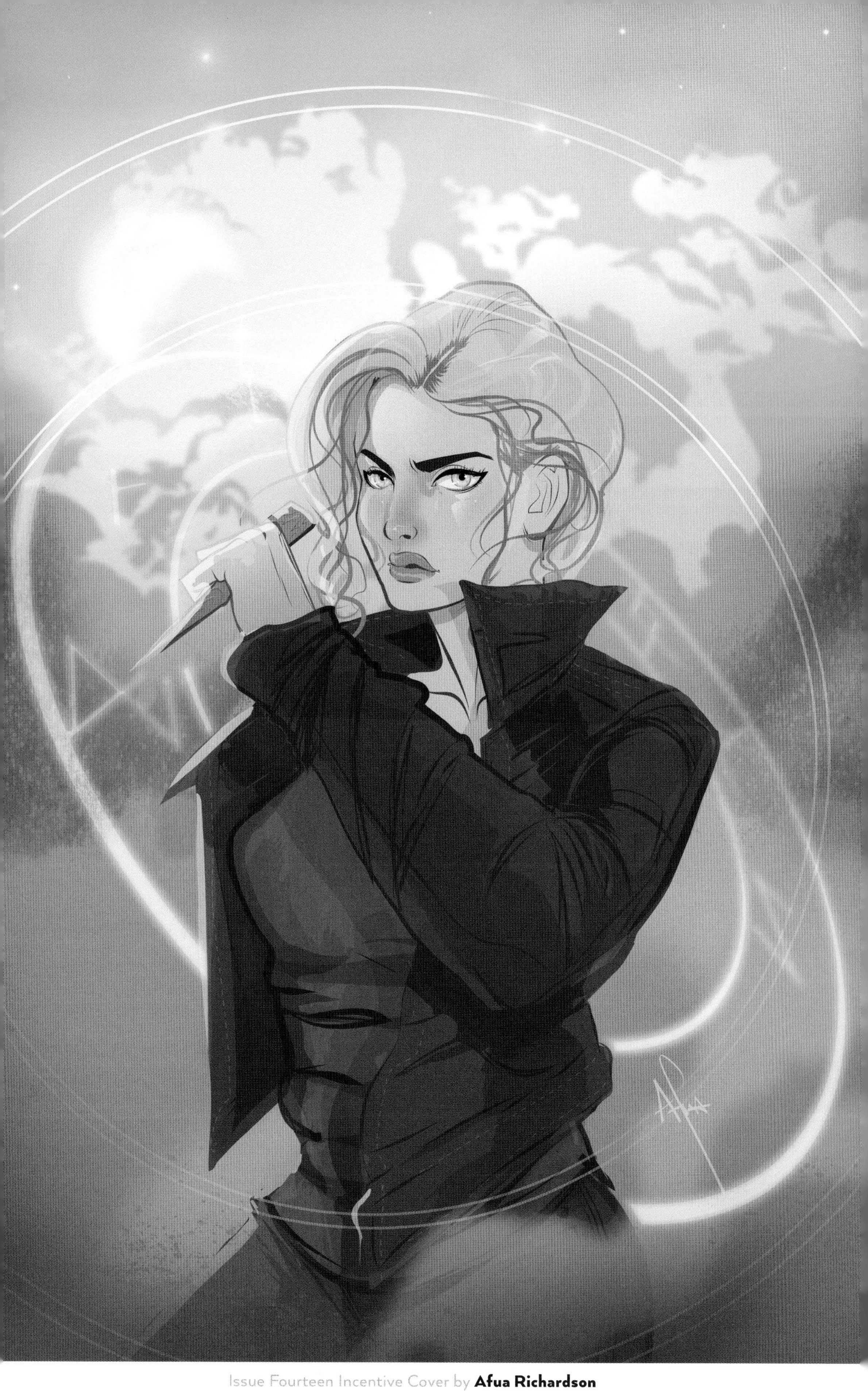

Issue Fourteen Incentive Cover by **Afua Richardson**

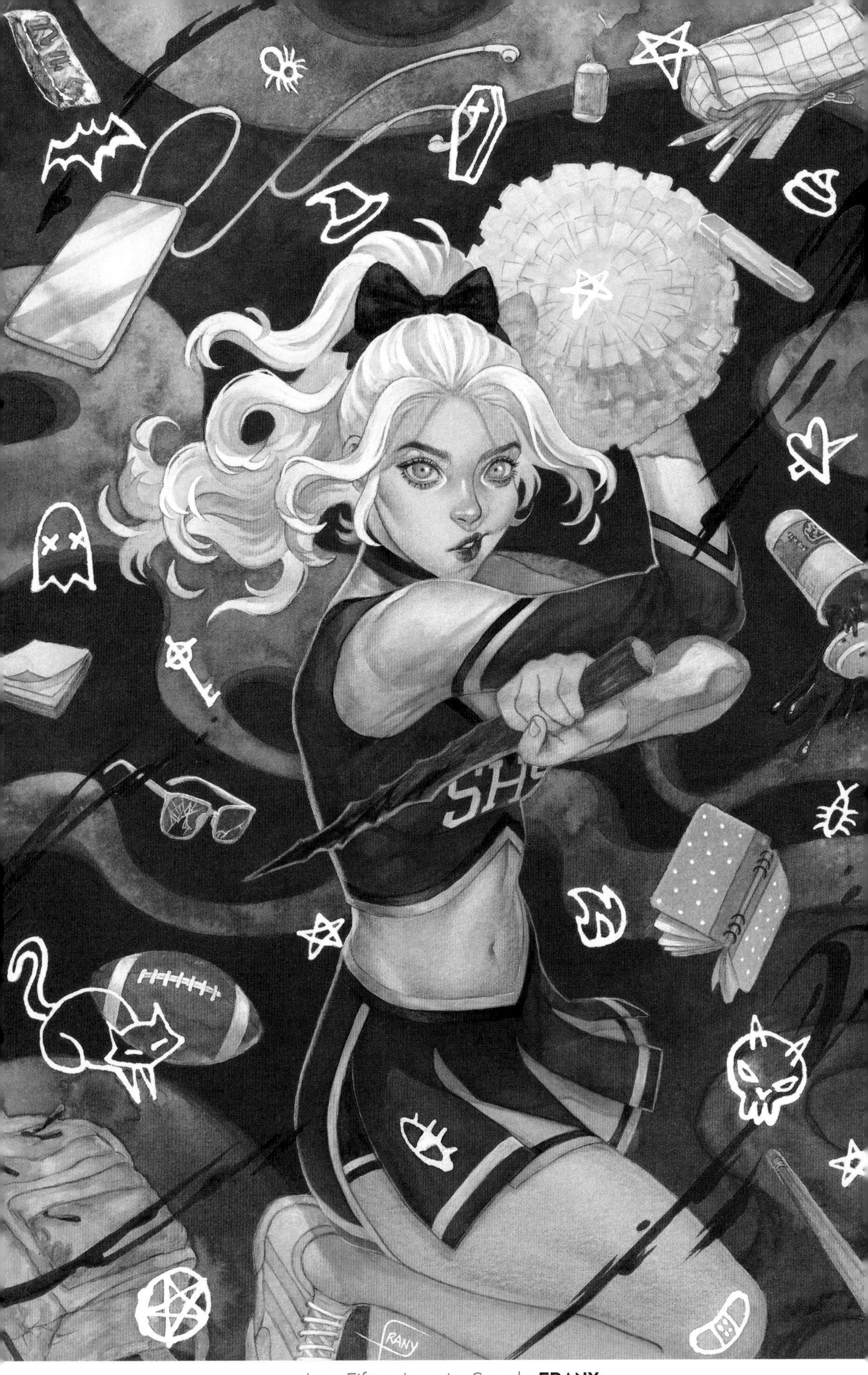
SH
FRANY

Issue Fifteen Incentive Cover by **FRANY**

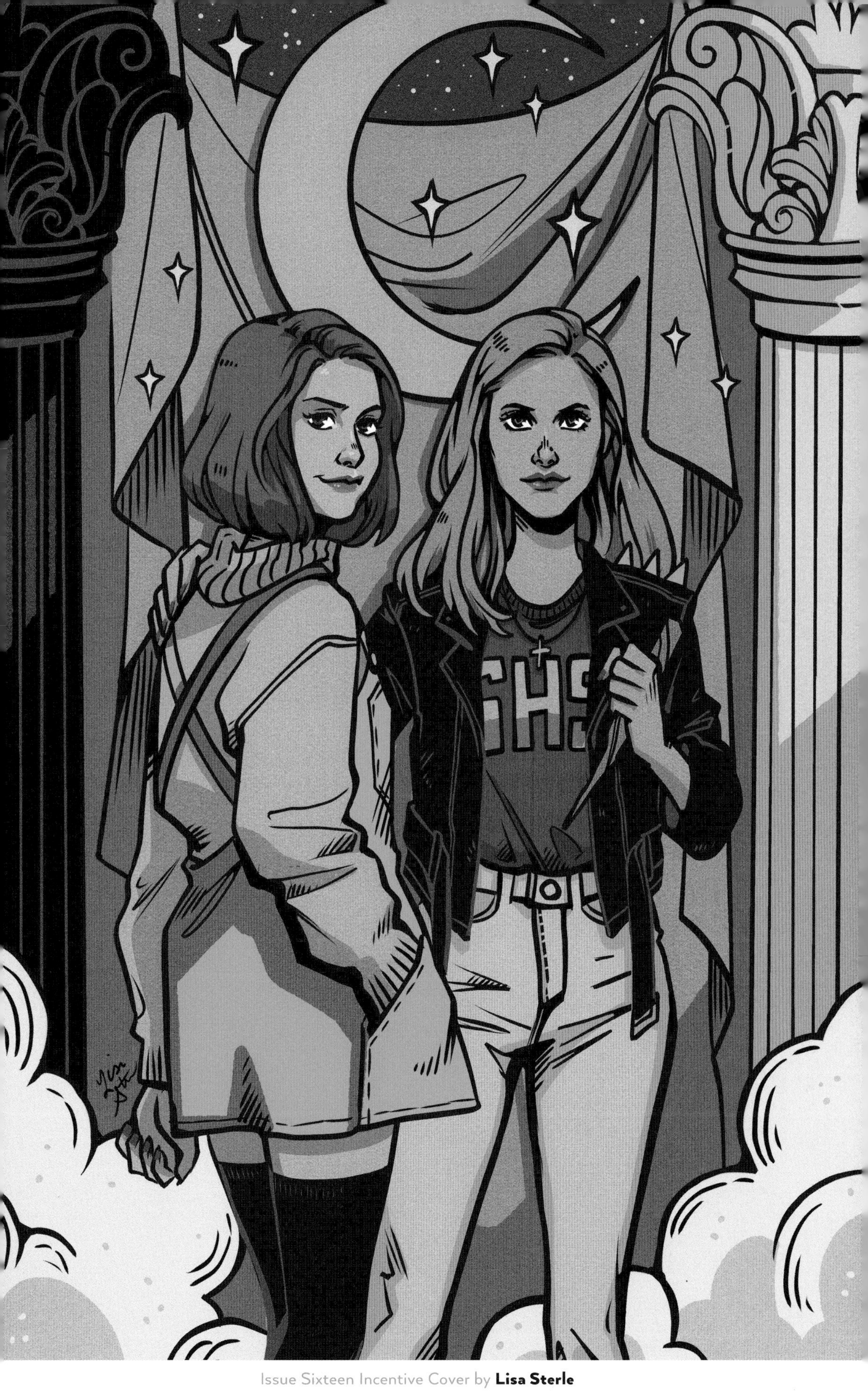

Issue Sixteen Incentive Cover by **Lisa Sterle**

DISCOVER
VISIONARY CREATORS

THE WOODS
JAMES TYNION IV • MICHAEL DIALYNAS
VOL. 1
THE ARROW

"The Spire is fantastic! My kind of genre free-for-all."
—BRIAN K. VAUGHAN (Saga)
THE SPIRE
SIMON SPURRIER
JEFF STOKELY
ANDRÉ MAY

MARK WAID • PETER KRAUSE
IRREDEEMABLE
AFTERWORD BY GRANT MORRISON

MARK WAID • JEAN DIAZ
INCORRUPTIBLE

MICHAEL ALAN NELSON
DAN MORA
GABRIEL CASSATA
HEXED
THE HARLOT & THE THIEF VOLUME ONE

ABNETT & CULBARD
WILD'S END
FIRST LIGHT
"IT'S REALLY, GREAT!"
JEFF LEMIRE

AVAILABLE AT YOUR LOCAL COMICS SHOP AND BOOKSTORE

To find a comics shop in your area, visit www.comicshoplocator.com

WWW.**BOOM-STUDIOS**.COM

James Tynion IV

The Woods

Volume 1
ISBN: 978-1-60886-454-6 | $9.99 US
Volume 2
ISBN: 978-1-60886-495-9 | $14.99 US
Volume 3
ISBN: 978-1-60886-773-8 | $14.99 US

The Backstagers

Volume 1
ISBN: 978-1-60886-993-0 | $14.99 US

Simon Spurrier

Six-Gun Gorilla

ISBN: 978-1-60886-390-7 | $19.99 US

The Spire

ISBN: 978-1-60886-913-8 | $29.99 US

Weavers

ISBN: 978-1-60886-963-3 | $19.99 US

Mark Waid

Irredeemable

Volume 1
ISBN: 978-1-93450-690-5 | $16.99 US
Volume 2
ISBN: 978-1-60886-000-5 | $16.99 US

Incorruptible

Volume 1
ISBN: 978-1-60886-015-9 | $16.99 US
Volume 2
ISBN: 978-1-60886-028-9 | $16.99 US

Michael Alan Nelson

Hexed The Harlot & The Thief

Volume 1
ISBN: 978-1-60886-718-9 | $14.99 US
Volume 2
ISBN: 978-1-60886-816-2 | $14.99 US

Day Men

Volume 1
ISBN: 978-1-60886-393-8 | $9.99 US
Volume 2
ISBN: 978-1-60886-852-0 | $9.99 US

Dan Abnett

Wild's End

Volume 1: First Light
ISBN: 978-1-60886-735-6 | $19.99 US
Volume 2: The Enemy Within
ISBN: 978-1-60886-877-3 | $19.99 US

Hypernaturals

Volume 1
ISBN: 978-1-60886-298-6 | $16.99 US
Volume 2
ISBN: 978-1-60886-319-8 | $19.99 US

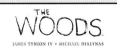

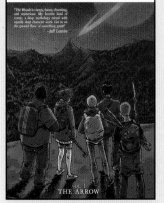

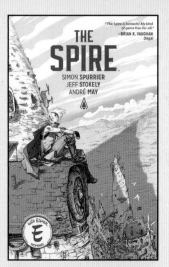

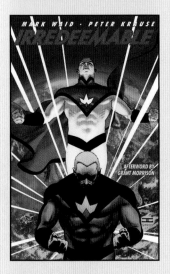

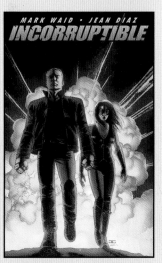

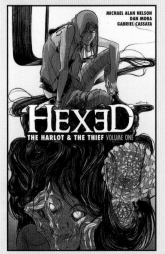

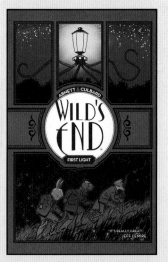

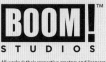